Jockey

JOCKEY

The Rider's Life in American Thoroughbred Racing

Scott A. Gruender

McFarland & Company, Inc., Publishers
Jefferson, North Carolina, and London

LIBRARY OF CONGRESS CATALOGUING-IN-PUBLICATION DATA

Gruender, Scott A., 1960–
Jockey : the rider's life in American
thoroughbred racing / Scott A. Gruender.
    p.   cm.
Includes bibliographical references and index.

ISBN-13: 978-0-7864-2819-9
ISBN-10: 0-7864-2819-8
(softcover : 50# alkaline paper) ∞

1. Jockeys—United States—Biography.
2. Horse racing—United States.
I. Title.
SF336.A2G78   2007
798.40092—dc22 [B]   2006033196

British Library cataloguing data are available

©2007 Scott A. Gruender. All rights reserved

*No part of this book may be reproduced or transmitted in any form
or by any means, electronic or mechanical, including photocopying
or recording, or by any information storage and retrieval system,
without permission in writing from the publisher.*

On the cover: Mathieu Adam drives for the finish
at Keeneland (© Cris Forney Photography)

Manufactured in the United States of America

*McFarland & Company, Inc., Publishers
Box 611, Jefferson, North Carolina 28640
www.mcfarlandpub.com*

ACKNOWLEDGMENTS

The author would like to express his sincere appreciation and gratitude to the hundreds of active and retired jockeys, agents, exercise riders, trainers, racing officials, clinicians and others who contributed their time, effort, stories and passion about the great sport of thoroughbred horse racing.

In particular, Chris Lamance and Kevin Mangold went above and beyond the call of duty in helping out with in-depth interviews and explanations.

Several professional and amateur photographers contributed to the book. Thanks go out to Cris Forney Photography, Thomas Thompson, Molly O'Brien, Debra Gruender, the New York Racing Association and retired jockeys Tom Chapman and Frank Lovato, Jr., for their help on the project.

Thanks to the following individuals and organizations for sharing detailed information, clinical expertise and professional opinions: Gary Wadler, MD, New York University School of Medicine; Brian Davis, MD, University of California, Davis Medical Center; David Baron, MD, Temple University School of Medicine; Anna Waller, ScD, University of North Carolina, Injury Prevention Research; Nancy Clark, MSRD; Jean Bradely Robel, ThD; Anorexia Nervosa and Related Eating Disorders, Inc (ANRED); and the National Eating Disorders Association.

Thank you to the Journal of the American Medical Association for permission to quote from *Jockey Injuries in the United States* [JAMA 283 (2000): 1326–28] ©2000, American Medical Association. All rights reserved.

Thank you to equiline.com for the use of jockey racing records.

CONTENTS

Acknowledgments   v
Preface   1
Introduction   3

1. Becoming a Jockey   7
2. Day in the Life   24
3. Winning Is Everything   38
4. Size Really Does Matter   77
5. They're Off!   94
6. Those Are the Breaks   145
7. Best of the Best   164
8. Out of the Saddle   192

Notes on Sources   201
Index   203

PREFACE

This book tells the dramatic story of thoroughbred racehorse jockeys. Often overlooked and undervalued as professional athletes, these diminutive men and women risk their lives day in and day out to make a living and chase their dreams.

Through the eyes of jockeys, agents, trainers, track officials and others in the racing industry, *Jockey* takes you inside the game and into the mysterious world of racing. In a lifetime of wonderment and two years of exhausting interviews, I have been overwhelmed with the genuine spirit, determination and heart of these jockeys as they shared their stories, troubles and wisdom.

I spent time talking with riders from all over the country, from Emerald Down in the great Pacific Northwest to Calder Race Course in sunny Miami, and from where the turf meets the surf at Del Mar to the pageantry of summer racing at New York's Saratoga. What I found is that it didn't matter if I was talking with the all-time money-winning rider Pat Day or the young apprentice Peter Artieda with just a handful of wins under his belt—they all share the same passion for the sport and the drive to win. The composite sketch of the life and times of the professional jockey you are about to read is truly a tribute to fine men and women who thrill us every day in the great sport of horse racing.

Introduction

The vital soul of thoroughbred horse racing is the intense bond between man and horse. The world's toughest athlete, that small warrior with hands of iron, sits atop that graceful thoroughbred and leads it into battle at breakneck speeds to win the day.

Jockeying is a way of life as much as a sport, and it demands discipline, courage and dedication. Through the tiring schedule, the struggles to maintain low weight and the constant danger of racing, jockeys push on as consummate professional athletes, driven to win every time the starting gate bursts open in front of them.

Racing, with all its majestic history, is an often misunderstood sport. The average racing fan enjoys a day at the local oval watching fast horses ridden by men and women wearing bright, colorful uniforms. Most of the viewing and betting public sees only the glamorous side of the sport—the pageantry, beautiful horses and thrilling excitement of racing. After eight or ten races, the fans go home, oblivious to the amount of time, work and effort it takes to put on the show. Few know of the risks, personal sacrifice, hardship and horrors that some jockeys endure. There's an entire culture at the track that's different from life anywhere else. There's a whirlwind of bustling activity behind the scenes that allows a 110-pound man to thunder down the stretch aboard a horse outweighing him tenfold.

Often viewed as second-class athletes, jockeys are grossly underrated for their pure athleticism, dedication and sacrifice to their profession. It takes incredible concentration, strength, balance and courage to ride a racehorse. The sheer dynamics of the sport are spectacular. With as many as a dozen or more horses racing in heavy traffic at speeds exceeding 40 miles per hour, split-second decisions separate winners from losers. As they fly around the track sometimes only inches apart, the slightest bobble can lead to tragedy. There's little room for error.

On the racetrack, rider and horse become one. They work as a team, neither one able to do without the other. The horse doesn't know how far the race is. He doesn't know how quickly he should run or where he should be within the body of the race to have the best chance. It's the rider's job to implement a winning racing strategy, measuring the effort and timing necessary to propel them to the front at the wire. The equine athlete's performance is driven by the judgment, horsemanship and physical abilities of his rider in a beautiful relationship unique to all of sports.

Riders must have strong legs to balance themselves in the irons and hold their position in the saddle. They must have the arm strength to pull the horse back from going all out at the start when the gate flies open; the endurance to push the horse in the drive to the finish, pumping his neck in rhythm with each stride; and the mental strength to deal with the pressure from owners, trainers and racing officials.

Jockeys must be able to guide their horses on the shortest trip from start to finish, steer them through racing traffic, accelerate at just the right moment and muscle their horses to a driving finish. Racehorses are not predictable machines. They are high-strung animals bred for raw speed and competitiveness. There are no brakes, lights or directional indicators to announce a change of lanes. With nerves of steel, it's all a matter of split-second timing. It's not easy to change a horse's intentions—yet jockeys make it look effortless.

Many a jockey tells the story of falling in love with the power of the horse. They often are hooked on the thrill ride the first time they saddle up. Most are driven purely by the love of the game, not the money. Only a handful of riders ever make it big time. Most of them struggle just to make a living at it. Many know of nothing else and will sacrifice everything to live the jockey's life.

There are no guaranteed million-dollar contracts like those that top athletes have in other sports. Most riders never make it past the daily struggle just to make ends meet. Only a few make a comfortable living at it and even fewer join the elite handful who earn seven figures per year. Jockeys are financially motivated by the incentive of earning more for winning races. It seems like that's the way it should be for all sports.

How about lucrative endorsement deals? Not much chance. Granted, you might catch a glimpse of Jerry Bailey, the icon of jockeys, pitching the *Daily Racing Form* on a TV spot for the Derby or Breeder's Cup, but that's going to be about it.

In racing, there's no such thing as a "no-cut clause." Deals are made with a shake of the hand and nod of the head. Being fired comes with the territory. There's no injured reserve, either. There's no second-string substitute to take over if the jockey is having a bad day. There's no sick leave pay or injury pay when he's unable to make it to the office. No doubt, it's one tough gig.

Jockeys must be thick skinned to handle the rejection and immune to the disappointment of losing. Being beaten only 85 percent of the time means you're doing good, losing 80 percent of you're your races means you're doing great. With only minutes between races, there's no time to be wallowing in self-pity after poor rides, for each race brings the hopes of a fresh horseman looking for a strong and willing rider to get the job done.

Jockeys must stay positive. They must emotionally survive the ups and downs of their roller-coaster profession and put on a happy face when making early morning rounds with trainers to secure new riding business.

Because racing is a year-round sport, there's no off-season. There's always a track racing somewhere. Therefore, jockeys typically become transitory, moving from city to city to follow racing meets at different tracks to ply their trade, often leaving their families behind. Too often, they live a solitary existence that revolves entirely around their life at the race track.

There's no rain delay in racing. It doesn't matter how bad the slop is; the show goes on regardless of racing surfaces only a hog could love. There's no rescheduling just because it snows or it's freezing outside, either. Racing goes on through the bone-chilling cold at Philadelphia Park and the sweltering heat of summer racing in Texas.

Centuries ago, horse owners simply put the lightest person they knew up on their horses. Today, jockeys ride following a scale of weights established to theoretically level the playing field for horses and give each a fair chance to win. Jockeys will literally starve themselves, if necessary, to make weight. Some risk their health and well-being with excessive use of diuretics, laxatives and weight-loss drugs. The battle against the scale is relentless, waged day after day.

Competing in a sport so dangerous that an ambulance follows them around the track as they race, some jockeys suffer paralyzing back and neck injuries. Some pay the ultimate price. Head injuries, broken bones and damage to vital organs are a constant threat. Danger lurks at every stride, and falls are inevitable. It isn't a matter of getting hurt; it's a matter of how often and how badly.

Jockeys don't think about accidents—they can't. They're supposed to be tough. No trainer wants a worrisome jockey in the irons. Owners want the best man for the job and the weak of heart just won't do. Because of this, most injured jockeys don't say they are banged up. They'd rather suck it up, block out the pain, and continue riding. If they leave their mounts, certainly someone will be waiting to steal their business away.

Riders are always under the scrutiny of the public eye. If they have a bad ride, everyone in the house sees it. Not just once, either. It's replayed on the monitors throughout the track over and over again, as well as in the jockeys' room where every mistake is magnified, analyzed and picked apart. A serious foul by the jockey may get his horse disqualified or bring an invitation to visit the racing stewards. Impeding or causing other interference may be disciplined with a fine or suspension from racing.

Unlike other sports, jockeys return to the same locker room, the jockey's quarters, after competing against each other. While they're fiercely competitive on the track, they are a tight knit group who typically enjoy each other's company. However, flared tempers can result in shouting matches, shoving contests and fistfights.

Even with all the risks of physical injury, the constant challenge of making weight and the highly competitive nature of racing, the mental side of the sport is underestimated. Winning riders must be cold-blooded with nerves of steel, smart enough to avoid the traps, daring enough to take risks and patient enough to know when not to.

For these self-employed, independent contractors in a dangerous industry, health and life insurance are difficult to obtain and expensive to keep. While many riders belong to the Jockeys' Guild, they have no organized representation, and the industry has done little to help them.

Racetrack politics run rampant throughout the industry. The stories of stone-cold lies, slap-in-the-face betrayals, broken promises and kickback schemes are countless. Learning how to play the game and avoiding the landmines often separates successful riders from the also-rans.

Horse racing and scandal have gone hand in hand through time, but the integrity of the game has significantly improved the last thirty years. With increased scrutiny by racing officials and the constant eye of the camera, modern racing is sound and aboveboard. There's still a joker in every deck, though, and there's always someone thinking he can beat the system.

Exposing the underbelly of racing, there is a dark side to the jockey profession. The bitter suffering with weight issues, agony of injuries and battles with drugs and booze are revelations most people are oblivious to.

Jockeys are different from other professional athletes in many ways. They are often seen as second-class athletes, not receiving the notoriety they deserve. But pound for pound, there are few athletes who can compare with the strength, drive, determined lifestyle and commitment made by jockeys. The physical risks, restrictive diets, mental anguish and out-of-whack risk-reward ratio combine to make jockeys the toughest professional athletes. They simply don't get the recognition they deserve.

Being a jockey is not just a job; it's even more than a profession. It's a way of life.

1

BECOMING A JOCKEY

For many would-be jockeys, the dream of winning the "Run for the Roses," otherwise known as the Kentucky Derby, gloriously run on the first Saturday of May since 1875, begins when they watch one of the big horse races on television. But the televised, commercialized version of racing, the one that shows all the excitement, thrills and big smiles that accompany winners, doesn't expose fans to the magnitude of hard work, dedication and sacrifice it takes to get there. Many dreams of being a jockey are born long before there's any understanding of the demanding lifestyle it takes to fulfill the vision.

The most common introduction to the working world of racing for young men and women desiring to be jockeys is through entry-level positions as grooms or hot walkers. Grooms provide basic care to horses, and hot walkers hand-walk horses for exercise. Many young horsemen graduate from these roles to become exercise riders, eventually obtaining their jockey's license. Starting from the ground up, the experience teaches them valuable lessons about horses, the racing business and how the game is played.

Sons and daughters of trainers and jockeys often make good horsemen and excellent jockeys. Drawing from a racetrack lifestyle, they are raised around horses and gain the comfort, confidence and touch with horses much earlier. Many of them learn how to ride a horse before a bicycle. Often times, they will be exercising racehorses in their early teens and are racing by age sixteen.

Frank Lovato grew up in Cherry Hill, New Jersey, a ten-minute drive from Garden State Race Track. His father, Frank, Sr., was a jockey. "As far back as I can remember, I was hooked on the racetrack," the junior Lovato shared.

Most kids were watching Saturday morning cartoons or sleeping in, I would be up and fully dressed before daylight. I would tap on my dad's bedroom door, trying to motivate him to wake up and get ready to go to the track for early morning workouts. Finally, Dad would get up and slip his boots on. I think I was about four years old when this started.

Although this was the regular weekend drill, it was like the first time every weekend, and I would still be excited to hurry up and get to the track. The ride to the track was in silence. My dad wasn't in a bad mood or anything he just was never a man of many words. So I sat alongside him, crouched on my knees so I could see outside the window. When we'd finally reach the track, we'd drive through the stable gate, exchanging waves with the security guards. Everyone was always happy to see my dad and welcomed him with a generous "Good morning, Frank."

Aside from my dad's mannerism, he also impressed me so much as a race rider in general. His personality and presence carried over to the actual race. I think you could describe him as being like Fonzy from the old show *Happy Days*. He was very cool and quiet, but when he said something, everybody seemed to listen. Even simple things like a handshake or walking into the winner's circle was very cool.

While the number of male riders dwarfs the females, it's the young ladies who often have the dream long before boys. There are many more girls riding horses as teens, with some parlaying a horse showing, barrel racing or other equine activity into a racing career. Considering all the dirt, muck and sweat that go with the job, there are many more tomboys than prissies at the track.

Growing up on a farm, young apprentice rider Jennifer Schmidt was up on her first horse at age two.

My parents always had a horse, or more like 20 horses, around in the backyard. I remember entering horse shows when I was around seven and competing in events all the time. As I got older, I started doing rodeo events. Any time I could, I'd be doing dressage, reining, barrel racing or anything else I could try. Every chance I get now, I still try and do some rodeo roping with the little bit of free time I do have.

I actually got started in the horse-racing business through the rodeo: A friend of mind there asked me if I'd be interested in exercising horses at the racetrack and I said sure. From there, things just took off.

From my experiences working with horses since I was little, I learned how to read the horse and to adjust my style to theirs. I learned how to listen to what the horse tells me. I'm too small to overpower a horse, so it's more of a peaceful agreement I make with them now.

Often ridiculed because of their diminutive stature, many future jockeys grow up frustrated when dreams of playing football, baseball or basketball fade away. Their options for an athletic outlet narrow, as other boys keep growing larger. Many turn to wrestling, where they can compete against kids their own size. It's widely accepted that pound for pound, wrestlers are as tough as any athletes around. The discipline of training, control and muscle development in wrestling prepares them well for the rigors of a riding career.

A young rider with great potential, Mick Ruis grew up as an All-American wrestler: "I started wrestling when I was seven. My father was really the motivator behind it. He encouraged me, pushed me to train hard and helped me become a good wrestler. He even put wrestling mats in the house and made a wrestling room, so I could train at the house. He kind of started his own wrestling club and we had guys coming to practice all the time."

By virtue of a second-place finish at the Youth World Championships in Reno, Ruis earned All-American status. As a freshman wrestler at Poway High School, he made the varsity and wrestled at the lowest weight class, 105 pounds, while weighing eight pounds under the allowance. "I finished second in the Conference as a freshman. Some of the guys were just bigger than me. But as a sophomore, I was right at 105 and came in a lot stronger. I finished 29–1, losing only in the state championship final."

Ruis walked away from wrestling and high school to start his riding career but carried with him a valuable lesson: "I think wrestling helped me tremendously. It taught me about balance and self-discipline, which help me a lot in this business. When I first came to the track, people told me it would take time to make the physical adjustments and get fit for racing, but with my wrestling experience, I came to the track fit so I was able to really focus on learning how to ride."

Top rider Corey Nakatani was another of the many riders who wrestled in high school:

> I was small, but very athletic when I was in school. I played other sports, like football, but with wrestling, my size wasn't an issue. With my warm-ups and letterman's jacket on, I probably weighed all of 93 pounds.
>
> I wrestled just one year and went 34–4 before a broken nose ended my season. After that, I went to night school to finish my high school education so that I could ride during the day.

A number of jockeys grow up as young cowboys on farms and ranches, unaware of the racing world. Many are drawn to rodeo events, but experience limited success because of their size. Four-time Eclipse Award–winning jockey Pat Day always wanted to be a rodeo star:

> I was raised in the hills of Colorado. I always wanted to be a bull rider and did the rodeo circuit for a while. I was having minimal success and learning the great art of falling. I really mastered how to fall and roll. In fact, it's probably helped me avoid injuries as a jockey in my career.
>
> People around me told me to try being a jockey, either because they

thought I was short in stature or because they knew I wouldn't make it as a very good bull rider. So, I went off to be a jockey, learning from the ground up. I didn't have much patience, though, and a few months later I rode in my first race."

Day brought home his first winner, Forblunged, in 1973 over a sloppy track at Prescott Downs in Arizona: "The purse was $600 and the winner's share was $360, so my 10 percent was $36. I didn't think it could get any better." Day is now the all-time leading money-winning rider with mounts totaling $297 million in purses.

Many of modern day racing's top jockeys started their riding careers outside the country and were recruited by American horsemen or came over on their own accord based on their success overseas. National Museum of Racing Hall of Fame riders Braulio Baeza, Angel Cordero, Jr., Laffit Pincay, Jr., Jacinto Vasquez and Jorge Velasquez all started careers outside North America. An increasing number of current riders are coming from Latin America, often coming stateside with jockey school and racing experience under their belts.

Like many riders who come from countries like Panama, Peru and Puerto Rico, Daniel Centeno came to America in search of a better career. Named the top apprentice rider of 1991 in his native Venezuela, jockey Centeno moved his tack in 2003: "I had a friend at Thistledown who told me I could do good here. He told me there's more purse money, the horses are better, the tracks are nicer and the people are good. The money is so much better here, probably double or more what I could make in Venezuela, so I came over here to ride, even though it meant starting all over again at the bottom because no one knew about me."

Many foreign riders learn the basic art of riding at jockey schools located around the globe. Unfortunately, there are few formal riding academies in America. At schools like the University of Arizona, where their Race Track Industry Program offers professional education, and the University of Louisville's Equine Industry Program, individuals can prepare themselves for a fulfilling career in the racing business, exclusive of jockey training.

At age fifteen, jockey James Graham left his Ireland home and quit school to attend an Irish apprentice school for aspiring jockeys. Following his grandfather's suggestion to become a jockey because of his size, he learned the foundational skills necessary to build a career upon: "The apprentice school teaches you everything you need to know. When you're done, you know how to take care of horses, how to ride and are ready for work. I was there 10 months, did all the groundwork and was sent to a trainer to work everyday."

Graham, now a graded stakes-winning rider in the United States, has been riding in the States for several years now: "I rode in Ireland for awhile, but things were getting on a little sour. I was one for 86 as an apprentice there, so I came over here for a change and did much better."

Ever since he was a little boy watching the races at home on television, Peter Artieda wanted to become a jockey. Several years later with his dream still alive, Artieda is poised to become an apprentice rider in California, although the road to get here has been a long and bumpy ride.

As a reckless youth, he got himself into trouble with the law: "I was young and stupid. I made a mistake and stole money from the store I was working at. They didn't have much trouble figuring out it was me, and I got hung with a second-degree burglary charge." With a felony on his record, Artieda was frustrated with the long, slow process of clearing his name so he could work on the racetrack. He often thought of calling it quits but continued to fight through the discouragements.

After appealing to the California Horse Racing Board, he was finally granted an exercise rider's license at Los Alamitos Race Track in California. Thanks to trainer Craig Robertson's help, he started exercising a couple horses every day, picking up riding tips along the way from veteran riders. After a few months of galloping horses, he was ready for the next step:

> Earlier this year, I contacted the stewards, who told me I needed to obtain signatures of approval from the track's outrider, three journeyman riders and the gate starter.
>
> At the gate, I had to demonstrate that I could break cleanly. I had to be solid coming out of the gate, controlled and keeping the horse in a straight line. After three or four weeks, I got the final sign off.
>
> I went back to the stewards and was given an apprentice certificate, which means they'll watch me closely for my first four races to be sure I'm safe and not putting anyone at risk out there. If I pass that test, they'll fully activate my license. Before I can race, though, I needed gear, so the Clerk of Scales helped me contact some of the guys in the jock's room who are helping me with an old saddle, girth straps, boots, pants and stuff. I can't wait to get started. This is like a dream come true for me, particularly after all the struggles I've gone through just to get this far.

After getting his first ride at Los Alamitos Race Track, Artieda finally broke through with his first win in 2005 with the Cat's Joanna at Pleasanton.

While there is no designated gateway into the American jockey business, working as a groom provides a solid base of horse knowledge for most riders. Under the direction of a trainer, grooms are assigned a set number of horses to care for, so they become very familiar with that particular horse's needs, habits and quirks. Seldom does anything slip by, and no one knows a horse better than his groom.

Grooms work long hours, getting the barn started early in the day and finishing the morning up once all the horses have been worked, bathed and fed. Afternoon rounds include another round of feed and watering. Evening rounds are done to check that everyone is safe and sound. Some grooms live on the track, either in tiny tack rooms sleeping alongside saddles, bridles and other racing equipment, or in small apartments on the backstretch. Arguably the hardest working folks on the backstretch, grooms are largely underpaid and underappreciated for their dedicated efforts to see that horses are well treated and cared for.

Jockey Joe Bravo, whose father and grandfather were jockeys, worked as a young groom until he was old enough to start riding:

> I was more of a barn bitch than a groom. With my family around all the time, they had me doing everything they could think of, and I think they enjoyed watching me work so hard. I got all the jobs that no one else wanted to do. It's funny that looking back at it now, though, because I realize how much I learned about horses and the racing business, both from the inside and outside.
>
> I know firsthand how hard these guys [grooms] work, and that they really earn their money. It takes a lot to get up that early every day and care for these horses, so you know they're dedicated. I make a point of it now to let them know how much I appreciate their help with the horses.

At many racetracks, horses are walked by hand for exercise or when cooling down after a workout. Walking hots, as they call it, is sometimes done by grooms or by someone hired specifically for that job. If not walked by hand, horses are connected by lead shank to a device called a hot walker, which accommodates up to four horses at a time. The walker has long arms extending from the center of the device, leading horses in a circle about 60 feet across. In the long haul, the machine is less expensive, but most trainers feel it's better for the horses to be hand walked.

Trainers value riders who've come up through the system learning about horses. As Kentucky-based William "Buff" Bradley puts it, they must know the basics: "I truly believe that a jockey should work from the ground up and know about the horse's legs and should have experience galloping and even breaking horses at the early stages of the game. I believe that to be a good jockey, you must be able to listen to the trainer who is around the horse everyday."

At some point in their development, nearly all jockeys have been an exercise rider. Exercise riders, or "gallop boys" or "gallop girls" as they're called, usually work for one trainer, taking horses to the track each morning for exercise. Galloping horses helps build the horsemanship skills necessary to become a jockey and exposes the exercise rider to the different trainers on the grounds. Usually starting with the easiest horses to ride in the barn, they graduate to those horses that might need prodding every step of the trip and then to the "hot" ones that pull so hard the rider's arms ache.

Graded stakes-winning rider Jesse Campbell learned valuable lessons from his days as an exercise rider: "From the repetition of exercising horses, you learn how to get comfortable with them. They're high-strung animals, and you can't just jump on and expect to know what you're doing. In the mornings, you're most often working horses by themselves, and in the afternoon the races are tight and crowded. It takes a while to become polished, so working as an exercise rider helps you get you prepared to move on."

Exercise riders spend their mornings at the track, usually arriving around sunrise and finishing up three to five hours later, depending on how many horses they get up on. Having the afternoons free, many pick up additional work at the track as valets, gate crew or as post-parade pony riders, escorting horses to the starting gate on race day.

Some exercise riders are former jockeys who've outgrown their profession, with most weighing in the 130–150 range. While the majority of exercise riders are young, aspiring riders, many former jockeys who've retired due to health reasons or simply aged out of competition, find exercising a rewarding way to stay involved in the business.

Retired jockey Angel Cordero, Jr., one of the all-time greats, doubles as a part-time exercise rider and jockey's agent: "I'm there in the mornings anyway, helping my jockey. I'll often work horses for top trainers like Bobby Frankel or Todd Pletcher. Working horses keeps me fit and healthy, and I still love riding, so it's a pleasure to do it."

Not all exercise riders desire to become jockeys, however. Karyn Rainey is a professional exercise rider, having worked at many tracks, including Emerald Downs, Pimlico, Meadowlands and Rockingham Park. "I usually work six or seven days a week and work 7–10 horses most mornings. If the barn is close to the track, you can do more. I was able to do 15 at Pimlico because they were right there," she explained.

Like most backstretch workers, exercise riders become attached to their horses. Typically earning $10 per gallop, they love it when one of the horses they ride wins a race. "We get a stake, or bonus, when one of our horses wins," Rainey explained.

After mastering galloping, a thriving exercise rider may be allowed to breeze horses, again starting with the short, simple works and building to the longer works on better stock. Depending on the trust level and working relationship, each trainer sorts out who will be up for the workout. Workouts are a key ingredient in the trainer's preparation of the horse for racing.

For Rainey, it depends on the horse and workout distance: "I usually breeze the horses up to three furlongs, then the jock takes over. Breezing

Exercise riders in Southern California enjoy picturesque working conditions (photograph by Thomas Thompson).

is way different than galloping because of the intensity of the workout. When the horse starts to get tired, it takes much more muscle to keep them going strong."

Other than having a strong jockey up for the more physically demanding workouts, there's an injury risk of the horse carrying extra weight at the faster pace. Not many horses break down galloping with the heavier rider up, but there is increased injury risk when a horse runs close to racing pace, so most trainers prefer to put the lighter jockey up.

Another common pathway to the racetrack is through thoroughbred training centers. At these venues, staff break yearlings and teach them the fundamentals, offer rehabilitation for horses coming off the track due to fatigue or injury and provide conditioning for horses returning to the rigors of racing. In most cases, the younger horses are built up through walking, jogging and galloping until they are fit enough to gallop a strong mile. Most are then handed off to the owner's trainer and brought in to the track for more galloping and breezing in preparation for racing.

Breaking horses teaches patience and builds trust between horse and man. Getting up on young horses sharpens a rider's sense of balance and handling skills and builds up the required muscle development and motor skills, the foundation of every good rider.

Particularly through handling yearlings and breaking horses, one learns to have soft hands. It's the first time these young horses have had a bit in their mouth, so a light touch is required so that the horse learns the bit isn't something to fear. Some horses have sensitive mouths and respond only to gentle handling. Anything more aggressive from the rider will likely result in resistance and bad behavior.

Another option for young riders to learn basic riding positioning, balance, handling of reins and whip maneuvering is by training on an Equicizer. The equicizer is a form of mechanical horse with a swiveling neck, which mimics the running action of a horse.

Invented by jockey Frank Lovato, Jr., winner of the 1980 Eclipse Award as the nation's top apprentice, the Equicizer has become one of the few legitimate jockey training alternatives to being up on live horses. As Lovato explained, young riders need all the help they can get building up their skills:

> It's always been a catch-22 with learning the basic riding skills. It's like "who is going to let you ride their horse until you learn, but how do you learn until someone lets you ride." Unfortunately, many beginners have always learned on the actual playing field when the safety of themselves and others is at risk. With an Equicizer, beginners can practice basic skills like reining and whipping techniques in a safe environment, where a mistake won't put someone's life at risk.
>
> When an apprentice jockey starts riding, they may only ride a few actual races a week. With an Equicizer, they can pretend they're riding a hundred races if they want.

In addition to training benefits, the simulated riding motion serves as a rehabilitation tool for jockeys returning from injury, helping them build up fitness without the potential strain and risk of jumping back in the saddle prematurely:

> When a jockey is trying to return to racing from an injury, they are most vulnerable because their strength and fitness are not at their best, [Lovato explained]. The risk and danger is obviously greater with real horses than it is with the Equicizer.
>
> Before the Equicizer, jockeys had to go from a swimming pool, exercise bike or running track, which doesn't leg them up for riding a horse, to riding the horse without the benefit of working on the muscles required to ride. With the jockey not really being fit, that obviously puts them at risk.
>
> Additionally, a doctor might not give you the OK to start riding a real horse until you were 100 percent healed for safety reasons. A doctor can permit you to ride an Equicizer, as it is safe and you are in control. You don't have to over exert yourself. You can take it as easy as you like.
>
> When I first developed the Equicizer in 1982, I made it out of wood and springs, trying to simulate the riding maneuvers of a horse when running. I had a broken leg from a racing accident and was still on crutches. It was over

After a successful riding career of his own, Frank Lovato, Jr., is the creator of the Equicizer, a popular training and rehabilitation device for riders (photograph courtesy of Frank Lovato, Jr.).

three more months before the doctor gave me the OK to ride real horses again. By that time, I had already built up most of my fitness needed for riding. I was able to race ride almost instantly once the X-rays were good. Without the Equicizer, I wouldn't have built up my fitness and would've started at ground zero.

Lovato cites testimonials from Hall of Famers Julie Krone and Angel Cordero among the many jockeys who've benefited from his invention in returning to racing fitness levels. According to the 25-year riding veteran, the device can be found at racetracks across the country, including some

1. Becoming a Jockey

Wearing a handsome suit, 7-year-old Frank Lovato, Jr., proudly joins his father, Frank Sr., in the winner's circle at Pimlico (photograph courtesy of Frank Lovato, Jr.).

of the bigger jockey rooms like Belmont, Churchill Downs, Santa Anita and Saratoga.

The action of the Equicizer is so realistic that it was used extensively in the filming of the movie *Seabiscuit*, where actor Tobey Maguire and jockey Gary Stevens rode the equipment in several close-up racing scenes.

Once a would-be jockey has mastered the breezing process on real horses, the next logical step is training, or "schooling," races. Most racing circuits offer some type of training race, where young horses practice racing. These are typically short races for horses that have not yet raced or need the extra practice breaking from the gate with other horses. The races provide a good opportunity for young riders to get their feet wet. Before granting a jockey license, the track stewards evaluate the prospective rider's ability to ride skillfully and, more importantly, safely. Once approved, they may obtain their conditional riding license.

Kevin Mangold, aboard On Leave, makes his way from the paddock to the post parade (photograph by Debra Gruender).

Expectedly, and naturally so, young riders are anxious to get into their first race. However, they're better off spending more time upfront learning and preparing so that when they start their apprenticeship, they are ready to win races. Getting off to a good start is important. Making bad impressions from rushing to get their career started is far worse than patiently waiting to showcase their finer, developed skills. The danger is that if they fall out of favor with horsemen early, they may never bounce back.

Most riders get into the business in their teens, while their bodies are small, young and capable, which makes Kevin Mangold's actor-turned-rider story unique. With a lengthy acting resume that includes television and movie appearances in shows like *Saved by the Bell*, *Ellen*, *Highway to Heaven* and *Seabiscuit*, a 32-year-old Mangold decided to give riding a try. Trouble was, he didn't have a clue how to get started.

One morning he drove to Santa Anita, one of the country's top tracks, and found his way to Clocker's Corner, the legendary hangout spot for owners and trainers to schmooze and watch the morning's exercise activity. He took a look around, took in the scenery, walked to the center of attention and made a bold announcement. "'If anyone is looking for someone to ride their horses, I'll do it for free.' Most of them told me to forget it or go do something else."

After a moment, one of the men from the crowd came to him and told him he was doing it all wrong. He explained that Santa Anita is the cream of the crop for riders. You can't just walk onto the Dallas Cowboys playing field and hope to play for them. The man suggested Mangold attend jockey school and learn how to ride. It sounded like good advice. He thanked the man and set off to do the research. He was clueless that the informative man was D. Wayne Lukas, the country's all-time leading trainer by earnings and member of racing's Hall of Fame.

So Mangold contacted the Frank Garza Jockey School, one of a few of its kind in the United States. A former jockey himself, Garza had over forty years experience in the racing industry, starting when he was young: "When I was 10, my father, who was a quarter horse trainer, put me up in 'catch weight' races. In these match races, there was no limit on what weight the horse carried, and I was really small. I loved it, so I got hooked on racing early."

Garza enjoyed a 27-year riding career, winning riding titles in Texas and finishing his career on the major California circuit. After hanging up his saddle, he worked his way up the trainer ladder, at one time working in the barn of Hall of Fame trainer Laz Barrera. He opened the jockey school in 1989 and has earned a solid reputation as horseman, instructor and friend.

Many local farms and trainers employ his graduates because of his credentials. "I teach them how to be a jockey from the ground up. They learn everything from basic grooming and stall mucking to race-riding techniques. The kids are exposed to trainers, exercise riders, jockeys, and other professionals in the business. Graduates are released into the industry workforce and are suitable as exercise riders right off the bat," he explained.

Most importantly, he teaches values and respect. Speaking with pride, he explained that graduates from the program enter the market well prepared for success: "They come with skills in breaking horses, galloping horses in company, breezing, breaking horses from the gate, pace and rating, racing tactics and track safety. Once the kids are ready, I take them to the track and introduce them to trainers."

At this jockey boot camp, Mangold learned the basics of jockey horsemanship. He went back to Lukas, who hired him to gallop his horses in Florida. When Mangold finally got his jockey's license, he may have been the oldest apprentice rider to start at age 34. Mangold now rides at West Coast tracks and is working hard to make a name for himself in the racing business.

Another Garza graduate is Francisco Duran. Duran was a very successful apprentice, winning 215 races and finishing as an Eclipse Award runner-up in 2002. He is doing very well on the Bay-area circuit now and well on his way up the ladder of success, making a six-figure income and recently buying his first house.

Growing up in East Los Angeles, the proud young man survived some rough times before learning the trade: "I used to hang out with some thugs when I was younger. I owe a lot to Mr. Garza. If it wasn't for him, I don't know what I'd be doing now. Lots of people have helped me get the opportunities that have made me successful. It takes time to develop your own style. You have to be versatile to ride any kind of horse—no two horses are alike. I was very fortunate to have done so well as an apprentice."

Apprentice jockeys are riders just starting their career. Apprentices, or "bug riders" as they're called because of the asterisk next to their weight assignment, are granted a weight allowance, or concession, for being rookies. Generally speaking, the apprentice is allowed a ten-pound weight allowance until he wins five races, meaning if the horse is assigned 118, the apprentice can tack 108. Depending on the individual state's rule, the apprentice rider is allowed seven pounds until he wins 30 more races. If he has ridden 35 winners prior to the end of his first year from riding his fifth winner, he's allowed five pounds allowance for one year from the date of his fifth winner.

The lighter weight allowance, or "bug," helps them attract business. With the weight break, apprentice riders attract business. Without it, there would be no incentive for horsemen to give the unproven rookies a chance.

Some school-aged apprentice riders set aside their education to ride full-time. Others pull double duty, attending school before racing in the afternoon. Some even make it to the racetrack for morning workouts before school.

One of the top young riders in the country, Brian Hernandez, Jr., won 243 races, including four stakes last year. He won the Eclipse Award as the nation's top apprentice in his first full season of riding. As a high school senior, he pulled triple duty to pursue his dreams:

> I'd get up at 5:00 in the morning to exercise horses at Evangeline Downs by 6:00. I'd ride for awhile and then leave for school, which started around 8:00. I was riding the evening card at Delta Downs, so after school I'd get ready and then drive with my dad, who is also a jockey, for an hour and a half to get there. By the time we finished racing and drive back, we didn't get home until 12:30 or 1:00 in the morning. It was very tiring and really got rough at the end.
>
> I didn't have time for a social life, and I missed out on all the dances and school functions. I was too busy to do anything else but ride horses. But I

love riding so much that it was the sacrifice I wanted to make. If it wasn't for my parents, who've been so supportive through all this, I wouldn't have made it.

Because some riders spend their life working on the backstretch, starting when they're very young, many are undereducated. Graded stakes-winning jockey Lonnie Meche left school early to chase his dream: "I quit school in the 10th grade to be around horses and start working at the track. I knew I could make good money at the track, and being a jockey is all that I ever wanted to do. Don't get me wrong, it's important to finish up school, but this is what I've always wanted to do." Meche was joined by his twin brother, fellow jockey Donnie, as the young duo ventured into the backstretch with hopes of becoming jockeys.

Speaking from experience, veteran riders recommend young riders complete their education, so that when their riding days are over, they have something to fall back on. With the high risk of injury and financial challenges that lay ahead of them, jockeys need a back-up plan. It's far easier to succeed with at least a high school diploma, if nothing else. There's nothing wrong with being an intelligent rider, either.

Hall of Famer Angel Cordero, Jr., emphasized the importance of young riders completing their education: "When you don't finish school, it's like you're lost and alone in the world. You need an education today for when you're done riding. With all the computer jobs, you need some type of education and skills. You can't ride forever, and someday your talent will go away. Most riders don't make enough money to last for a lifetime. When you're out of riding, you're out of business and need something to fall back on."

If an uneducated rider struggles in casual conversation with an owner, the impression he makes may hurt his business. Perceptions can be misleading. If the owner feels the jockey isn't smart enough to carry a conversation, maybe he's not smart enough to ride his horses. Owners would much rather have faith that their intelligent rider is capable of making quick decisions and changing plans in the heat of battle than risk their expensive horse with someone they don't trust.

A lot of young riders just getting started are unprepared for the potential rapid income increase they can experience as a successful apprentice. Having a mentor, or nurturing agent, can help them invest and spend their monies wisely. Too often a youngster is taken advantage of because they lack the worldly wisdom to seek help or shelter some of their money for the hard days that typically follow losing their bug. Particularly if they don't speak English or have someone looking out for them, they can get blindly shafted.

Apprentice Brian Hernandez, Jr., went from schoolboy to a highly paid, sought-after jockey nearly overnight: "I went from earning $400 a week exercising horses to making $4,000 a week racing. It was overwhelming at first, but my mom helped me out a lot. She'd sit me down and helped me understand things and sort out my finances. She helped me open up a checking and savings account and hooked me up with a financial advisor for investments."

Typically, the harder a young jockey works to get up on horses in the morning, the better his afternoon business will do. Occasionally problem horses or chronic losers are skipped over by veteran riders and the only ones willing to pick up the mount are the apprentice riders. While many of today's young jockeys work hard to be successful, not all agree with their work rate.

Trainer Ian Jory, who had $5 million earner Best Pal in his barn, feels many of today's up-and-coming riders are underachieving: "I don't think today's jockeys are as good as they were 15 years ago. I mean guys like Tyler Baze, who works real hard and has done well, are great, but I've seen lots of young guys come up that just don't cut it. I think it's the work ethic that's different. They might tell the stewards they're not feeling well, then go off and play golf. The guys in the past wouldn't do that. They don't work as hard anymore. It's too easy for them. They make too much money."

A riding career can last as long as the jockey feels he can physically handle the physical demands on his body and as long his weight and health allow him the opportunities. While many riders race for twenty years or longer, most step out of their boots in 12–15 years. So many riders are tired and broken down by the time they hit forty, that even though their heart is still in it, their body just can't deliver.

When aging reflexes limit their physical capabilities, veteran riders draw from wisdom and racing savvy to remain competitive. Just like a good wine, some riders like Laffit Pincay and Pat Day keep getting better with age. In a classic example, the legendary Bill Shoemaker won the Kentucky Derby at an amazing 54 years of age with a masterful ride aboard Ferdinand in 1986.

As a 50-year-old jockey with 31 years riding experience under his belt, Perry Ouzts is still one of the top riders on the tough Kentucky circuit. With a combination of good luck and good health, he rides competitively against kids less than half his age:

> I've been lucky to not have any weight problems in my career, and I think it's the key to my longevity. I'm not fighting to pull weight every day or riding weak because I'm starving myself, and I think that's helped me stay competitive so long. I've been lucky to avoid major injuries, too. The longest I've been out is two months.
>
> I still get a thrill out of riding. It's hard to explain, but there's nothing like

the feeling of crossing the finish line first. I still enjoy going out in the mornings, too. I go around and visit all the trainers I ride for, even if they're not sending someone out to work. It's important to just drop by and say hello. They like seeing me every morning, and I'll help them out if I can. Some guys who get older stop going out in the mornings and after a while, their afternoon business drops off.

 I'd like to ride for another 10 years, if I can. I'm closing in on 5,000 wins and I'd like to reach 6,000.

2

Day in the Life

The day is long, hard and challenging for jockeys. The personal sacrifice a jockey makes to follow his dreams controls his lifestyle and affects the lives of those around him. Dominating that life is the hectic schedule of his workday.

For example, jockey Francisco Duran's schedule all but dominates his life: "I have very little family time. I'm often working when everyone else is off, like on weekends and holidays. I'm up and gone to the track, riding horses before most people even wake up. It's taken lots of hard work to get where I am today."

While their schedule has some regular predictability, specifically morning workouts, their afternoons and evenings are dependent on what time the track's race card is held and which races they are signed up for. On an early afternoon racing day, they may be at the track from sunrise to sunset.

With the frantic pace of their lives, personal time management is critical. Family support can play a major role in keeping them on track. Being late or missing workouts in the morning sends a negative message to the expectant trainers. Missing a racing assignment without a bona fide excuse is punishable by racing officials and obviously leads to lost business. Caring and loving spouses capable of helping them with schedules, nutritional management and general health maintenance help make this complicated life equation easier to plan and solve.

Chance Rollins, a graded stakes-winning rider, feels fortunate to have his family's support: "My wife knows how difficult it is for jockeys to keep such a low weight. She cooks healthy for us so that I eat right. Both her and my daughter will eat what I eat to show their support for me. I'm lucky in that I don't have to take drugs, flip or anything, but I do have to eat the right kind of foods and stay with small portions."

Stakes-winning rider Terry Stanton treasures the time he spends with his family: "The biggest downside for me is that my weekends are Monday and Tuesday, while my wife has the traditional weekends off, so we don't have as much time together as regular couples do. I'm a family man, so spending time with her and our two-year-old daughter is important to me."

Choosing to settle down in Texas to be near family has come with some sacrifices for the Stantons: "As is it is now, I make a comfortable living, and we have our own place to take care of, but I probably could've made a bigger name for myself riding somewhere else. But I wanted to be close to my family and chose to stay here. We live about 35 minutes from Sam Houston racetrack. The meet runs for six months here, and then I go to Dallas [Lone Star Park] for a couple of months and stay with my parents. Then I go to San Antonio [Retama Park] for their meet."

When not busy at the track, Stanton spends most of his days keeping up with the ranch: "We've got 21 acres and there's never a dull moment. We've got horses, cows and 16-acres of hay to take care of."

Like most jockeys' wives, Stanton's wife, Michelle, always carries a bit of fear when he takes to the track

> I've seen several accidents that put him down, including one where we thought he might never walk again, but he always bounces back. One time, he took a fall right in front of the grandstands where I was standing and it was just terrible. I can't stand out in front to watch the races anymore. It's just too much for me to handle.
>
> They [jockeys] work so hard. I watch him get up and go out to the track early in the mornings and he gets home real late sometimes after night racing.
>
> As a school bus driver of nineteen-years, she enjoys having him home between runs.
>
> He's a different person on race days than when he's not racing. If he's racing, he'll sit around and rest during the day, then head to the track early, around 2:00 p.m., even though they don't start racing until 7:00, so he can visit with people and get ready to ride. There's a lot of pressure on him. He always wants to do well for the trainers and owners. Even when he doesn't win, he's even-tempered and doesn't get down, or doesn't show it if he does.
>
> On his off days, he's always busy, usually outside working on the place, and it keeps him from eating. If he weren't busy, he'd probably be inside and eating. Like when I'm cooking and he's just sitting around, he'll munch on a bag of chips, knowing that he shouldn't. I've tried talking with him about what he eats, but he's hardheaded sometimes.
>
> He sometimes flips, and I don't approve of it. He doesn't do it often, and I understand why he does it, but I don't like him doing it. It's his life, though, and I've just learned to live with it.

If riders have school-aged children, their quality time with the kids is frustratingly limited. Other than the two or three dark days when the track is closed, they come home after morning workouts and don't likely see the children until after the race card is finished. If it's an evening card, they may be gone before the children get home from school and not return home until after they've gone to bed. On weekends, when the races are typically held in the early afternoon, they may be gone from sunrise until 6:00 p.m. or later.

When hard-working jockey Rene Douglas was riding at Hollywood Park, he was often gone from 5:30 in the morning until 8:00 at night. "It was very hard on my family. Because of the traffic, I couldn't risk leaving the track in the middle of the day. I didn't have enough time on break to make it home and back. I thought about how much I was missing my family every day."

Douglas, winner of the 1996 Belmont Stakes aboard Editor's Note, now primarily rides the meets at Arlington Park, located outside of Chicago, and Keeneland in Lexington. His family stays with him during the summer, then he heads home to Florida in time for his children to start school. He heads south to join them in the fall, picking up stakes assignments, allowing him the luxury of quality family time that most riders miss out on.

When a track opens each year, the racing season is called a "meet." The group of jockeys riding regularly at the track during the meet is called the jockey "colony." Many riders return to the same meets year after year, either because it's close to home, the meet schedule matches up well or they simply enjoy successful riding there. Others move on to bigger and better tracks, which may offer bigger purses. Some go the other way in search of success.

As racing meets close down and new ones start up, many riders begin the migration to new tracks. Most commonly, a few riders at the top of the standings stick around because they're getting all the best horses. Many of the second tier riders move on to other tracks in hopes of getting a head start at their next destination. Those on the lower end of the standings typically pick up more rides in the closing days of the meet because there are more openings. Riding against more talented riders helps developing riders improve their skills, but it's hard on their wallet, unless they win a few races along the way.

In some instances, tracks in the same geographical location run overlapping race meetings, and it's possible to ride at two tracks in one day, if the card doesn't run simultaneously. For example, the late Chris Antley rode a record nine winners on Halloween Day 1987, scoring wins at Aqueduct and Meadowlands.

Jerry Parenti, Jr., who has ridden all across the country, once rode winners at three different tracks in a single day. He explained, "I rode the first couple races at Delaware Park in the early afternoon and won, then shot over to Pimlico and rode the last couple of races and won again. Then I drove to Penn National for the evening races and won somewhere in the middle of the card."

The hectic pace of racing caught up with him, and he's slowed down now, riding just a few horses each week and spending more time with his family. When not at the track, Parenti is busy in the construction business, although his heart remains in racing, "I still have opportunities to ride all over the place, but I just can't travel anymore. I've got a house, wife and kids to take care of. I make good money in construction, but I could make more riding. As a rider, I'd love to do it, but as a husband and father, I just can't."

In the Midwest, many tracks are further apart, and it makes it tougher to travel track to track. In places like Southern California, Kentucky and New York, riders can set up shop generally in one area and ride the major circuits year-round.

Winning races at one track doesn't guarantee a jockeys' success elsewhere. Moving to different tracks can be very challenging. Breaking into a new jockey colony is difficult, because trainers and owners may have no clue about the rider's abilities. So many riders try to follow trainers they already know when moving to another location.

Riders are always on the lookout for racing circuits where they may be more successful. If a top rider gets hurt or retires, the opening may attract riders from other tracks to move in and win business in new territory.

Jockeys will move to wherever they think they'll be successful. Veteran rider Gary Boulanger started his career in 1987 at Tampa and then moved on to meets at Delaware, Thistledown and Aqueduct. "I hoped to find more success out west and drove across country with my buddy, 'Cowboy' Jack Kaenel. I did real well at Longacres, winning a couple of titles there. I also rode well in the Bay area and then tried my luck in Southern California at Santa Anita, Hollywood Park and Del Mar."

Again moving across the country, he later established himself at Calder, Gulfstream and Hialeah in Florida. He spent time riding at Belmont and Meadowlands before a nasty fall broke his back. "The doctors told him me I'd never ride again and would be lucky if I walked. I went through nine hours of surgery and with support from fellow jockeys and close friends Jose Santos, Jerry Bailey and Shane Sellers, I returned to racing 18 months later." After a short stint at Woodbine, Boulanger successfully returned home to Florida where he's been a leader on the circuit for many years.

He was seriously injured again on January 30, 2005, when his horse, In Hand, broke down during the running of the Mac Diarmida Handicap at Gulfstream Park. The veteran rider suffered a serious head injury and underwent surgery the following day to relieve pressure on his brain and remove his spleen. While his condition has stabilized, it's doubtful Boulanger will ever return to the game he loves.

Depending on where they're racing, some riders will move at the end of one meet to a track that's already been up and running for awhile. On circuits where racing occurs year round, trainers are more interested in building consistency with one or two riders they can rely on. Unless they're a top rider or have ridden that circuit before, it will be difficult for them to break in.

When riding at tracks far away from home, jockeys often live out of apartments and hotels, frequently buddying up with another rider or their agent. Long-distance relationships are difficult and challenge any relationship.

During the off-season when the local track is closed, most riders will move on to another meet elsewhere. Married with two preschool-aged children, jockey Rodney Prescott lives in Bethel, Ohio, on the outskirts of Cincinnati. He typically rides at five different tracks during the course of the year. Living 20-minutes from River Downs, commuting is a snap for him. He's 35 minutes away from Turfway Park and makes the daily drive for morning workouts and afternoon racing. When he rides at Indiana Downs, which is 90 minutes from home, he shares an apartment with his agent and another jockey. When the meet at Indiana overlaps with River Downs, he's on the run all day: "I'll breeze a few in the morning at River Downs, stay and ride the day card there, then drive to Indiana Downs for night racing. It gets pretty tiring, but at least I get to go home on the days they're not racing."

When the fall season starts at Hoosier Park, a three-hour drive from home, Prescott rents an apartment and the family joins him for the two-month racing season, although they'll need another plan when the children start school.

The summer meet at Ellis Park lasts six weeks and allows him more time with his family, granted it's far from home:

> I rent an apartment there, and my wife and family stay with me. It's about four or five hours from home, and they race six days a week there, so on the off day we have to drive back and take care of things around the house, like mowing the lawn and stuff, then turn right around and head back. When we're away so much at Ellis and Hoosier, we have to find someone to watch the house for us.
>
> People who don't know racing don't realize how many hours we spend at the track and how much time we spend on the road traveling. Many don't understand that there are a lot of expenses, too, with traveling, lodging and fees we have to pay for agents and valets.

Married jockeys Rosemary Homeister and Jose Ferrer ride on different circuits half the year but still manage to see each other weekly, seldom going more than four days without getting together.

They take turns flying each way from Florida, where Rosemary rides at Calder and toys with her new real estate license, and New Jersey, where Jose hangs his tack at Monmouth. Both Ferrer and Homeister are well established and highly successful at their home tracks and don't want to leave behind the hard work they've put into building up their business. While Homeister is trying her luck in the real estate business every chance she can, Ferrer, a Grade 1 stakes-winning reinsman, explained how the couple makes their long-distance relationship work "I ride the meet at Monmouth while Rosemary is riding in Florida. We take turns flying back and forth. When the meet is over up here in September, I'll go home for a couple of months and ride down there."

Some riders take time off between race meets to spend with family, rest up or work in other areas of the business. One of the more financially rewarding experiences is breezing horses at one of the premier Horses in Training, or HIT, sales. At many of these events, horses are sent at full speed through short workouts. Riders can make $100 per breeze and, in some cases, earn incentive pay for fast times. Some receive additional pay up to one percent of whatever price the horse brings through auction. A busy rider with the right connections can make $5,000 or more in a couple days.

The typical morning for an established jockey starts at the track often before the sun rises. For young jockey Tara Hemmings, the long hours are the hardest part of her schedule: "When I'm working horses at Philadelphia Park, I have a two-hour drive from home, so I have to leave around 4:00 or 4:30. If I'm riding races the night before, by the time I get home I might only get four hours sleep. It's really tiring."

For veteran Grade I stakes-winning rider Joe Bravo, his morning alarm clock goes off at 6:30: "I'll stop by Starbucks for a mocha on the way to the track and usually get in by 6:45. I visit the trainers, horsemen and check on the horses I'm riding. I've had the same agent for over a dozen years, so I don't really have to do too much checking in with him. I'll breeze a few horses most mornings and finish up by 9:00 or 10:00, depending on how much visiting I do."

For most riders, if they haven't already touched base with their agent, or business representative, before they reach the track, that's often first on their agenda. Depending largely on how the jockey and his agent have set up their business, the agent may have already lined up morning workouts for the jockey and will review the schedule with him, or the jockey starts checking in with all the trainers he usually rides for to see which horses are heading to the track for workouts.

Walking the shedrow, or area between barn stalls, jockeys try to sell their business to trainers every morning. Jockeys and their agents hustle trainers to drum up as much riding business as they can. Jockeys must present themselves as being light, fit, wise and strong, while on the inside they may be suffering from dehydration, fatigue, self-doubt and unrelenting stress. If you're not working harder than the next guy, they'll steal your business away in a heartbeat.

A young rider can benefit from the coaching and mentoring of a seasoned jockey agent. When agent Craig O'Bryan, a 30-year veteran, handled the book of Mick Ruis, he helped the young apprentice earn the respect of Southern California horsemen:

> I worked with Mick to help him learn how to work with people, show them respect and make sure he didn't get too cocky with all his success.
>
> As a former wrestler, Mick had a really good work ethic. He had a commodity that everyone wanted, his five-pound bug allowance. We were able to get into good barns and ride some nice horses. I wanted him to work on building good relationships that would last after his apprenticeship was over. After he lost his bug, he had to compete on level terms with guys like Nakatani, Solis and Stevens. It was tough, though, and I felt it was best for him to go somewhere where he could get up on five or six horses a day, because it just wasn't going to happen here. So, he went to Turf Paradise and has been doing great there. I would think he'll be back here in a couple of years and should do real well.

As a young apprentice rider trying to break in at big tracks like Aqueduct, Hawthorne Park and Arlington Park, jockey Tim Thornton feels that getting his foot in the door with trainers is key:

> As a young guy, I have to work harder than everyone else to make it. My agent will initiate contact with the barn first, give them an idea about my racing background, like where I've ridden, top horses I've been on and stakes I've ridden in.
>
> When talking with trainers, you can't be shy. If I was shy, they'd think I'm just some young kid, so I tell the trainer what I can do for them on their horses. I tell them I'm willing to get up on anything. They might have a tough horse, one who is hard to gallop, bucks a lot or tries to run off with the rider. I'll take him, though. I want the trainer to see that I've got heart.

Jockeys try to get mounts on horses that are breezing, or working, that morning. By showcasing his ability to master the horse, he tries to earn the trainer's call on the horse by working, or breezing, the horse. Running near racing speed, the "work" serves many purposes. In addition to the obvious conditioning benefit for the horse, it serves a gauge of the horse's fitness and race preparedness.

For the jockey, the next best thing to having racing experience on a horse is riding him in workouts. They need to understand how the horse moves and how he behaves in certain situations. Riding tough horses in the morning is most important because it gives the jockey a chance to learn the horse's behavior in an attempt to unlock the door to the horse's potential. Certainly a good rider can win first time up on a horse, but there's no substitute for experience with the animal. Despite a thorough description from the owner or trainer of things to expect from the horse, nothing verbal reaches the memory bank like hands-on experience.

Graded stakes-winning jockey Steve Hamilton learns a lot about young horses he breezes: "I work with the trainer to help build up the horse. Because horses are creatures of habit, we want them to be prepared for what happens when they race. They'll have to break out of the gate well, settle into stride, run behind other horses and get dirt thrown in their face. So, when I'm breezing a young horse, I'll put him in those kinds of situations. I always try and save something for the end of the work and will open him up the last eighth, hoping he'll learn to carry that over to his races."

Many jockeys will ride for one or two large barns in the morning. Others may pick up a few workouts from several barns each morning. A jockey may breeze five to ten horses, looking to learn as much as he can about the horse and putting to memory everything he can about the experience. He'll sort out the horse's temperament, gait and stride movements, running tendencies, quirks, likes and dislikes while piloting him around the track.

The trainer must work the horse hard enough to get him fit without overworking him and risking injury or fatigue. How fast the horse works depends greatly on how much the jockey lets him run. With untested horses, many trainers feel the jockeys push the horses a bit too much, believing the jockey wants to know how much "gas," or speed, the horse has prior to accepting a riding assignment on him. Trainers already have a good sense of what kind of horse they have without the need for an all-out effort in the morning.

Some trainers keep close tabs on the weather forecasts so they can move schedule workouts up or back a few days if they desire to keep their horses on dry footing, while others want to take a young horse around the block to see how he handles the slop, or wet track conditions. Many trainers put in a blowout, or short and fast workout, a few days before their horse races.

Handicappers who draw conclusions from the speedy times of some workouts are often mistaken. If the jockey weighs 110 pounds and his horse lights up the track while running hard, how can you compare it with another horse breezing under a 150-pound exercise rider? The times may be two seconds apart, but the horses may be identically fast.

As graded stakes-winning rider Greta Kuntzweiler knows, workout times can be misleading: "There are lots of things that can influence how fast a horse works. How fast he goes depends on what the trainer asked for and how hard the horse is working. If he's working in company, in race-like conditions, he's certain to go a lot faster than if he works by himself. I can tell, even if the time is slow, if the horse is going well, getting tired of struggling with the racing surface. The time isn't as important as how well the horse travels."

While most workouts are uneventful, some are lightning fast and catch everyone's attention. A bullet work, or best time of all the horses working that particular distance that day, from a big horse in preparation for a top stakes race is always exciting news. Sometimes too much of a good thing, however, can be bad. When Funny Cide blitzed five furlongs in :57.8 seconds four days prior to the 2003 Belmont, many blamed the quick workout for his loss. Did the taxing work take too much out of him too close to his Triple Crown bid? It just as easily could've been the aggressive stretch run to draw away from the Preakness field, the sloppy racing surface of the Belmont or its grueling 1½ mile test. We'll never know.

Stakes-winning jockey James "Chris" Herrell has worked many horses throughout his thirteen-year riding career and values the experience of breezing horses:

> Most often I'm asking the trainer what he'd like me to do in the work, like how far and how fast. He might ask me to go a certain distance and keep the horse well in hand. He may ask me to watch for something that he's checking on, like the horse's breathing, soreness or gait. With some trainers, like Steve Flint or Dallas Stewart, guys at the top of the standings, you don't ask any questions, you just do what you're told. They may tell me to go five-eighths in 1:01 and that's exactly what I'll try and do.
>
> If I go out and blow it, go too fast or something, I might not get to ride the horse back. Like the trainer, I want to ride the horse when he's fresh and on his toes.

Trainers value getting constructive ideas from riders after they've worked a horse for them. They rely on the rider's assessment of how the horse was traveling. Jockey feedback on the horse's running action, soundness or unusual tendencies is critically important information for the trainer to aid in charting the right course for the animal. Wise trainers want jockeys to be honest with them after a workout. If the horse doesn't have much ability, they want to know it so that when it's time to race the horse, they can enter him into a spot where he's going to be competitive.

Midwest-based trainer Jere Smith, Jr., recognizes the importance of jockeys' suggestions: "Well, you want honesty, which can be hard to find in some riders. Trainers know the weakness of their horse, for the most part, but if the jockey can give you an edge on equipment, like blinkers, bit changes or other small things, it can make a big difference."

Trainer Bruce Kravets, a perennial standings leader in Pennsylvania, is looking for riders with a good attitude in the morning: "I want them to be on time in the morning, so we can keep on schedule with everything. I want them to have some knowledge about horses. I want to hear from them how the horse is going and if they think there are any problems with the horse and where the problem might be so I can check on it. I don't like it when the rider comes back and tells me the horse is OK when he's not. I know a lot of riders with mediocre skills who have a good attitude and have done a lot better than riders with more skill and bad attitudes."

Jockeys don't get paid for "working," or breezing, horses and some who are struggling to get mounts may also gallop horses in the morning to increase their exposure and make some money. Conversely, some trainers try and save a few bucks by coercing jockeys into doing the morning gallops for free as well—work usually reserved for the paid exercise riders. The double duty of riding gallops and workouts can leave the jockey tired and overworked.

As a high-percentage rider with over 70 stakes wins to his credit, John Grabowski regularly rides at New York's Finger Lakes, where it's common practice for jockeys to gallop horses for free

> It's almost mandatory here to gallop horses in the morning if you want to ride in the afternoon. It started many years ago. Back then, some jockeys would do anything to get in with the barn. So, they started doing gallops, which saved the trainers money and got the jockeys' foot in the door. In order to compete, other guys started doing it and before long, everyone was galloping. It's been that way for as long as I can remember.
>
> To me, it's abuse of the rider because it wears us down. But I can't blame anyone but ourselves [the jockey colony]; we've set a bad precedent. For many of the riders, they'd be making just as much money if they were paid exercise riders somewhere as they do riding just a few races here every day. Even though our purse structure is better now, we're not getting the best riders because of it.
>
> Despite my success, to be told that if I don't come over and gallop someone's horses, they won't ride me in the afternoon is frustrating for me. If I don't go out and gallop, I won't be a top rider. But to go out and risk your life for it just doesn't make sense. It's just part of the way horsemen have control over us. If I don't want to gallop a bunch of horses every morning, I'll send someone to gallop the horses for me, and I have to pay for it. At the end of the season, I might have paid $4,000 in gallop fees. This just isn't right. My job is to race in the afternoon, not gallop horses.

Like racing, working horses can be dangerous. Breezing young horses, in particular, can be risky, as they lack the experience and often spook at the unexpected. Young horses are required a couple of breaks, or starts, from the gate, including one official workout, before being allowed to race.

The area where the horses enter the track from the barn area is typically the most dangerous area during the mornings as horses are both coming and going. With so many high-spirited animals excitedly approaching the track, there's a lot of misbehaving in the high-traffic area, placing horse and rider at risk of accident and injury. A jockey always has to be alert for loose horses.

Horses being ponied sometimes break loose from their handler and occasionally dump their rider, which can really scatter the chickens. The loose horse often tries to find his way back to the barn and may dangerously make a mad dash, against traffic, to find his way back home. Most tracks have some form of alarm system, like sirens and flashing lights, to alert riders of the impending danger. The outriders do a great job of providing safety and corralling the runaway horse.

Loose horses are a serious danger to horses and their riders, and every effort is made to protect all parties, whether it be in morning workouts or during races. On August 26, 2000, jockey Stacy Burton was permanently disabled when her horse collided with another. Burton, a former teacher who chased her dreams to become a professional jockey at age 36, was aboard Lot O Love in a $2,000 claiming event at Prescott Downs. After another entrant, Pacific Wind, fell on the sloppy racing surface, the disoriented horse got up and started running the opposite way into traffic. The two horses collided in a head-on collision. The accident left Burton in a coma for three weeks. She tragically suffered severe brain damage and now requires constant medical care.

The typical morning routine for jockeys usually lasts three to five hours. Most will try and take at least one morning off per week, usually a nonracing day, to rest and heal from aches, pains and weary muscles. If it's a nonracing day, once the morning's work on the backstretch is done, the jockey has the rest of his day free.

The backstretch, the area of the racetrack seldom seen by public, is a warm and friendly place. It's often home to a thousand head of horses or more and is usually located behind or beside the racing oval, well separated from the racing fans.

"Life is different on the backstretch than anywhere else," says Grade I stakes-winning rider Shaun Bridgmohan.

> The people that work there—the grooms, exercise riders and trainer—are very dedicated to taking care of the horses they're charged with. Work on the backstretch occurs seven days a week all year long. The racing business doesn't sleep.
>
> Having worked as a groom and exercise rider before, I know how hard those people work, too. After I win a stakes race, I'll stake the groom and exercise rider. At one of the bigger barns that I work for, I won about 20

races for them during the season and to show my appreciation, I brought in food and threw a little party for them.

To begin with, the racetrack environment is different from any other. The backstretch community is a unique culture within the racetrack environment. The connection between horses and the people who care for them is a tight bond. The lifestyle of backstretch workers revolves entirely around the industry. For some workers, the racetrack is more than just a job; it's home. Some grooms live right at the end of the barn row in tiny apartments, overlooking the stalls they are responsible for.

Backstretch workers live a tough life, with long hours and low income. Fortunately, there are many programs available to support jockeys and other racetrack personnel. One such program is the Race Track Chaplaincy of America, or RTC. Formed in 1971, the RTC services the racetrack community at more than 70 tracks across the country.

Former jockey and the only Eclipse Award–winning reverend in the country, Ed Donnally, is the director of development for the organization. Donnally won the 1984 Eclipse Media Award for his work with the Dallas Morning News. He joined the ministry in what he describes as "the best career move I ever made."

Mike Smith is a full-time pastor and part-time chaplain at Emerald Downs racetrack near Seattle. With 25-years ministry experience, he spends much of his time away from the church at the racetrack, working firsthand with grooms, exercise riders, trainers and jockeys.

Grooms make up the largest population of backstretch workers. "I think 90–95 percent of them are Hispanic, and many of them barely speak English," Smith estimated. Concerned, he feels many are there illegally: "I'd guess with confidence that one-third are not U.S. citizens. They probably have false ID, and many are very young, just in their teens."

In most cases, the chaplain provides an initial evaluation with clients. Counseling is provided for those with personal, emotional and spiritual needs. Some clients are referred back into the community for more complex issues. He further supports the racetrack community by providing social alternatives to the long days and the hard lifestyle. He's organized pool, dart and horseshoe tournaments and the very popular Cinco de Mayo dinner dance. He coordinates the ESL (English as a Second Language) program. Sitting on bales of hay, he helped one backstretch couple with pre-marriage counseling and performed the ceremony right in the winner's circle.

Finding healthy activities is better than the alternatives. "It helps keep them busy when they're not working. It helps keep them out of trouble," Smith explained. "For some workers, the downtime between shifts leads to temptations. Alcohol, drugs and gambling are all threats to these people."

Some RTC chaplains hold prayer sessions in the jockeys' room before the day's races begin, although Smith finds the jockey colony a tough nut to crack: "They're a strong-willed group. They're very competitive, and it's a challenge to build relationships with them. They're sometimes as high strung as the animals they ride."

It's in the best interest of all horsemen and the industry to get racetrack workers and their families involved in programs like Chaplaincy, Winners Foundation, Backstretch Employees Assistance Team, Grooms Elite, Kids to the Cup and similar programs whenever possible.

At most tracks, the backstretch barn area is large, and movement from barn to barn can be time consuming on foot. Many jocks ride bicycles or hop aboard golf carts to scoot from one trainer's barn to another.

Most tracks have some sort of backstretch café that provides a relaxed atmosphere and resting place for jockeys during their morning routine, between workouts or prior to heading to the jocks' room for the day's racing. Racetrack kitchens are known to offer great food, reasonable prices and as many stories as patrons are willing to hear.

On an afternoon racing day, riders may head to the jockeys' room straight away after morning works are done. Time permitting, they may hit the jockeys' quarters bunkroom for a nap. If it's evening racing, they might head home to rest or run errands. Either way, if they need to reduce, or lose weight, before weighing in for their first ride, they must build time for it in their schedule. Depending on how much weight they have to "pull," or lose before riding, it could take hours, and there's no time to spare.

Jockey rooms across the country differ greatly in size, quality and comfort. At their worst, they are small, cramped, short on accommodations and uncomfortable. At their best, they provide all the amenities and comforts of home with plenty of space for all.

For decades, jocks' rooms across the country were an afterthought and provided only the basic locker room necessities. According to Pat Day, he's seeing improvements: "Jocks' rooms haven't been on the top of the priority list, but it's getting better now. New tracks and rebuilding of old ones has improved the quality of jocks' rooms. Arlington Park's is top notch with all the amenities, although it's long and narrow. Belmont Park's is also large and spacious."

The jockeys' room is an interesting melting pot of cultures, excitement, disappointment, hope and frustration. It's a world unto itself. Everyone from young, baby-faced teenage boys to gray-haired, grizzled veterans spend countless hours confined together, as they battle each other race after race. Unique to the racing world, these gladiators return to the same locker room after competing against each other.

Dean Sarvis is a graded stakes-winning rider who likens the jockeys' room experience to that of other professional sports:

> Imagine two baseball teams going into same dugout after every inning, sitting next to guys they're competing against, and imagine the problems that could bring on. That's what it's like in the jockeys' room. Ask any other pro athlete if they could handle it, and I'd bet they couldn't.
>
> We share locker space five feet away from the guys we compete against, 10 times a day. There can be up to 40 guys in a small area. Although we joke around and try to keep things on the lighter side, nobody likes to lose. Only one guy comes back a winner after every race, so there's 10 guys who just lost. Our adrenaline is pumping and emotions are high; there's lots of emotions at stake. We're all trying to get the best mounts. Someone might steal my horse, and I'll steal another mount away from someone else, but on the track we really try to take care of each other, because it's such a dangerous sport. I think we do really well together, considering the situation.

The relationship between jockeys is truly one of camaraderie and friendship. While they are fierce competitors on the track, the atmosphere in the jocks' room is usually relaxed and jovial. Certainly, things can get stirred up in a hurry when someone feels they've been unfairly slighted. As Sarvis explained, tempers flare when someone has been cut off or feels like they've been put in a bad spot: "Sure, tensions can get high when guys get upset with each other. If someone feels they were cut off or put in a dangerous position, he might say something to the rider, but there's really very seldom any physical confrontation. If somebody gets out of control, it usually cools off pretty quickly. Everyone just treats each other with respect like professionals should. It's a tribute to jockeys that we get along so well, given the small space we have to share."

By the time the day's racing is done, the jockey may have put in a grueling 12-hour day at the track. When he leaves, weakened, tired and dehydrated, sunrise is just around the corner. Racing never sleeps. Day after day, the grind continues with hope and promise of tomorrow's winners.

3

WINNING IS EVERYTHING

The most talented athletes in every sport possess three common attributes—raw talent, unquestionable passion for the sport and relentless determination. The jockey profession is no different. There are plenty of good riders out there with raw talent; sometimes it's wasted because they don't have the passion or drive to excel.

While a great jockey can't make an underachieving nag win, a bad ride can certainly seal the fate of a good horse. Simply put, a jockey must do more good than harm. After all, it's called horse racing, not jockey racing. Jockey Francisco Duran summed it up nicely: "Win and you are the hero. Lose and you're the bad guy."

From their initial win, the taste of victory leaves the rider endlessly thirsty for more. Winning becomes an addiction. There isn't a jockey alive who doesn't love the thrill of entering the winner's circle each and every time. It doesn't matter if it's a $4,000 claimer or a million dollar stakes race, their first win or their thousandth; for a moment in time they are in the racing spotlight. After all, winning is what it's all about.

"Jockeys are fierce competitors," described retired stakes-winning rider Mike James. "As a rider, you've got to hit the home run every time up. There's only one winner a race, and no one remembers the name of the rider who finishes second."

Jockeys describe the thrill of winning as the most incredible feeling in the world—an adrenaline rush like no other. As graded-stakes winning rider Jon Court shared, "If you like thrill rides, it's like the feeling of riding the greatest roller coaster ride ever made when you bring home a winner."

Jockey Casey Fusilier described the sensation of winning as an unbelievable adrenaline rush: "It's just a thrill to be racing, whether you're trail-

3. Winning Is Everything

Christophe Soumillon, aboard Shirocco, celebrates the thrill of victory after the 2005 Breeder's Cup Turf (photograph courtesy of New York Racing Association. Adam Coglianese, photo contributor).

ing the field or out in front. Winning is just icing on the cake. It's hard to explain the feeling and difficult to put into words, but when you enter the winner's circle, the adrenaline rush is just overwhelming."

When a rider breaks his maiden, or wins his first race, the victor is ceremoniously welcomed by his racing compatriots by getting "creamed," as they call it. The traditional initiation usually includes anything from eggs, ketchup, mustard, Vaseline and shaving cream to whatever else is handy. The celebratory welcoming typically happens somewhere between the winner's circle and jocks' room and is often accompanied by cheers from racing fans in witness. Jockeys are notoriously known for "painting" first-time winners, by yanking their trousers and coating them in shoe polish.

One of the hottest young apprentice riders in the country, Eric Camacho, won his first race April 18, 2004, aboard Love Game at Pimlico. On his way back from the winner's circle to the jocks' room, he was met by a horde of jockeys waiting to welcome him into the winner's club: "Even though I heard something like this could happen, it caught me by surprise. They hosed me down, dumped eggs on my head, threw baking powder on me, sprayed me with shaving cream and painted me with shoe polish. I guess they used just about anything they could get their hands on."

All jockeys dream of riding in the Kentucky Derby, the most exciting two minutes in all of sports, and when that dream becomes a reality, it's an emotionally charged time in their lives. With $50 million in lifetime purse earnings, Gary Boulanger is no stranger to the winner's circle or big races.

When Boulanger took a leg up for his first Kentucky Derby ride in 1998 about Chilito, he was overcome with a euphoric feeling unlike anything he'd experienced, "You hear about it, you can read about it, but you really can't even imagine it. When you make that last turn from the paddock to the track and see the huge crowd and hear them all singing that song (My Old Kentucky Home), it just overtakes you. The hair on my arms was standing up and I had a lump in my throat. Tears were running down my cheeks."

Winning races isn't easy, though. With most race fields carrying six to ten horses, losing is the norm. In fact, winning at a 20 percent clip is the sign of a top rider. The national average for riders is near 9 percent. Winning one of four over the length of a race meet is a rarity and 30 percent is unheard of. Hall of Famer Kent Desormeux won an amazing 598 races in 1989, setting the single season mark for races won. Desormeux was an apprentice rider at the time, riding day and night and winning on 26 percent of his mounts. If not for a season-ending injury in December, he certainly would've won well over his goal of winning 600 races that year.

One of the country's top athletes, and arguably the best jockey, in the 19th century was an African American rider named Isaac Murphy. "Honest Ike," known for his high integrity, rode without the benefit of a racing whip and motivated his horses with his voice and riding style. While racing records from that era are incomplete, Murphy won a staggering 44 percent of his recorded mounts and was the first jockey inducted into racing's Hall of Fame. Each year, the Isaac Murphy Memorial Award is given to the country's highest percentage winning rider.

Completely dominating northern California racing over the past two decades, jockey Russell Baze exemplifies the high-percentage riding champion. He's won record numbers of jockey titles at Bay area tracks with winning percentages consistently in the high 20's and won the Isaac Murphy Award the first nine years it was awarded, losing for the first time in 2004 after winning 27.1 percent of his races.

3. Winning Is Everything

With over 9,000 wins to his credit, Russell Baze, shown here interviewing with TVG, is closing in on Laffit Pincay, Jr., as the winningest rider of all time (photograph by Thomas Thompson).

The veteran rider simply typically visits the winner's circle several times a day:

> I really like winning. To hang up the numbers I have, you have to put in the time, though. You have to be determined, and I have the drive to excel. I work really hard to keep it up. I work six mornings a week and I'm at the track for 12 hours on race days. I just ride better in the afternoons if I'm up on horses in the morning. It helps me keep my timing and internal clock in tune. I have to stay in shape and mentally sharp all the time. I don't drink, smoke or carouse around. I really watch how much I eat, too. One thing I know for sure, it's a lot easier to get to the top than it is to stay at the top.

As far as identifying the key to winning, the Hall of Famer feels it has to do with staying sharp and riding with confidence: "The horses can feel it. The confidence I give them might help them go through a hole, rather than balking at it."

Like other sports, riders endure hot streaks and cold streaks. Even a top rider can fall out of the groove and struggle. Riders typically think of their work in weeks. For example, a top rider might hope to win ten races a week. For lower-end riders, one trip to the winner's circle a week may be a more reasonable target.

Graded stakes–winning jockey Chris Emigh, a winner of 176 races in 2004, shared that the emotional rollercoaster of winning and losing goes with the territory: "Hitting a losing streak gets you a little bit down. If I go a week without winning, maybe riding 30–35 horses, that's a bad week. You don't make any money riding losing horses. I try and stay positive and do positive self-image thinking of winning races. You can't let yourself get down or hang your head; you've got to get yourself up. You might be feeling down one day, then snap back and win a $100-grander and be on top of the world again. It's like one day you're a zero, and the next day you're a hero."

Because year-round racing nowadays has worn down racing stock, the average number of horses in each race, about eight, continues to shrink. Shorter fields mean fewer opportunities for jockeys, making it tougher for the low-end riders to get mounts because the majority of rides go to the track's top-10 jockeys.

When a rider gets hot, it can do magic for their career. The more they win, the more they get noticed. The increased recognition leads to better horses. Better horses means more wins. Conversely, struggling low-end riders can see their business all but dry up if they aren't getting quality, or "live," mounts.

John McKee, one of the country's best young riders, benefited from a hot streak last fall: "Like most guys who lose their bug, I went through a bit of a drought after losing the weight break. But I got hot last November and started winning bunches of races and my career just took off again. Winning caught the horsemen's eyes and got me up some really good horses that I might not have otherwise ridden. Thanks to the streak, I've been blessed to having some great opportunities now."

Sometimes horses and riders come together to form an unbeatable partnership. Such was the case for veteran stakes-winning rider Perry Ouzts, "In the 1970s, I rode this filly named Hy Carol. She won 26 races in her life, and I was up for every single one of them, including 19 stakes wins. There were times when someone else rode her, but she never won with anyone else, just me."

For Hall of Famer Chris McCarron, building relationships with horses and sharing in their development was one of the highlights of his brilliant career:

> One of the most enjoyable parts of my career was being involved with the young horses and watching them develop into something special. Getting up on a youngster and watching them learn and grow, showing their class and staying with him as his racing career progressed was a thrill.
>
> I rode Precisionist as a two-year-old and had the pleasure of riding him throughout his racing career. He was a tricky horse because he was so sensi-

tive. All I had to do was move, just twitch a muscle, and he'd take off, thinking it was a signal of time to go. He had such an explosive move, it was really a thrill to be involved with horses like that.

The key to making it big in the jockey game really isn't about being the most skilled rider; it's about getting the best horses to ride. Every top jockey shares credit for success with his jockeys' agent, whose job it is to get the jockey up on those live horses. When a jockey hires an agent, the agent acquires the jockeys' "book" and assigns the rider to horses at the time of entry, done a few days before each racing day. Most agents represent two riders and top-level jockeys are usually a one man show.

Hall of Fame jockey Earlie Fires attributes his former agent as being one of the keys to his early success: "I had Paul Blair as my agent for over 25 years. He helped me immensely. He was really on top of his game and kept me on live horses over the years. I wouldn't have had this kind of success without him."

Some outstanding jockeys never get the chance to reach their true potential because they don't get the top horses a strong agent should bring them. Each jockey feels he should be getting up on the best horses, and the jockeys' agent works hard to secure what he thinks are the best spots. No doubt, there are some very good riders hidden behind mediocre agents, who could be doing a lot better if they were only getting more chances on better horses.

For decades, jockeys were taken advantage of by trainers and owners prior to agents entering the equation. Historically, jockeys could be hired and fired many times over while the trainer looked to secure the services of the best jockey available. When a lesser jockey made the commitment to ride the horse, the trainer may still have been shopping around, leaving the rider stranded without a mount if the trainer landed a better rider at the last minute. Now, with a middleman in their corner, jockeys focus on riding while the agent works the business. However, the best agent won't be successful unless he has a rider capable of getting the job done on the track.

Understanding racetrack politics and how to play the game for maximum opportunity is critical. Unwary riders with lousy agents may end up working every horse in the barn in the morning and get stuck on every 30–1 longshot without a prayer in the afternoon. This is very frustrating for jockeys and runs some of them out of the business. It's even harder to make a living at it when you don't have much chance of winning races. There's an old saying in the business: "Good riders aren't made, they're born." To this, most jockeys wonder why they're working so darn hard to make it.

Agents line up workouts for their jockeys with trainers most every morning. Most jockeys will be up for five or six workouts each day, arriving to the track at sunrise and working for three to five hours, depending on how many horses they get up on.

Agents can play a variety of roles with their jockeys, depending on how deep and strong the interpersonal relationship is and what the jockeys' needs are. In some aspects, the agent serves as coach and manager, helping guide the jockey to making wise decisions for the good of his career. They can also provide a sounding board for the jockey and serve as their best critic.

The agent might need to pick the rider's spirits up when he's in the dumps or suffering through a dry spell. He might help the jockey keep his head on straight when he's been sat down, or suspended, by the stewards, or get the rider focused when he's busy riding eight or ten horses day after day.

Agent Randy Wiseman handles the book for a couple of young riders. When the going gets tough, it's his job to help them stay positive: "It's my job to put the jockey in the position of riding good horses. If he's not winning, I'll compliment him when he gets off the horse, tell him he's doing a good job and to keep riding well. If the jockey is having a bad day, or not getting enough good rides, I'll try and pump him up and reassure him that we're going to get through it. To help our business, I might try and get better horses from our customers or convince new people to give this kid a shot."

Many agents help guide their jockeys through life's challenges outside of racing. Because their profession takes such a demand of time, effort and concentration, some riders don't have the time, energy or knowledge of what to focus on when they're not at the track. A jockey may need help acquiring lodging, guidance with financial matters and staying on track with a healthy and wise lifestyle.

Occasionally, a retired jockey will step into the agent's role as a second career. After a 15-year riding career and working as a trainer for several more, Steve Goldsmith became a jockeys' agent: "It's a natural progression for the profession. It was an easy transition for me because I know what riders go through, I know how to talk with trainers and I know how the business works. I think my experience helps me do a better job handling book for my riders."

Like most aspects of the racing industry, most agents are male. One of the few exceptions is Cathy Leuszler, who calls Ohio's Beulah Park home. Leuszler proclaimed she's done every job on the backstretch: "I've been a groom, exercise rider and trainer; why not become an agent? I got started four years ago when I was asked to take on a female rider as a favor."

Having spent most of her life at the track, she's paid her dues along the way: "I've dealt with prejudices all my life. I had to learn to put up with sexual remarks and innuendos for years. But really, you're either a good agent or a bad agent; gender doesn't matter. Most horsemen respect me because of my knowledge and experience."

A good agent knows most horses at the meet, which could be one thousand or more, and keeps tab on every barn's progress. They need to know which horses are going to be running and how well they might do. They pay close attention to the condition book, looking for spots where they might place their riders on live horses. With good predictability, they can speculate which barns are going to produce winners next time out.

As a top agent for over forty years, Tony Matos has worked with some of the country's best riders, including Angel Cordero, Kent Desormeaux, Corey Nakatani, Laffit Pincay, Pat Valenzuela and the late Chris Antley. He finds that keeping open and honest relationships with his jockey and trainers to be key ingredients to success: "Over time, you get to be close with your jockey, and it becomes more like a family relationship than just business. I try and maintain a good relationship with the trainers by keeping track of their horses. I check in with them and find out what everyone is doing."

"I have the pleasure of handling book for Victor Espinoza now." Espinoza is best known as the rider of War Emblem, near Triple Crown winner of 2002. Matos further explained how they keep their customers satisfied: "We stay in touch with people, and it's important for us to honor our commitments. We try and make people as happy as we can. After we win, we'll stake the exercise rider, groom and foreman to show our appreciation for their hard work."

An early morning trip to the backstretch will find jockey agents busily at work. Most can be seen peering over their condition book and glued to their cell phone, walking from barn to barn trying to secure business for their riders. Agents and trainers scrutinize over the fine print of the book, trying to find horses that best fit the race conditions. Distance, grass or dirt racing surface, conditions and weights are all key factors to be considered.

As an agent for over 35 years, Harry "the Hat" Hacek has seen it all. Hacek, who obtained the nickname from friends who enjoyed his wide variety of hats, has worked with many of the country's best riders—Steve Cauthen, Eddie Delahoussaye, Chris McCarron, Alex Solis and Gary Stevens. He currently hustles book for Hall of Fame jockey Kent Desormeaux.

As a racetrack fixture, Hacek gets an early start to his day:

> I'm usually up at 4:30 and at the track by 5:15. I'll talk with trainers, owners and friends while pitching business for my rider. It really pays to do your homework. I keep charts, make my own notes and keep extensive records. I

use the records to try and match up the best spots for horses in the condition book. I'll go the trainer and make suggestions of what I think are good spots to run. Some get offended, but most appreciate the help.

I'll look to find where other riders might have a conflict. If they're overbooked with two or three options in a race, we might want to pick up one of the horses. Depending on the trainer, I'll accumulate the entries and take them to the race office. After we're done with entries, I usually go home for lunch, then I'm back the track for the afternoon racing. At the races, I'll socialize with our contacts, and make notes on the racing. At the end of day, I've probably put in 12–14 hours.

Handling the book for a new rider can prove to be a challenging proposition. Agent Steve Goldsmith is now hustling book for Travis Wales at Turf Paradise:

> If you have a new rider, like my situation with Travis, where few people know him, I have to work harder than if I had a veteran rider. With Travis, he's got a ton of talent, but he's new to the area. So, I need to convince others that he's as good as I know he is. I have to help him get into good barns so that he gets a chance to ride good horses.
>
> For riders who've been here for 10 or 15 years, riding for the same barns, it doesn't matter how good my guy is, we won't be able to break in there because the veteran jocks are pretty much locked in with the barn. But I like to hustle for a guy who can really ride and this kid can ride. I don't doubt that the cream will rise to the top.

Contrary to popular belief, riders may choose one horse over another not necessarily because they think that the horse has a better chance of winning, but because of what that decision represents in future mounts. If they're riding for two trainers and one has a stable of 10 horses and the other has a barn of 50, the choice is easy. They often choose the larger barn, even if this particular horse might not measure up to the smaller stable's horse in this spot. Now, depending on the jockeys' relationship with the trainer, it might not matter that he takes the other assignment. The last thing a jockey wants to do is fall out of favor with his best customer.

Making long-term decisions at the cost of short-term opportunities is a difficult bridge to cross for most people, jockeys included. Sometimes a jockey has the option to ride one of two or more horses in a race. He may have the option, as first-call rider to a certain trainer, to ride horse A. Horse A might be a quality horse the rider has won on before, but for the race being entered for today, he's a cut below the competition and an unlikely winner. Horse B may be the live horse and one to beat in this race. The jock may have even won on him before. Horse B, however, is from a smaller barn.

While the jockeys' chances of getting his picture taken this time out are better with Horse B, the wise play is Horse A. The jockey has an alliance with the trainer of Horse A. If he passes up the ride here, he may not be given a chance to ride this horse back again. More so, he may lose opportunities to ride other horses in the barn if the trainer gets upset. Horse B's trainer is understandably trying to land the best rider. As a trainer with a smaller barn, he may be more pressured to win and may go back to the better rider next time, even if the jock passed this time to stick with his top barn.

Even if they pick the right horse for the race at hand, jockeys must consider the future ramifications of the selection. Is the horse coming up to his best race, or is he tailing off? Is the jockey likely to get future rides on this horse? Does the horse have "conditions," or allowances for wins at certain prices or within certain time frames, left to fill? Jockeys, and their agents, must keep one eye on today and the other one, smartly, on tomorrow.

Some agents are so sharp with their knowledge of the horseflesh on the track that they know the most productive racing spots for a trainer's horses. If their relationship with trainers is healthy, his suggestions may be encouraged and welcomed. The agent has the advantage of working with several trainers and often has the inside scoop on what's happening in other barns. He may know which horses are going to be entered in certain spots and which horses are going to be sitting on the sidelines. Some trainers, however, feel the agents are blowing smoke and are just trying to get their rider more mounts.

Some insiders see jockey agents as a nuisance, particularly trainers. Some horsemen perceive them as part-time, self-employed hustlers making a good living off the success of others. Compared to most other occupations on the track where people work very long hours and make little money, many feel agents have it pretty easy.

Jeff Greenhill, a stakes-winning trainer from Kentucky, feels many agents don't have the right work ethic:

> Some agents must've been born to tell lies. Most trainers don't even like talking with them. The bad agents seem to come out just to play cards, sitting around waiting for their phone to ring and the good ones are worth their weight in gold.
>
> There are a few guys, like Steve Elzey, the agent for the top two guys here [Turfway] in Dean Sarvis and apprentice Rodolfo Ignacio, who really do their homework. He knows which horses are going into which races and which ones are most likely to win. He can spin you and still leave you laughing when he's done. All he wants to do is win.

As he explained, Greenhill would like to see agents take a more personal approach to their business: "My horses are kind of like my kids because I spend so much time with them and watch them grow up. It would behoove agents to ask me about how they're doing once in a while, rather than just poking their head to ask if they can ride him next time. There must be a better way of doing it."

With agents receiving a 25 percent to 30 percent cut of the jockeys' winnings, there's plenty of incentive for both jockey and agent to visit the winner's circle often. After wins, some agents follow the tradition of bringing donuts to the trainer's barn the next morning, demonstrating appreciation for the barn's work in getting the horse prepared to win.

Shelly Moran, a veteran jockey on the Kentucky-Ohio circuit is in the minority of riders working without an agent: "I don't have an agent and haven't had one for several years. I've had a few over time, but didn't have much luck with them. It seemed like I was already outworking them and getting more rides on my own. In fact, they may have hurt me rather than helped me."

As she explained, Moran finds having full control beneficial to her career: "I already know my schedule every day when I get to the track. I carry around my condition book, keep track of which horses should be racing soon and stop by all my trainers each morning. I think they respect me more now that I'm making contact with them personally every morning. It is a bit time consuming and it's hard work. Some mornings, I'm working up to a dozen horses, riding the day races in Ohio and the night program at Turfway or Mountaineer."

Similarly, jockey Joe Steiner, a Grade I stakes–winning rider, recently went two years without an agent before recently hiring Marcus Guidry to hustle book for him: "Some of the guys I've had in the past didn't even want to work and they weren't helping me at all. I've been doing as well, if not better, on my own. I was able to be more selective on the horses I rode and enjoyed working for people who raced their horses where they belonged."

The trainer–jockeys' agent relationship is one of the most politically charged settings at the track. Deals are made with a handshake and a smile. There's no written agreement and zero job security for anyone. Even for jockeys who are fortunate enough to be tabbed as the primary rider for a trainer, the security of regular rides comes without promise or guarantee.

The agent tries to convince the trainer of the jockeys' skills and abilities. He'll boast how well the jockey fits the particular horse, especially if the jock has breezed the horse before. They often push the limits of suggestion, sometimes actually begging for business.

Scotty McClellan, an agent for 32 years, currently handles book for top Southern California jockeys Alex Solis and David Flores. He values the relationships he's built with trainers over the years:

I've worked with really good people over the years. Even though the jockeys I represent have changed over the years, I've been lucky to have great customers in guys like Charlie Wittingham, Bobby Frankel, Ron McAnally, Richard Mandella and Bruce Headley. I have riders that fit most of their horses.

For trainers with 40 or 50 horses, it's hard for them to keep track of everything, so I help them find spots or remind them of stakes nominations and closings. I get rewarded when they put my riders up in the big races.

Agents often take heat from the trainer and/or owner for unexpected losses, bad rides and missed opportunities. Undoubtedly, agents must be thick skinned. While taking the heat, the agent plays middleman, as sometimes it's the jockey who is upset that the horse didn't run well and feels like he was misled into riding a "dog" when he was told he was getting a tiger.

Some agents have the luxury of helping their jockey sort out which of two or three horses to pick in each race, while others pound the pavement looking to pick up any three horses for the day, no matter if they're all hopeless plodders that can't run a lick.

When it's time to make decisions over which horse to ride, jockeys and their agents sort through all the factors of the race at hand. It's not just a matter of which horse is better. They must consider which horse fits the race best. Which horse will handle the distance best. What if the track turns up sloppy? Would one of them likely be scratched if the track were off? Could the race be moved off the turf and onto the dirt? Will the pace be favorable for a particular running style?

Building upon his Triple Crown success, jockey Stewart Elliott is getting better horses nowadays and relies on his agent to help steer him in the right direction. After splitting with his former agent of four years, Ray Lopez, he's branching out into new areas:

I've had Joe Rosen as my agent for almost a year now. He helps me get new business and keeps my racing business straight. It's his job to keep me out of jams and try not to upset anyone. He keeps in touch with everyone we work with.

> If I have first call with two trainers and things are equal, like they both have 20 horses in their barn, the agent will check with both of them see if they're going to go in this certain race. If they're both in, Joe and I will make the decision of which horse to take together. Sometimes I'll ride the horse we think is better and other times we might take one horse to avoid upsetting the people. Maybe the trainer already made a commitment to the owners and we'll choose that horse, even if he doesn't have as good a chance as the other one, just to keep the peace.

Trainers may have a particular jockey they like to use as their primary, or first-call, rider. Most trainers have one or two others they use as back-up when their main man isn't available. In this way, they may be working with one jockeys' agent for the barn's top rider and one or two others for riding assignments not taken by their ace.

Todd Pletcher, 2004 Eclipse Award–winning trainer with a barn full of stars, names rising star jockey John Velazquez on many of his horses:

> We use Johnny a lot. It's not like he's a contract rider, but we use him like a first-call rider. We use him because we've had so much success with him on our horses. He's a versatile rider, meaning he does a good job with both front-runners and closers, racing short or long and on either turf or dirt. He doesn't need to be on a particular kind of horse. He just fits our horses really well. If Johnny isn't available, we're fortunate enough to have many world-class riders here in New York. Guys like Jerry Bailey and Edgar Prado take horses for us all the time.

Sometimes the decision of which jockey to ride rests with the horse's owner. While most owners turn full decision-making authority over to their trainer, some prefer to call the shots. While the majority of owners wouldn't have a clue what type of training regimen their horses need, they certainly see the jockeys frequently enough to form their own opinions.

Occasionally it's the jockey who's working the owner directly to get more business. They'll play golf together, go to family cookouts and parties or whatever it takes to get inside with the owner. If the owner wants to ride the jock, it might not matter what the trainer wants because it's the owner who's writing the checks. Jockeys and agents know that as well as anyone.

Mike Luzzi, 1989 Eclipse Award winner as an apprentice, spends time talking up his business:

> I do a lot of politicking with people—owners and trainers—at the barns or clocker's stand. Sometimes we talk about stuff that has nothing to do with racing, or we may talk about particular horses or races.
>
> I try to sell myself as being the man for the job. I want to come across as confident, experienced and a versatile kind of rider; one that's not built for just one kind of horse, but one who can ride a speed horse, come from the inside or outside, the turf or dirt. I want them to know I'm their man for all kinds of horses and races.

The power struggle between owner and trainer over who gets to ride the horse begins when the owner wants to use a jockey the trainer doesn't usually ride or doesn't want to use the trainer's top gun. While most people are understanding of the trainer's need to please the owner, sometimes the truth gets a little bent and feelings get hurt. Some trainers will promise an agent that he'll use one of his jocks. But when the entries are made, he'll pull the old bait-and-switch trick, naming someone else to ride. The trainer may have even already told the jockey he was going to use him before going with someone else. The trainer may pull the switch because he's found someone who better fits the horse. Knowing this, the majority of riders don't get too excited about promised rides and wait until the overnight sheet comes out with their name in print before making plans.

Riders find the politics of riding assignments an unpleasant necessity they'd rather do without. For many young riders and those struggling to land quality mounts, it gets frustrating. Jockey Kevin Mangold is angry when riders are taken advantage of:

> A trainer may take a young, green, ambitious rider to work a bunch of horses based on the promise that they'll ride them in the races, then the trainer enters the horse with a different rider. It happens all the time. Every jock will tell you not to burn your bridges and that you've got to put up with it. I've been lied to so many times, I've come to expect it. Many times, they intend to ride me and then can't for whatever reason, but also many times, they are outright and knowingly lying to my face about putting me on the horse.

There are times when the agent is the one playing cat and mouse, making a commitment to ride for a trainer, then pulling out before entries are drawn to take call on a better horse. Pulling out of a commitment, or "spinning," frustrates the trainer. It leaves him scrambling to find a last-minute replacement. Whether it's the trainers or agents who break more promises on riding assignments is too tough a race to call. Each side feels the other is to blame for the problem.

The politics of riding assignments at the top level of the sport is one of the games within the game. For example, as horses begin sorting themselves out each spring down the Kentucky Derby trail, agents begin lining up their top jockeys for riding assignments across the country to get aboard top three-year-olds in preparation for the Triple Crown races.

The big name trainers have their big name riders tied up early in the process. Lesser-known trainers may have their top man taken away by a bigger stable, or may simply lose the rider to a better horse.

The country's top riders—Jerry Bailey, Gary Stevens and John Velazquez, for example—are sought out and usually get first call. However, in many cases the trainer keeps the horse's regular rider up, even though he may be a notch below the nation's best. If the jock has worked his way up on the horse and proven he's capable, it's a great reward for his hard work.

Sometimes you go through life hoping and dreaming of that one chance when you'll be the blessed one with all the luck. When Smarty Jones made his remarkable run up the ladder of success in 2004 from rather humble beginnings, trainer John Servis stuck with his regular man, Stuart Elliott. Certainly they could've hired a big name rider to take over the reins, but he stuck with the man who knew his horse best. Elliott rode two brilliant races before losing the Triple Crown bid in a heartbreaking loss in the Belmont.

While Elliott made the most of his golden opportunity, he deeply appreciated the loyalty he received from his corner: "It felt really good that they supported me. I'd been riding for John [Servis] for many years and had been up on some of his better horses and I knew he felt comfortable with me. When Mr. and Mrs. Chapman kept me on Smarty, that vote of confidence made me feel great—it meant the world to me."

As the number of Derby hopefuls thins out, the number of riding opportunities, likewise, diminishes. If the agent has done well, hopefully his rider will have the option on a few horses as they enter the final weeks before the Derby. As delicate as horses are, many get hurt along the trail. Others just don't have the ability to handle the grueling schedule or possess the constitution to carry their speed the longer distances and drop out as Derby Day approaches.

As the final days dwindle down before the entries are drawn, most riding assignments have been committed. Some years, however, large fields complicate matters, and the final list of entrants isn't known until just before entry deadline. Sometimes a top rider will find himself without a Derby ride when his horse pulls out or doesn't qualify for the field. Occasionally, one of the horses with lower credentialed earnings gets moved up just in time, and a mad scramble to find the best available rider ensues.

Whether it be for the Derby or any of the other 58,000 races held each year, finding the right rider for the horse is important. Trainers seek out the jockeys who will give their horse the best chance to win every time out. They want jockeys who will push the horse hard down the stretch all the way through the finish, even when the horse isn't going to win. Purse money drops off considerably after the top slot, with pay for second through fifth place finishes also generating purse monies.

Belmont Stakes–winning trainer Kenny McPeek likes hard-working jockeys: "My favorite rider is a guy named 'Hungry.' It's a guy who will work hard for you. The guy who will take the horse through a hole and give you a shot. I look for continuity and will give the rider two, three or four tries on the horse so they can learn about each other. I prefer a patient rider, someone who is a good passenger. Pat Day, for example, is great because he keeps it simple and lets the horse do the running."

West Coast–based trainer Doug O'Neill runs one of the largest, and most successful, stables in the country. He likes to utilize riders who fit into the program well:

> The longer you're in the game, the more you build a rapport with certain agents and jockeys. I like to use jockeys who try really hard and seem to fit the type of program we have. We don't use any of the guys who are hot headed.

Sometimes we have a horse that really needs a good, hard warm-up. I've found that the guys who are hungrier than the top riders usually work best on that kind. Some of the big name guys shy away from that type of horse. I stay away from riders who won't hard for us, whether it be in the morning or afternoon. I get disappointed if someone stops trying on one of our horses. I like the guys who try hard every time out, not the kind who quit working on the horse at the top of the stretch just because he knows the horse won't win."

I usually stick with just a handful of riders. Some guys are good gate riders and some are good finishers, but we're really blessed here in Southern California to have so many good riders who can do it all. I can put any of them up with confidence that they can handle whatever kind of horse we have.

Some riders and trainers do particularly well when partnered, like jockey Jon Court (left) and top trainer Doug O'Neill (photograph by Debra Gruender).

Trainer-jockey relationships can last a lifetime, or can end over one poorly ridden race. Earning the trainer's trust and respect is the key. Kathy Mongeon, a trainer on the Florida–New Jersey rotation, understands the importance of finding the right jockey for her horses: "The relationship between trainer and jockey varies. Sometimes you hardly know the jock and other times you are good friends with them. You try and use a rider that you have a good rapport with. I try and find the rider that will fit the horse. Like if the horse is a front-runner, or a come-from-behind closer, I may choose a particular rider."

Trainer Jeff Greenhill has strong opinions about his relationship with jockeys:

> I like a jockey who really tries. If he can't be first, be second; if he can't be second, be third; if you can't be third, try and get fourth. Particularly if it's

someone who is high profile, jockeys don't seem motivated to try harder for the place money. To the owner, the difference between third and sixth might be a $1,000 and that's what pays the bills. I think some of these guys don't try hard enough to get there. There's a saying around here [Kentucky circuit] that good jockeys don't need instructions and the bad ones can't follow them if you give it to them. The relationship with jockeys is tenuous, at best.

In the 10 or 12 minutes the jockey is actually up on the horse, he makes as much money with the horse as I do, and I'm with the horse all month. And the groom, who spends more time than any of us, makes even less. Maybe some of them [jockeys] aren't hungry enough.

For Kentucky-based trainer Joan Scott, dependability is high on the list of credentials she's looking for when selecting a rider: "I have to have confidence that my jock is going to give my horse a good ride every time. I want my jock to have confidence in my ability to have a horse ready, so he can be confident about riding the horse. No use collaring a leading rider or a big name rider that ships in for the day unless you know they are going to show up to do their best."

One of the attributes trainers look for when selecting jockeys is horsemanship. Veteran rider Russell Woolsey, who describes himself as a horseman who happens to be a jockey, rather than a jockey who thinks he's a horseman, grew up with horses and feels his knowledge can be helpful to trainers:

I remember this one horse, American Prince, who was a skinny and skittish two-year-old. When I got up on him the first time, I really thought he was just another piece of crap. I got stuck on him because no one else wanted up on him.

Because he was so easily spooked, I suggested we try blinkers because I thought it would help him pay more attention to his training. The horse started trusting me more, started training better and, with time, eventually got more aggressive in his workouts. I ended up winning a $100 grander on him, and he ran second in the Tampa Bay Derby.

Jockeys often earn rides from their work aboard horses in morning workouts. If a rider likes a horse from breezing, or has ridden the horse and believes he's capable of performing better, he may stick with the horse even when it appears on paper that he's overmatched. While sometimes you'll see a rider on a no-hope longshot if it's a horse from his top barn, sometimes the long-term play pays off when the horse gets hot. If he'd given up the opportunity to ride the horse earlier, he might not ever get back on the horse.

For jockeys, riding a first-time starter after breezing them for months is a reward for their hard work. Getting on good bloodstock with racing potential provides promise for the future. You never know which one might be the next stakes winner.

Riders are often able to tell when they're up on something special, even before the young horse makes it to the races. Winner of the 2002 Eclipse Award as the country's top apprentice rider, Ryan Fogelsonger recognizes talent from his work with horses in the mornings:

> All horses are different, but you can tell when a young horse is going to be really good. You just get to know about their personality and behaviors from how they work. The good ones usually act like an older horse and behave more like a professional racehorse, even when they're young. The maturity helps them learn their lessons.
>
> I remember being on a filly named Pompamento quite a bit before she first raced. I knew she had a lot of ability. The first time out, I think she was something like 15–1, but I knew she could run and would be tough to be beat.

Fogelsonger was right, as Pompamento went on to break her maiden impressively and continued on to become a stakes horse.

One of the oldest tricks in the book is when a trainer has a monster in the barn and doesn't want to let the word out. If the horse has been tearing up the track in workouts and the trainer thinks he can win with him first time out, there's a few things he might do to keep things quiet. In workouts, he may have the jockey "choke" the horse for the first furlong or two, and then let him run on late.

Rather than showing up with a work tab full of bullet breezes, his times fit in with the rest of the group. To further conceal his ability, he may throw on a low-end rider first time out, or an apprentice rider. If the jockey knows of the horse's ability, he's likely been instructed to keep things hush. The trainer may even risk entering the horse at a few levels lower than he thinks the horse belongs, particularly if the horse wasn't an expensive purchase. By camouflaging the horse's ability, the trainer and owner hope to drive up the odds and cash in.

Grade I stakes–winning jockey Dennis Carr was a young rider when he had the pleasure of riding eventual multiple Grade I stakes winner Turn Back the Alarm:

> She showed a ton of ability in training and did everything real easily. She'd drag me through five-eighths in :58. Sometimes we'd work her in the dark to keep her under wraps, hoping to fool the clockers or make it hard for them to pick her out. It was hard to conceal her, though. Although they called her grey, she was as close to white as they get.
>
> It was obvious to all of us in the barn to keep things quiet or they'd be wanting to know who leaked about her. Bill went back and forth about where to run her and finally entered her in a maiden $50,000 claimer. I never saw someone sweat as bad as he did in the paddock. He knew that she could've blown the doors off straight maidens, or just about anything else.
>
> She blew away the field and won by 17 lengths. I rode her the next three starts and won a stakes on her at Saratoga. She was the best filly I ever rode.

Young horses go through growing and development spurts, just like teenage children do. They may one day put it all together and blossom, clear out of the blue. Sometimes the trainer or jockey may see the horse's potential through all the disappointments, and his patience may be rewarded. Once a horse figures out what racing is all about, they can get real good in a hurry. Other times, everyone in the barn is clueless why the horse finally woke up.

If you see an expensive first-time starter, one purchased for $100,000 or more at one of the yearling sales, show up in a maiden claimer for $50,000 or less, it's a safe bet that the horse doesn't have much to offer. By the time the owner shelled out six figures to buy the beast, plunked another $20,000 to get him trained for his first race, he's not about to give a good thing away for half price.

A switch in racing surface or racing distance may also trigger a horse's improvement. Some pedigrees are better suited for grass racing or running longer distances. Some horses enjoy racing advantages on off-track conditions, relishing the slop and mud. Even the subtle difference between the types of dirt and grass surfaces at different tracks may generate better finishes. Perhaps a horse enjoys a deep, tiring dirt track or a lightening fast, hard-as-rock turf course. Oftentimes, the jockeys' feedback on how the horse handles various racing surfaces leads the trainer to the best course.

When horses don't run well, or don't win when they're expected to, the axe may fall on the jockey. Getting fired for a bad ride goes along with the territory. It could be due to a bad ride, poor work habits or owner's preference. Some trainers will stand behind the jockeys they've hired when an owner wants to pull him. Others are either less supportive and buckle under the pressure and pull the rider. What burns most jockeys is being replaced for no apparent reason and without explanation.

"There isn't a lot of loyalty between jockeys, agents and trainers," trainer Doug O'Neill explained. "All our agreements and deals are done verbally. I might think we have a rider all locked up, but if he thinks he can get off our horse that might be 8–1 to get on something that might be 5–1, he could jump ship at the last minute."

Trainer Kenny McPeek has been in the situation of having to let a rider go for his behavior off the horse: "I fired a rider last year because he was temperamental and unreliable. He failed to show up for morning workouts and didn't communicate well with me. He just didn't have the good attitude I'm looking for."

Graded stakes–winning rider, and 1997 Eclipse Award–winning apprentice, Phil Teator knows the hardship of getting the pink slip:

> Getting fired happens to all the riders. It doesn't matter who you are; even Jerry Bailey gets fired once in awhile.

The majority of the time, it's the owner that decides to change rides. The owner might be disappointed in the way their horse race and tell the trainer to try someone else. It might not even be my fault. Maybe the horse got into trouble and had a bad trip, but if the owner thinks we went too fast early, or waited too late to make our run, they'll want to change.

I always make a point of asking the trainer why he's making the change, so that I can try and learn from the experience. Sometimes, though, I can't tell if the trainer is telling the truth or not. He might be saying it's the owner, but it might be his call.

It's tough, no matter how you look at it. I'm out there just trying to make a living. If I get pulled off a horse, I have to bite my tongue a bit because I still want to ride for that owner or trainer. The worst time was when I was taken off a horse just before the Preakness two years ago. I had ridden the horse [Magic Weisner] to four stakes wins and was his regular rider. I'd already bought tickets for my family coming in from New York when on the day the entries were taken, I was told the ride was going to someone else.

The process of selecting the track's races starts when the track's racing secretary writes the races and publishes them in the "condition book." The condition book typically lists the possible races for the coming two weeks. There are more races written than are run each day, given that some races will not have enough entrants to fill them. Nearly always the lower-end races and maiden races overfill. Maiden races are those held for horses that have not yet won their first race.

Roughly following the scale of weights, races are written with the intention of evenly distributing racing opportunities to all types of horses—providing equal opportunity for the male horses, colts and geldings and the females, fillies and horses. There's also a balance of sprints to routes, dirt to turf, maidens to winners and fair distribution of claiming price ranges.

Some trainers seem to get all the luck in finding the right races for their horses. They may find a race written for their nonwinner of two races, a four-year-old filly getting a written-to-order 5½-furlong sprint on the lawn. The race may be written when the trainer's horse is just coming into top form. Somehow the trainer may even know which horses are signed up before entries are released. Some horsemen feel it's not by accident that races are carded that so perfectly fit "favored" trainer's horses so often.

Race weights are assigned based on a scale of weights and the conditions of the race as it's written. Centuries ago, races were run with no consideration of the rider's weight. Over the years, owners sought the lightest jockey with adequate riding skills to guide their horses. Eventually, attempts were made to level the playing field, and racing moved from "catch weight" to "give-and-take" weights, which was based on the size of the horses. The bigger horses carried extra weight. Over time, weights were assigned to handicap the faster horses. Eventually, the industry evolved in to the modern day scale of weights, which is a guideline for horses of different ages racing varying distances with escalating weights each month of the year.

Within the conditions written for each race, the weight to be carried by the horse is specified. For example, a field of $10,000 claimers may be assigned 118 pounds. However, if the horse hasn't won a race this year he may be given a five-pound condition or be allowed to tack 113.

Depending on the conditions of the race, weight in stakes races are assigned by the Racing Secretary. Based on the horse's demonstrated abilities, he assigns weight with the intention of making the race fair and equal. In the eyes of the secretary, the best horse is assigned top weight, 122, for example. In this way, the horse is handicapped. He will run slower carrying that weight than he would if he were assigned 115. The secretary will assign a less talented horse a lower weight, hopefully bettering his chances than if he carried equal weight with the best-credentialed horse.

The weight a horse carries in a race obviously affects the outcome. The more weight he carries, the heavier the burden. Although horses are big, strong and powerful, an extra five pounds over a mile route of ground will slow him down a fraction of a second, costing him a length or two. The length of a horse's body from head to tail is the standard used to measure distance between racing horses.

Some horses enjoy an additional weight allowance awarded apprentice riders, often five pounds. Recognizing the difference five or ten pounds can make in a race, many trainers are willing to trade experience for a break in weights and put the young lads up.

Once apprentices lose their "bug," getting work can be difficult to nearly impossible. Nearly every rider struggles for some time after they've lost the apprentice allowance. In fact, some never rebound from it. They might go from having ridden eight or nine races a day to maybe picking up one mount. Their income plummets and some riders just get sour on the business, or simply can't tough it out.

A trainer might ride an apprentice on a horse the entire meet, but once he loses the weight advantage, he's likely to be replaced by a veteran rider. It might not matter that the rookie won on the horse, either. Whether it's the trainer's preference, owner's call or racing politics, it happens to every young rider at every racetrack. It's one of the painful realities of paying your dues in a business steeped in tradition.

Born and raised in the Virgin Islands, Kevin Krigger was a successful apprentice on the tough Southern California circuit. Like most, he struggled after finishing his apprenticeship: "When you're a bug rider, you get lots of good horses, but after losing the bug, the hardest thing is getting good mounts again. It's like everything changes overnight. It's taken me awhile to get good business back."

As a rookie, mistakes are part of the learning process, and Krigger had his fair share of early suspensions. Racing stewards try to correct young riders' mistakes by setting them down or suspending their riding privileges for short spells as a sort of warning.

Like many before him, Krigger moved away from the top racing circuit to get back to his winning ways. Once a jockey starts winning again, trainers and owners will start paying attention, and their career can take off.

Many apprentices want so much to do well, they try too hard, meaning they don't ride with patience. They force the issue. Rather than sitting off a hot pace, they may rush the horse into contention, fearful that they're out of the running if they're not mixing it up early. If they're on a closer, they may move their horse to the outside and "send" him prematurely down the backstretch to gain racing position, only to run out of steam inside the final sixteenth.

With plenty of naysayers around, it's easy for rookies to get discouraged. They must draw upon their determination and passion to get over the hump. Paying attention and learning from veterans is critically important and can help young riders gain self-confidence. The veteran horsemen have seen it all and are delighted to share their stories and wisdom.

As a young apprentice rider who's left regular high school to ride full-time, Kyle Kaenel tried breaking into the tough-as-nails Southern California racing circuit:

> It's hard to break in here because so many riders are already established in good barns already. I went to Phoenix [Turf Paradise], where no one know me, and I'm able to get on some good horses. When I come to California, I'm trying to get rides away from some of the best riders in the world.
>
> I work three of four horses every morning, and in Phoenix I'd usually get to ride those horses back in the afternoon, but here I usually work them, and then the trainer puts a more experienced rider up for the race. It's a little frustrating. I've breezed the horse ten times, how can you get any more experienced? Some of them must be thinking that for the same price, why ride a bug boy? Most of the horses I do get are like 15–1; they're just throwing me a bone.

While cracking into one of the toughest circuits around is daunting, the young rider sees the benefits of paying his dues and learning from the ever-present Hall of Famers: "The first time I rode down here, I was in the starting gate and looked to my left and there was Gary Stevens. I looked to my right and there's Mike Smith. It's really pretty cool. The guys are willing to help me out with advice on how to become a better rider and a safer rider."

Similarly, apprentice rider Eric Camacho finds the hardest part about competing against older riders is the high level of competition: "It's kind of a pro and con at the same time, I guess. There are a lot of really good riders here at Pimlico. I'm competing against guys like Ryan Fogelsonger, Ramon Dominguez and Mario Pino—all great riders, so it's tough. On the other hand, I'm learning from some of the best. I learn by watching their riding style and how they get horses to respond. But if I mess up, they'll tell me right away. I just have to take it constructively, though, because I still have a lot to learn."

At some point in a rider's career, hopefully sooner rather than later, they will accept the fact that they are going to make mistakes and not blame others for their weaknesses and faults. Some young riders experience success as an apprentice, win lots of races on good horses because they can make the lower weight and make some big money. Some inherit a jumbo-sized ego along with it. No doubt it's difficult for some teenagers to handle the fast money and pressures of grown-up life.

Hungry to get rides and make a name for themselves, many apprentices will take any mount that's offered them. Sometimes they pick up rides on behaviorally challenged horses other jockeys refuse to ride.

Stakes-placed apprentice jockey Liz Morris specializes in taking horses others may pass over:

> It's my cup of tea, I guess. I do my homework, study up and try and learn as much as I can about the horse. I'll communicate with the trainer and try to prove that I can handle the horse.
>
> I try to respect the horse and really get to understand him. I'm blessed with patience, so I don't fight them. I try to give them confidence by stroking and rewarding them for things they do right. I try to bring out their positive personality.
>
> I've had really good luck with some nervous horses. I've ridden one that was a $5,000 horse and by working with him, helped him move to up being a $30,000 allowance-class horse. I really loved doing that.

With the unpolished riding style of most apprentices, many veteran riders are worried about rider safety at times. Like any other profession, it's important for rookies to learn from their mistakes. Earlie Fires, the country's top apprentice rider himself in 1965, is concerned about the dangers of reckless young riders: "Racing really needs to fix the problem with dangerous young riders. For example, some of these young riders are like kids learning how to drive a car. They seldom look back before they change lanes. If young riders don't look around before recklessly changing running lanes, it's dangerous and they should be taught a lesson. They should be given days. Officials need to take more responsibility."

At the time apprentice rider Freddy Fong, Jr., was 55 mounts into his career, he'd already moved from Calder to Arlington Park and was working with veteran agent John Hoffman. Able to make 105 pounds, the 19-year-old Fong was picking up about three riders a day on the strong Illinois circuit: "At the start, I didn't have much luck winning races, but when I moved up here, the hard work started paying off. I'm now riding for some good trainers and getting on some live horses. Things can only get better now."

As a rookie rider, mistakes come with the territory. Shortly after arriving at Arlington, Fong received his first suspension. He was racing near the lead when the field turned for home: "I was making a run on the lead and really race riding. During the stretch run, I was hitting my horse right handed, and he didn't feel like he was drifting in, but he did."

The infraction warranted a trip to the office upstairs: "I met with the stewards, and they gave me three days because I didn't keep my horse straight." While he finished third in the race, he had his number taken down for causing interference and was sat down with a three-day suspension, a slap on the wrist intended to teach the young rider a lesson.

As a young rider, Liz Morris likens herself to being a sponge: "I have to learn from everything I do. I accept criticism, learn from it and try to turn it into something positive I can apply to my riding. I have to eat, sleep and dream about horses to become the best rider I can. Racing is always on my mind. You can never learn all there is to know."

Knowing that scrutinizing eyes will be watching every move they make, female riders have it rough at the start. If a trainer, or owner, has resistance to putting a woman in the saddle for whatever reason, they are going to be looking for the first sign of weakness or hesitation. They'll be looking for any excuse to blame her riding as the reason for not putting her up, not her gender, although it might not be further from the truth.

To the contrary, a male apprentice who shows ability might be hyped as the next coming of the great Bill Shoemaker if he picks up a couple of early wins. His mistakes may be overlooked and taken for granted as part of the learning process. If he's in the hands of a top agent, he could be getting live mounts and big chances during his apprenticeship.

Many insiders say it takes five to ten years to hone the skills necessary to be a top rider. It takes that long to master the finer elements of judging pace, reading the race as it unfolds around you, getting the most effort from the horse and taking the advantage of opportunities presented during the heat of the battle.

Regardless of whether the jockey is a fresh-off-the-farm apprentice or a grizzled veteran rider, everyone is out for themselves in the race for the riches that come with victory. Tracks put forth purse money, which is awarded to the owners of the top-placing horses.

The purse, or prize money, is awarded to the top-finishing horses in every race. While there is variation by track of how the purse monies are split, the common division is 60 percent to the winner, 20 percent to second, 10 percent to third, 6 percent to fourth and 4 percent to fifth.

How big the purse is depends on many factors. Purse structures are built from the track's take of the handle. Depending on the state, about 8 percent of every betting dollar goes toward taxes and 7 percent goes back to the horsemen, or owners, in the form of purses, after taxes, track rate and special program deductions are made.

Purse value ranges widely from track to track. For example, Yavapai Downs in Arizona has daily purses totaling around $35,000 a day. Big tracks in California, Kentucky and New York give that much away every single race. At "racinos," or tracks where casino or slots have been added to the package, purses are skyrocketing. With more money on the table, many jockeys are relocating to grab their share of the increased handle.

Purse monies put up by the racetracks come from the track handle, or amount wagered by bettors. In reality, it is the gambler who supports the revenue stream that supports the entire industry. It's the primary reason why tracks spend so much time and energy improving bettor comforts, education and wagering options. Without the gambler, the house of cards would come tumbling down.

Average race purses in the United States are approximately $20,000 and about 40 percent of the races nationally offer purses under $10,000. There are roughly twenty races each year in America with purses at one million dollars or more.

Jockeys get paid a minimum fee for riding races, with additional pay for placing in the top finishing positions. At most racetracks, there's a sliding scale of jockey mount fees, based on the purse, or value, of each race. For example, a race worth $5,000 often carries a nonplacing jockey mount fee of $45. As the purse values increase, the jockey fees step up. For a $20,000 race purse, a losing ride nets the jockey $60. In a $50,000 race the minimum mount fee averages $80.

If the jockey hits the board, the fee goes up. In all races, the winning jockey receives 10 percent of the winner's purse. So, in the $20,000 race, which carries a winner's share of $12,000, the jockey will receive $1,200 for the win. Running second will earn him $200. A third place finish in this race is rewarded with $100. Fourth and fifth place finishes typically pay just slightly more than the losing ride minimum.

If the rider is good enough to compete at big tracks, where the earning potential is so much better, that's where he should be. As you can imagine, getting mounts against the top jockeys in the world at places like Belmont Park, Del Mar and Churchill Downs is no easy task. Young riders who've found success at smaller tracks and attempt to break in at major circuits are chewed up and spit out every year.

Most tracks run eight to ten races per day, often more on weekends. Riders at the top of the standings board typically ride nearly every race. The lower-end riders sometimes struggle to pick up one ride a day. Races are usually held four or five days per week.

In order for a jockey to be successful on any circuit, he must have a shot to win the big ones. One stakes win can earn him as much money as a season's worth of small check wins. Most jockeys will work countless numbers of horses for a trainer, and suck up when he has to, to keep his foot in the door in hopes of picking up the mount on the stable's stakes horse.

Stakes and handicap races offer the biggest purses at tracks. Small tracks may run a stakes worth $10,000 while the big tracks give away hundreds of thousands, sometimes even a million or more. Winning a $100-grander puts $6,000 in the jockeys' pocket. Winning a million dollar race puts $60,000 in the bank, but only a handful of the country's top riders ever get a chance to race for the big payday.

When a top-level rider is brought in to ride in a stakes, how he's compensated depends on how the trainer or owner has extended the offer. As jockey Pat Day described, there's much to think about when taking the show on the road: "I may be offered upfront money, or guaranteed money, it really varies. I always get 10 percent of the winning purse, but for out-of-town assignments it's also 10 percent of the place and show purse money. All my travel expenses are reimbursed, too."

Day's agent considers all the traveling stakes offers as they come in, making connections and coordinating details with trainers and owners: "My

Recently retired Hall of Famer Pat Day is the leading money-winning rider of all time, with over $297 million in purses (photograph by Debra Gruender).

agent and I talk over the major stakes, of course, but otherwise it's his job to pick out the best spots."

Ron Anderson, who handles book for Hall of Fame rider Jerry Bailey, knows a thing or two about big races: "I'm proud to say my jockeys have won 14 Breeder's Cup races and 9 of the last 30 Triple Crown races."

When considering options for the decade's top rider, Anderson has free rein:

> I've had Jerry's book for six years and I make the calls about where we go. Once in awhile we'll talk about how things could play out. He'll give me input on when he thinks a horse might have more ability or might be on the improve.
> When we're taking riding assignments in the big races, we usually don't ask for, or receive, upfront money. For example, Jerry's been riding Yearly Report all over the place and recently flew out to ride her in the Sunshine Millions for Bob Baffert, so we don't even think about upfront money. But if some obscure guy we don't know calls and wants us to fly out and ride, he might guarantee $5,000 of the purse money to show his confidence in the horse.

How much money a jockey earns from racing depends on several factors. A rider struggling to get rides at small tracks with a low purse structure is making a couple of hundred dollars a month. Top riders getting quality mounts in big stakes across the country are comfortably in the seven-figure bracket. For the majority of riders in between the extremes, it's largely dependent on which meets they are riding at and how well they're doing.

Depending on how well their horses are finishing, six digit incomes are common on the big circuits. Approximately 12 percent of licensed riders are making that kind of money. Trouble is, most riders aren't on the big circuit and aren't on the top of the leading rider list. Most struggle to make a decent living. Nearly 70 percent of riders make under $30,000 a year, before expenses.

Jockey Danny Sorenson, a 27-year riding veteran, feels riders are often stereotyped and misunderstood regarding their financial situation:

> There isn't one of us that doesn't want to win every time out. So many people simply don't understand how racing works on the inside. They might see the earnings of a top jockey listed as something like $7 million, but that's what the jockeys' horses earned, not the rider. If the jockey wins a race, he gets 10 percent of the winner's share of the purse. But for second and third, it's 5 or 6 percent and for losing rides, it's even less.
> From what the jockey actually makes, he has to pay his agent 25–30 percent, and his valet and the stable help and then pay taxes. For every $100 I make, only $22 makes it into my pocket.

Using Sorenson's example conservatively, for the rider whose horses earn $7 million, the rider would gross approximately $420,000. By the time the other expenses and taxes are paid, the rider would be taking home approximately $180,000. For the record, only 21 riders had more than $7 million in purse earnings in 2005.

Hall of Famer Kent Desormeaux acknowledges most people don't understand how jockeys get paid: "Fans sometimes give us a bad time if we won't win races. Believe me, we feel as bad as anyone when we don't win. For the racing fan who might lose $2 or $5 if their horse doesn't win, it might cost us thousands. We get paid a lot more for winning than losing, so we're all out there trying to win every race."

A long overdue opportunity for top billing riders to generate revenue on the backs of their success is through advertising. Many racing "hard boots," or old school loyalists, have opposed jockeys wearing of advertisements and corporate logos on their racing uniforms. The issue of advertisements is very important to jockeys, and it deals with their self-worth and place in the industry.

Jockeys fought for the right to wear advertising on their racing pants in the Kentucky Derby in 2004. One of the leaders of the charge, Shane Sellers, wore the Jockeys' Guild patch and an advertisement for Wrangler Jeans after taking the issue to federal court. With support of the Guild, only an 11th hour ruling allowed the jockeys to make the breakthrough.

> Here's a chance to bring corporate America into horse racing, so why wouldn't we want to do it. I'm not a businessman, but why not increase advertising of the sport. It's ridiculous that we had to go to Court over this. We asked why we could wear VISA, the official sponsor, but Churchill wasn't willing to pay us to wear it. They wanted us to do interviews, sign autographs and promote the Derby, but they don't pay us for that, either. Unless you hit the board, you're only making $55 for the race. I'm happy to promote the sport of horse racing, but why can't the tracks reciprocate and do something for us. We're the ones out there risking our lives.
>
> Horse racing used to be the biggest sport in the country, bigger than football, basketball and baseball, but we're struggling right now. Where would we be today without the slot machines at the tracks or without simulcasting? Again, the jockeys aren't getting any share of the revenue, but we're the ones out there risking our lives and killing ourselves to do it.
>
> The judge didn't think much of Churchill's argument and sided in our favor. In the end, I was able to secure a last-minute endorsement from Wranglers and got paid to wear an advertisement.

Kelly Wietsma, president of Equispone, Inc., a sports marketing agency exclusive to equine sports, was instrumental in helping lead the change:

Our primary goal all along has been to rise the profile of these great athletes. The great horses in racing are around for a couple of years, then go off to the breeding shed, and horses can't talk to the media, but our top jockeys are going to be around for many years, and we need to help them become recognized and valued. In most other sports, they go out of their way to promote their top athletes.

We sued and won for the jockeys' rights to wear advertisements. I know it comes as a bit of a shocker to the industry, because they haven't seen this kind of thing before, but it's the fair thing to do. The industry is starting to open their eyes now and seem willing to work with us. We're looking for a really big push this year with the Triple Crown races.

Her group represents high profile riders like Jerry Bailey, Stewart Elliott, Jose Santos and John Velasquez, managing their media relations and endorsement deals.

There's tremendous endorsement potential out there for jockeys. For example, we were able to secure a $200,000 endorsement deal for Stewart Elliott in the Belmont Stakes last year.

In California, jockeys can wear logo endorsements, but in New York, they need written approval from the owner, which is virtually impossible. In Kentucky, where racing traditions run very deep, we've struggled. We work closely with tracks and the NTRA [National Thoroughbred Racing Association], and we'll be working with Churchill Downs earlier this year. We're hoping to have Jerry Bailey in a week before to do signings for his upcoming book release.

Rather than the industry coming together collectively to address the attractive advertising opportunities, it appears that jockeys, owners, racing associations and racetracks are headed for more arbitration over the issue. At times, it appears the racing industry is out of touch with modern day advances and struggles to keep up with the pace of ever-improving technology. The future of racing would be enlightened if only the industry would promote the human equation, parlaying the jockeys' incredible gifts to the sport in marketing, promotions and advertising.

The average jockey earns about $30,000 a year from racing, before paying their help, which includes 25 percent for their agent, plus valet fees and tipping the barn help. Considering their day begins at sunrise and often ends long after sundown, you can see they're not in it just for the money. In addition, jockeys must supply their own riding gear.

Riding equipment costs typically trickle in over the course of a year. Other than high start-up costs to secure the basic starter set, expenses are quite manageable for most. Helmets cost $125, and riders need at least two for the jockeys' room and one for morning rides. Primarily made of fiberglass, helmets last for years, although the harness and strapping need replacing yearly. The helmet is insulated with impact-resistant padding inside and can literally save a rider's life.

Every jockey needs a couple of saddles for racing, with at least one ultralight-weight saddle, which weighs around two pounds and serves little purpose other than to hold the stirrups in place. In the mornings, trainers provide the saddle for workouts, usually a much heavier version. Saddles start around $250.

Safety vests, or flak jackets, run about $200, and the rider needs at least two, again with one for morning and afternoon. The vests can get sweaty, so many keep or use a third in the jocks' room. They last a couple of years. Jockeys are required to wear safety vests when racing. Made with high-impact foam, the vest weighs about two pounds and provides minimal protection for the rider through shock-absorbing material inside the vest.

Whips, sometimes called racing crops, start at $30, and most riders own a dozen or more. They come in all kinds from flimsy to rigid, about 30-inches in length with a 2-inch leather popper at the end. Whips come in a rainbow of colors, and many riders try to match their "stick" to the silk colors they're wearing. Like most other pieces of racing equipment, whips are subject to inspection by the stewards.

Plain white trousers, or "breeches," are $45 each, and the rider needs ten or more pair. If he wants his name on them, that costs a little extra. The pants are thin and wear out quickly, rarely lasting more than a year.

Slip-resistant racing boots run $140, and two or three pair are needed. They last a year or two, depending on how they're cared for. Most riders have an ultralight pair that's really more of a sock than a shoe, along with a heavier set that's more durable.

Racing goggles start at $5 a pair and haven't changed in design for years. Jockeys usually ride with their best pair on top, progressively layering down to their worst pair, the one with the most scratches on it. They usually last up to 100 races or so, depending on how hard the track's racing surface is on the thin and lightweight goggles.

While racing is still a male-dominated sport, women are starting to catch up. Female jockeys are gaining more respect all the time but generally remain underappreciated in the sport. They're winning stakes races and occasionally winning riding titles across the country.

It's still a rarity to find a female rider getting enough quality mounts to compete for jockey titles, despite their keen ability to handle horses with a soft touch. Greta Kuntzweiler, who won a riding title at Turfway in 2002, acknowledges the difficulty of the job, "It might look easy, but it's really complicated to be a good rider. It's not as simple as just jumping on the back of a horse and riding. It takes a lot of hard work over several years to become a good rider and gain the respect of others."

In 1969, Diane Crump became the first woman to ride in a thoroughbred race when she took a leg up at Hialeah. Prior to that, women hoping to race pleaded with trainers for the chance to prove their ability. They were rejected, ignored and discriminated against.

Crump explained that getting to that historical day took lots of hard work and upset many: "After Kathy Kusner took her case to court so she could race, I was able to get my jockeys' license. But the riders were up in arms and boycotted the races, even though they'd been riding side-by-side with me for years in the mornings. Even the Jockeys' Guild complained."

When the American Civil Liberties Union supported Kusner's bid for a jockeys' license, the male-dominated industry eventually relinquished their stronghold. Male jockeys at Tropical Park boycotted to stop Barbara Jo Rubin from riding in January. At one point, her trailer was stoned. Finally, on February 7, 1969, Crump became the first female jockey when she rode Bridle 'n Bit to a 10th-place finish in front of a divided crowd of admiring feminists and staunch male loyalists. Two weeks later, 19-year-old Rubin became the first female rider to win. One after another, tracks caved in to jockeys' complaints to keep women off the track. Later that year, Crump became the first female rider to win a stakes race.

Despite the breakthrough, getting business was an uphill battle for the women. Oftentimes, the only rides they could get were at small bush tracks or aboard hopeless longshots: "It was never easy to get rides. It was very hard for the first ten yeas. We really struggled to get accepted," Crump explained. Competing in hostile environments, the women occasionally required police escorts just to cross the path from the jockeys' quarters to the paddock.

Crump broke another barrier when she became the first woman to ride in the Kentucky Derby aboard longshot Fathom in 1970. "If he'd not been coupled in the field, we'd have been 100–1," she explained. She kept Fathom in the running and was within striking distance at the eight pole before fading in the late stages. The highlight of her career, she fondly remembers her limelight: "Of course, I was thrilled. It's an awesome feeling to be a part of something like that. I loved every aspect of it. Riding in the Derby is the greatest feeling in the world."

Since Crump's heyday, women continued an uphill battle to gain respect from horsemen. Many trainers and owners feel women riders didn't have the physical strength, athletic ability or fighting determination to compete with the big boys.

In most parts of the country today, local jockey colonies include a few female riders. In other regions, like Southern California, it's hard for them to break in. Jockey Tara Hemmings unsuccessfully tried cracking into the male-dominated jockey colony of southern California, "I worked horses in California and raced at Santa Anita, but it's really hard for a woman to

3. Winning Is Everything

Julie Krone is the all-time leading female jockey with 3,704 wins, including the 1993 Belmont Stakes aboard Colonial Affair (photograph by Thomas Thompson).

break in there against the best riders in the world, so I came here to Philadelphia to get a fair shot. Some men still don't think we're strong enough to ride, but I guess I'm always going to be fighting against that."

There are very few professional sports where men and women compete against each other on a level playing field. While most male riders are well adjusted to competing against women, there are some who still take issue with it. In some cultures where women unfortunately still play a less than equal role to men, riders have grown up expecting to have dominance and control and have a hard time adjusting to modern reality.

The best way for women to make a name for themselves is to simply win races. Nothing earns respect like bringing home a winner. Put a few numbers in the win column and people will start taking notice. Winning often has a snowball effect, as winning races earns the jockey better horses, which should lead to more winning.

Vicky Baze, third-winningest female rider of all time, understands how tough it is to break in: "I would have to earn the respect and trust of trainers by galloping and exercising their horses, often for much longer than a man would have to. Especially if I was new to the trainer."

She fought through discrimination and had to convince others of her abilities long before she was accepted as a top rider: "There was a perception that this 90-pound woman couldn't be strong enough to ride that big horse. Some men just seemed uncomfortable communicating with a woman rider. Even for some trainers who believed in me, if the owners didn't want to ride me they'd switch. After all, it's the owner paying the bills."

Over the years, female riders have had so many obstacles to overcome. While few talk of it, sexual favors in exchange for riding opportunities have been a reality. A few of these cases even went to court, while most seem silently hidden in the dark side of racing.

One of racing mysteries is trying to figure out why some horses win at huge odds. Truth be told, there's plenty of logical reasons to explain why an illogical horse won at a big price. For example, when a horse is claimed from a race and moves to a new barn, his world changes. Moving to a different barn means different feeding patterns, a new training regimen, and new fixes to old problems. This change of scenery can go either way, moving a horse up a few lengths or taking him the wrong way.

Like nearly all riders, Mike Luzzi gives his best effort on every horse, regardless of their odds: "In the paddock, the trainer may say he's fixed something that's been bothering the horse, or he may be just blowing smoke, I won't know for sure. But when I put the goggles down in the gate, my approach is always the same, and I feel like I've got a shot to win every time out, whether we're even money or 100–1. If the trainer has fixed a problem, sometimes the longshot can jump up and pull a big surprise."

Sometimes a change of racing tactics does the trick. A horse that has been employing the "pop and stop" practice may wake up when pulled back off the pace and rated. Once he finds the trick to winning, some of these types can climb the ladder quite smartly.

When good horses suffer losses, there are often legitimate excuses. There are so many things that can happen to a horse once he enters the starting gate. With well-matched fields, any type of racing trouble may knock him out of contention. The horse might break awkwardly, or get tangled up in traffic in the cavalry charge out of the gate. The rider may misjudge the pace and move too soon or too late. He may experience traffic jams while trying to navigate his way through the field or may get forced wide on the turn. These scenarios, called "bad trips," are commonplace and occur in nearly every race across the country.

Racing luck goes both ways, of course. Whether it's the heavy favorite who trips coming out of the gate, bolts on the turn or doesn't handle the racing surface, breaks even out over time. In fact, most races are not won by the best horse and oftentimes not by the fastest horse. Races are usually won by the horse that gets the best trip. Its the jockeys' top priority to try and get that dream trip every time out. Break well, get position, save ground and save something for the stretch. Great plan, only trouble is it's the same game plan for every rider in the race. So easily said; so hard to do.

Unfortunately, some people will try anything to gain an advantage, even when it's illegal. While the industry has implemented numerous procedures, policies and tests to keep racing honest, winning is not always the priority; in rare cases losing is. Unfortunately, there are times when the rider is instructed not to win. Cheating is very rare, but a reality of racing. The risks of getting caught are so severe nowadays that very few even think about it. Severe punishments up to lifetime bans from racing are levied for serious offenders.

There are times when a trainer will instruct a rider to take it easy on the horse during a race, however. Retired rider Chris Lamance was never told not to win a race but was instructed not to break the horse trying:

> Trainers have told me to take it easy on the horse, maybe because he's not fit or something. If the horse is sore and the trainer wants to get him claimed, he may tell the rider to just get him around the track in one piece so he can sell him.
>
> In one situation, I was instructed to stiff a horse because the groom had accidentally given the horse two doses of bute. The trainer already had two offenses, and the next one would cost him 30 days. He told me he didn't want the horse to get tested.

Veteran horsemen and retired riders often spin tales of horses not being given a fair chance to win. From their stories, most cheating was associated with known shady characters and most often occurred at smaller tracks, where racetrack security and scrutiny often took a backseat to the track's bottom line.

Races can be thrown rather easily during a race, although it's arguable that this rarely happens because of the high risk of being caught and the stiff penalties associated with cheating. If a horse is to be "stiffed," or not supposed to win, there are a number of ways to fly under the radar. The first opportunity occurs at the break, the moment the horses thunder out of the starting gate. Grabbing a short, tight hold of the reins will limit the horse's ability to get out quickly by restricting his head movement. It puts tremendous pressure on the bit in the horse's mouth and is very unkind to the animal. It may cause the horse to toss his head or dangerously rear back in the opening strides. Or the rider can turn the horse's head to the side when the gate pops open. The horse naturally wants to lunge out with his head driving forward.

Intentionally miscalculating the pace is another way to toss a race. Certainly, judging the pace is a split-second decision that is often misread; if a jockey forces his horse to run a much faster or slower early pace than the horse is used to, it will compromise his chances. Particularly if the horse breaks slowly and is then immediately pushed hard to chase the leader, it leaves the horse with an empty tank when the real running counts down the stretch.

Conversely, if the jock gradually eases the horse back out of contention early and swings wide around the field on the turn, it will leave the horse with too much work to do down the stretch. Running the horse into tight quarters and forcing him to "check" is dangerous and easily questioned by the stewards.

If the jock is up on a contender and the stewards are puzzled by the rider's efforts, he may be called into the office and asked to explain. Again, there are so many things that can happen to put a horse into racing trouble that there are nearly always logical explanations to explain a horse's sub-par performance.

Despite the risks, in the heavy fog of fall racing at Delta Downs on January 11, 1990, jockey Sylvester Carmouche tried to play hide-and-go seek with his mount, 23–1 mutuel reject Landing Officer. With fog so thick you couldn't see more than a few yards, Carmouche pulled his horse right to the back of the field as they broke from the gate going a route from the chute located at the head of the stretch as the horses raced past the stands the first time.

Apparently the rider, parked at the top of the stretch, waited for the hoofbeats to approach through the fog before taking off at a full sprint down the stretch in front of the field. Unfortunately his sense of timing wasn't very good, as Landing Officer roared past the finish line more than 20 lengths in front. Alarms went off when none of the riders remembered seeing the winner anywhere during the course of the race after being asked about the horse's near record-setting time for the mile. The jockey was issued a 10-year suspension for his poor judgment.

Another illegal way to attempt winning races on the track is by use of a device called a "machine," or battery-charged zapper. While few active jockeys are willing to talk about these devices, retired riders shed light on the practice of "plugging the horse in," as it's often referred to. While this used to be a more common practice than insiders care to talk about, the use of machines is a rather outdated technique seldom utilized in today's high security racing.

Sometimes referred to as a "buzzer," the machine is a small, electrical device held in the jockeys' hand and applied to the horse's neck or shoulders while racing and gives the horse a small, electrical shock. The machine typically consists of two small batteries, a coil and two prongs held together in a small package of materials about the size of a cigarette lighter. Theoretically, the charge jolts the horse into running faster.

Machines are most typically used on horses that are ironically described as "cheaters," because they don't give a full effort. Often, the machine is first tested on the horse during morning workouts to check his reaction before use in races.

To conceal the machine, jockeys would tuck it under their racing shirt sleeve before heading out to saddle up in the paddock. Because they use rubber bands to hold the length of their sleeves in place so that wind doesn't blow up, there was little chance of the device slipping out accidentally.

After the race, the jockey might toss it into the bushes or drop it somewhere along the track. Rather than risk tossing the device, a jockey may slip it into his boots or tuck it back under his sleeve on the post-race cooldown. When jockeys have been caught red-handed cheating, it's usually a combination of video evidence accompanied with the locating the device after it was discarded by the jock.

After Valhol, a 30–1 maiden, won the 1999 Arkansas Derby, videotape evidence showed jockey Billy Patin dropping a small black item shortly after the finish. Patin was found guilty of using a buzzer on the horse and was eventually suspended from racing for five years: "I'd always wanted to ride in the Derby; it's everyone's dream. Riding in the Arkansas Derby was a big opportunity for me and hoped it would lead to a Derby ride. But I made a mistake and went about doing it the wrong way. They saw me drop something on the film and found the buzzer on the track. It cost me five years. I've served my time now and learned a lesson. I'll never do anything like that ever again. I'm so thankful to be back racing again."

Unlike most riders who never make it back, a remorseful and determined Patin successfully returned to the track last year and is gradually regaining his reputation.

Prompted by a questionable photo published by the Miami Herald, Churchill Downs officials investigated what appeared to be a mysterious dark spot in Funny Cide rider Jose Santos's hand as they pulled off the Kentucky Derby upset in 2003. Santos was soon afterward cleared when the blown-up photo revealed the spot to be nothing more than jockey Jerry Bailey's silks aboard Empire Maker.

Rarely, horses are "fixed" before they take a step on the track. This can be accomplished a couple of ways. Usually a horse's training is eased in the last few days leading up to a race. If he's trained hard and not given a chance to recover from strenuous work beforehand, his race performance will suffer.

Horses are usually fed a light meal and little water on race mornings. But if the horse's feed and water intake are limited the day before and then he's allowed to chow down on race morning, running on a full tummy and bladder will certainly affect his performance.

While a few trainers have been busted for stuffing a sponge into the horse's nostrils, thus limiting his air intake and leading to dreadful finishes, these shameful events are truly the exception. There's far too much at stake for trainers to be risking their livelihood and intentional cheating has become nearly obsolete.

Why might someone want to lose a race on purpose? Money, of course. Some subtle forms of payoff for throwing a race can be handsomely rewarded. Stories of $10,000 bribes for jockeys to lose races were commonplace in the 1970s. With there being so many ways to lose a race and go undetected, most likely got away with it.

Known to enjoy a good party now and again, jockey Ron Hansen was a kind and talented rider with a penchant for being in the wrong spot at the wrong time. He had been linked to some rather shady characters, and his name popped up frequently regarding accusations of fixed races, including one story where he wasn't supposed to win but found himself alone in deep stretch when the leading horse broke down in front of him. Hansen, desperately trying not to win, swerved his horse into the path of another, apparently hoping to have his number taken down. Unfortunately for him, and his backers, the stewards didn't change the order of finish.

Hansen disappeared in 1993, although his car was found on San Francisco's San Mateo Bridge. Several months later, his badly decomposed body was found in a nearby marsh. While it's likely we'll never know exactly what happened, it's probable that he either jumped off the bridge or misjudged the depth of the water, or he was pushed off.

In more recent years, some horses have raced with the benefit of a "milkshake," a concoction made with a mixture of sodium bicarbonate, sugar and electrolytes. It is believed that the milkshake helps prevent the buildup of lactic acid in the horse's muscles, possibly retarding fatigue and leading to dramatically improved performance. Commonly administered through a feeding tube into the horse's stomach, it may also be administered through the horse's regular feed in various forms of paste or tablets. While most states prohibit the use of milkshakes, few are currently testing for them. As more industry research is being done, and the concoctions become more defined, it's certain that testing processes and enforcement will increase.

The performance-enhancing cocktail is suspected as being a likely contributor to some horses' dramatic form reversals. The New York State Racing and Wagering Board filed an 88-count indictment against 17 persons of interest in 2005 revolving around the horse A One Rocket, whose smashing 10-length win in December 2003 reflected a significant improvement from his prior races, and the offshore betting activity surrounding this and other races over the last five years.

Through this experience and similar cases, more and more states are beginning to test for alkalizing agents, the key ingredient in milkshakes, and other suspected performance-enhancing drugs.

When foul play is suspected, tracks often call in the Thoroughbred Racing Protective Bureau (TRPB), racing's investigative branch. Formed in 1946, the TRPB works with tracks to maintain high standards, enforce the rules of racing and protect the integrity of the sport. In the past, the TRPB has investigated claims of race fixing, major narcotic activity and inappropriate industry licensee behaviors.

With racetrack cameras everywhere in modern racing, jockeys have too much at stake to bite on the temptations to cheat. Many illegal practices that tarnished racing for decades are no longer a risk to the industry. For the greater good, race track workers, trainers and jockeys are very hardworking people and as honest as the day is long. It's very rare that a jockey is found guilty of race tampering, and most will honestly tell you they try their hardest to win each and every race they ride.

With the high stress levels associated with weight reducing, the constant risk of injury and unrelenting pressure to win, it's no wonder that some jockeys are unable to cope with the daily rigors of their chosen career.

While few jockeys will name names, most admit there is far more alcohol and drug abuse problems among the group than they are comfortable with. Some with dependency issues find themselves gravitating towards the "dirty tracks," as they are called. Here, they can race without the threat of testing positive for drugs. Clearly, clean riders are in the majority everywhere, and most would prefer some form of random testing be done.

Some tracks require jockeys to undergo drug screening, but most do not. Of those that do, some consistently test regularly, while others will test randomly or whenever they suspect testing is warranted. If a rider tests positive, most tracks will dish out some form of a penalty or suspension.

No jockey wants the added burden of racing against someone who may not be at his or her physical or mental best. The sport is tough enough as it is, let alone for someone who's been under the influence of alcohol or drugs. The Jockeys' Room can become a lonely place for a rider without friends. The riding colony has ways of telling a jockey they're not welcomed, both in the jocks' room and on the racetrack.

While a number of today's most notable riders—Jerry Bailey, Pat Day and Stuart Elliott—have rebounded from battles with booze or drugs, jockey Mark Guidry's return to stardom has been remarkable "Growing up in Louisiana in the 1970s, lots of people were doing drugs, and it just seemed like the thing to do. I was young and foolish, and it just became a part of my life. In 1989, it all came crashing down."

Already in downward spiral, Guidry took his $10,000 racing paycheck and simply disappeared. As his family and local police searched for him, the disenchanted rider was in hiding and binging on drugs. After plowing through the money and running out of drugs a week later, he mustered up the nerve to call his wife for help.

Rather than taking him home, she courageously took him directly to jail. After spending time in the slammer, he went straight to a drug-treatment facility, where he faced the demons and won.

After leaving the rehab center, he made a humble riding comeback at Evangeline Downs. From there, Guidry has ridden the long, slow train back up the ranks of leading jockeys. After virtually losing his career to drugs 15 years ago, Guidry's horses earned nearly $4 million last year, and he is back on a major racing circuit. "I guess I'm one of the lucky ones who made the most of his second chance. I've worked very hard to make it back to where I am today, working and riding every horse I could get on along the way to regain people's trust. I feel very fortunate to have been blessed with riding talent and given a chance to prove myself again."

While Guidry's story has a happy ending, the late Chris Antley's story does not. Antley, a two-time Kentucky Derby winner, had long history of substance abuse and tragically died from a drug overdose in 2000. It was originally thought that he might have been murdered, as his body was covered with numerous cuts and bruises when he was found in his home. The house showed signs that a violent struggle had taken place. However, toxicology reports led investigators to conclude the death was an overdose of multiple drugs.

Antley had a history of being manic depressive and bipolar. Heavy boned, he had long struggled with weight issues and had a string of substance abuse issues.

As troubled as the talented, young rider was, the sight of Antley dismounting Charismatic after the horse broke down in the 1999 Belmont Stakes is one of racing's most touchingly unforgettable moments. Charismatic was attempting to win the Triple Crown and courageously fell just short after becoming injured in deep stretch. Shortly after the finish, Antley jumped off the gallant horse, calmed the scared animal down and held his injured leg up to protect further injury. Tears were running down Antley's face.

No doubt, his actions saved the horse's life. When a horse fractures a leg, they are frightened and will attempt to move away from the pain. In the struggle and thrashing around, further damage is done to the bones and ligaments. In most cases, the damage is catastrophic and the horse is put to rest.

Certainly, the stressors of the jockey profession can lead good men, and women, to make bad decisions. The psychological component of the sport is demanding and unappreciated by many outside racing who simply can't relate to the unique challenges jockeys endure.

4

SIZE REALLY DOES MATTER

Is there any other job where one big meal can put you out of work? Many jockeys literally starve themselves, depriving their bodies of vital nutrients, to make weight and earn a living. They must present themselves as light, fit, wise and strong on the exterior, while on the inside they may be suffering from dehydration, fatigue, self-doubt and unrelenting stress. Because revealing their weight struggles would most certainly lead to lost business, most riders are secretive about their battle with the scale and refuse to talk about it, often sharing stories of pity for their fellow riders who must make unthinkable sacrifices to play the game they love.

The never-ending battle with the scale drives some to make extreme sacrifices to pursue their dreams. Most riders will do just about anything to keep riding, including making a deal with the devil that jeopardizes their health, safety and sanity. While the long-term health effects from extreme weight-loss measures are not scientifically known, many punish their bodies with marathon sessions in the sauna, heavy doses of medication and self-induced vomiting of the little food and drink they dare take in. The strain eventually takes a toll on their bodies, leaving many of them worn out, visibly aged well beyond their years, and dealing with life-long health problems as a result of their war against weight.

Like the majority of jockeys, stakes-winning rider Jeff Bloom battled weight throughout his career: "Nothing else compares to the struggle of weight. Jockeys think about what they eat and drink every single minute of every day. It's all consuming. It takes such a toll on your body for life.

I had to reduce 7–9 pounds most days and now I suffer from kidney stones. It's such a tough grind."

Depending on the track and conditions of each race, most jockeys are required to make weights of 112 to 118 pounds for races. The scale of weights varies somewhat from track to track. At one location, riders may be assigned a low carry weight of 118 while at others it's 112. That six pounds is huge to many riders and makes the difference when choosing which venue to pursue.

For jockey John Grabowski, weight concerns are part of the equation in his decision to stay at New York's Finger Lakes Race Track, where he is a six-time leading rider: "I've ridden well in New Jersey and California, but I have a weight problem and I can tack 120 here without much trouble. If I went somewhere else, I'd really have to reduce hard every day to make the lower weights, and I don't want to do that to my body. When I'm 50, I don't want to look and feel like I'm 60."

Most riders start their careers in their teens, and they find making weight increasingly challenging as their bodies grow and mature. As a skyrocketing Eclipse Award–winning apprentice rider, Steve Cauthen was a teenage phenomenon when he won the Triple Crown aboard Affirmed in 1978. However, as Cauthen's body grew up, increasing weight forced him to move his tack to Europe, where higher weights are allowed. His success continued, as he was three-time leading rider in England before he became tired of battling to make the heavier European weights. Cauthen remains the only rider to win the Kentucky, Epsom, French, Irish and Italian Derbies.

When graded stakes–winning jockey Vann Belvoir began riding at age 16, he tipped the scales at a mere 100 pounds, but as his 5'2" frame matured, he knew things were going to get tough: "I was heavy boned and as I got older, I got taller. I just outgrew the sport. By the time I quit riding at 23, I'd grown four or five inches and was fighting every day to make 120. It got really frustrating at the end."

Belvoir, who now stands 5'8" tall and weighs 165, tried to stay in the game as long as he could: "I was pulling six or seven pounds in the hot box every day, mostly water weight. I was like a sponge—I could only ride if I was all ringed out. If I drank anything, though, I just sucked it up and kept it on, so I tried not drinking anything, but it would keep me up at nights and my heart would race. I was hospitalized twice for dehydration."

For men and women typically ranging from 5' to 5'6" tall, they must make weights 15–20 pounds lighter than the scale suggested by the American Medical Association. It's estimated that up to 80 percent of riders must endure some form of daily weight loss regimen to make their assigned weights. For some, "reducing," or losing, five to ten pounds every day is just part of the routine. While it's a constant struggle, they say it just comes with the territory.

A perennial leading rider at tracks like Boston's Suffolk Downs, Josiah "Joe" Hampshire is a 5'5" tall, thin-boned jockey. The 25-year riding veteran is able to tack 115 pounds most days and feels fortunate that he doesn't have the drastic reduction issues many of his brethren face: "You wouldn't believe what some of the things these guys go through every day. I know guys who drive to work with a rubber rain suit on with the heater turned up and when they get to the track, they're dripping wet. Some guys pull 7–10 pounds every day. It just becomes a part of their life. These guys are amazing athletes to go through the things they do just so they can ride every day. It's such a tough game; people have no idea."

When he's racing at Tampa Bay Downs, stakes-winning rider Terry "TD" Houghton jogs in the Florida sunshine and humidity in a truly inspiring sweat suit:

> It takes twice as long to pull weight in the sauna as it does when I go running, but I have to do it in a sweat suit. First, I put on regular long underwear, top and bottom, then I put on a rubber-like sweat suit that really locks in the heat. Over that, I'll wear a sweatshirt and sweatpants. Sometimes I'll go running after morning works right on the turf course at the track. Usually I'll go two or three miles, and longer if it's a nonracing day. The suit really makes me sweat, and I can usually drop two or three pounds in a half-hour run.

Many riders adopt a mind-over-matter approach while fighting off hunger pangs when their body cries out for sustenance. They refuse to admit that making incredibly low weights affects their athletic performance. Losing weight causes them to lose strength, endurance and balance. Going into races already weakened by restrictive diets and reducing, they oftentimes come back from races physically and mentally drained, struggling to make it back to the jocks' room where they may enjoy a few sips of water.

A former leading apprentice rider in his native Peru, David Lopez eats one meal a day and struggles against the desire to eat all the time: "Sometimes I don't get hungry, but normally I just get more and more hungry the longer it is between times when I eat. When I do eat, it's usually a salad. If I've got to have something else because I get so hungry I can't stand it, I'll have a little piece of bread and lots of water, just trying to trick my stomach that I'm not hungry any more."

Making weight is constantly on the jockeys' mind. Compulsively weighing themselves up to 50 times a day, they watch their caloric intake closely to stay as low as reasonably possible. As Hampshire described, riders must keep a close eye on everything they take in: "It's hard to keep my weight at a certain level. I have to watch what I eat every day. For breakfast, I might have two scrambled eggs, then not eat again until dinner at 7:30 or 8:00. Dinner is usually something low carb, like a turkey sandwich. I still have to pull two, three or four pounds every day in the box. I'm usually in there an hour or more every single day."

Starving their body of vital nutrients, eating disorders expose jockeys to serious long-term health risks with blood disorders, kidney and liver damage, heart problems and gastrointestinal tract problems. Bones and teeth denied of calcium become brittle, leading to painful bones and joints. From the constant grind to lose weight, many riders look years beyond their age with premature facial wrinkles and dark circles under their eyes, a telltale sign of their plight.

The near-starvation diets that many jockeys practice can be classified as anorexic behavior. According to the National Eating Disorders Association, there are significant health consequences at stake:

> Eating disorders are real, complex, and devastating conditions that can have serious consequences for health, productivity and relationships. In anorexia nervosa's cycle of self-starvation, the body is denied the essential nutrients it needs to function normally. Thus, the body is forced to slow down all of its processes to conserve energy, resulting in serious medical consequences.
>
> The health consequences are significant and include the following: abnormally slow heart rate and low blood pressure, which mean that the heart muscle is changing. The risk for heart failure rises as the heart rate and blood pressure levels sink lower and lower; reduction of bone density [osteoporosis], which results in dry, brittle bones; muscle loss and weakness; Severe dehydration, which can result in kidney failure; fainting, fatigue and overall weakness [Reprinted with permission from the National Eating Disorders Association. For more information: www.NationalEatingDisorders.org].

Internationally known author and sports nutritionist Nancy Clark has experience with jockey clients:

> I've had two that I can remember. One was bulimic, and I saw him just once. I saw the other jockey a few times, and he basically wanted to know how to starve himself to make his weight goal. Most jockeys don't want to hear the bad news.
>
> The trick is that's really hard to get as low as these guys want to get. A male who is 5'4" tall should weigh more like 130, not 110. The taller the jockeys are, the harder it is for them. For someone 5'7", they should weigh 148, give or take a bit depending on their body frame. The trick is that it is really hard to get that low. As a nutritionist, we would want jockeys to have high protein in their diet to help maintain muscle. But, if you're starving yourself, it would just get used for energy.
>
> The long-term effect of this lifestyle must be psychologically exhausting,

but the human body is amazingly resilient. My advice is that jockeys get professional help. There's great benefit for them in working with a sports nutritionist, because they really need a personalized food plan that works for them.

Although short in stature, you can see that jockeys do come in various sizes, typically ranging from 4'10" to 5'6" (©Cris Forney Photography).

The body fat percentage recommended for the average man is 15 percent and 25 percent for the average woman. Clinical literature shows that recommended minimum body fat for jockeys should be 5 percent body mass. In situations where the body fat falls too low, such as when jockeys are virtually starving themselves to make weight through extreme measures, the human body will begin breaking down its own vital organs to survive.

According to Dr. Brian Davis, director of sports medicine at the University of California, Davis, Medical Center, jockeys put themselves at serious health risk with their extreme weight maintenance measures: "A crucial component for the athlete is the body–fat ratio and whether or not it's suitable for their sport. The lower the fat ratio, the more likely they are to have higher endurance. Endurance-based athletes, like marathon runners and triathlon athletes, typically have body–fat ratios in the 7–11 percent range, with some percentages as low as 3–5 percent."

With most jockeys being in the 3–5 percent body fat range, Dr. Davis feels they would have little fat in the form of reserve: "We probably don't have enough data to draw any conclusions about the long-term effects of competing at those low rates over time. The real issues are what are causing the low body fat rates. That's where the concern is."

As glycogen stores are used up, the body relies on fat reserves to provide a greater portion of the required fuel for energy. When this happens, the intensity causes metabolic changes in the body. "Once we use up our immediate energy storage, we start using our glycogen stores," Dr. Davis explained. "After that, the body turns to reserved fat storage. If there is not enough there, the body starts tapping into proteins, meaning muscle mass. Certainly if you're breaking down the muscle tissue, the jockey is going to be less competitive."

Jean Bradley Rubel, ThD, president of Anorexia Nervosa and Related Eating Disorders, Inc., can understand the emotional pull jockeys must face:

> As a competitor myself, I know the seductive power of winning, but in the long run, winning is not as important as staying alive and being healthy.
>
> If not stopped, starving, stuffing and purging can lead to irreversible physical damage and even death. Eating disorders can affect every single cell, tissue and organ in the body.
>
> The cruel reality is that persistent undereating, binge eating and purging may lead individuals to any one of the following psychological complications: Depression; anxiety and self-doubt; guilt and shame; hypervigilance and fear of discovery; compulsive behaviors and rituals; and feelings of alienation and loneliness.
>
> Eating disorders bring pain and suffering not only to the people who have them, but also to their families and friends. The problems may disrupt the family relationship with fights over food and weight. Family members may also be struggling with guilt, worry, anxiety and frustration. Nothing they can do seems to make things better.

4. Size Really Does Matter 83

Jockeys are forever trying to find a tolerable diet that works for them. Graded stakes–winning jockey Gary Baze has battled the scale for decades and, like most riders, finds weight issues the most unpleasant part of his profession: "Dieting is miserable. I've tried all the different programs—low carb, low fat, high protein, fruits and vegetables. I would say the only thing that really works is just not eating much."

While there's no magic beyond good common sense in dieting, modern day jockeys know more about nutrition than their predecessors. Aaron Gryder is one of the new breed of jockeys who seek out professional help in managing his weight and fitness:

> I have a dietitian and personal trainer. I've been working with Mark Bertrand, who used to be a body builder, for a few years now. I'm on a consistent eating plan and I exercise a lot. I do yoga, weight training, pilates, run on the treadmill and work out with my trainer. I still have to pull a few pounds in the sauna every day, but I'm able to stay away from diuretics and things like that. I'm lucky because I'm getting really good help now. So many young riders need more education about weight issues, so they don't get into trouble with things they're going to regret later.
>
> For breakfast, I typically have two egg whites and maybe a slice of tomato. I might have a protein shake and water for lunch. Between races, I might have a slice of orange or a bite of a power bar. For dinner, I like to have fish, usually steamed, broiled or grilled. I usually have veggies or salad on the side with lots of water. I also take 22 vitamins during the course of a day to make sure I'm getting all the nutrients.

Frank Lovato, Jr., a rider for 25 years, used a somewhat unorthodox method to make weight:

> Making weight is a desperate way of life for many jockeys. It runs your life as a jockey. You're always thinking about it. When you are in that state of mind, you would do or try just about anything to see if it would work. For me, it wasn't the hunger that bothered me as much as the thirst.
>
> What worked best for me, strange as it sounds, was drinking beer. For dinner, I'd drink a couple of beers because they would really dry me out. If I drank water or anything else, I'd balloon up. After the beer, I'd eat healthy, like vegetables and protein, when I got hungry. But after I was done eating, I'd go flip it up. I know it wasn't healthy, but there were guys doing a lot worse things than me.

In the case of Debbie Hoonan, a better diet gave her a second chance. Hoonan was a modestly successful rider at Longacres Race Track near Seattle, when the track shut down in 1992. Like so many others, she struggled with weight and health issues her entire career and called it quits for good when the track closed, at least she thought so at the time.

Twelve years later, at the age of 37, she made it back to the track: "I hadn't really planned on coming back to race riding, but I thrive on a good challenge. I eliminated the things that were bad for me in my life, went on a low carb diet and started galloping horses again. I just feel stronger now, both physically and mentally, and people kept encouraging me to keep going." About a month after her remarkable comeback, she won her first-ever stakes race.

When unbearable food cravings become too much, riders may turn to anorexiants, appetite suppressants or amphetamines for help, trying to fix one problem, but creating others. These drugs may cause elevated blood pressure, irregular heartbeat and ultimately some degree of psychosis, if overtaken. Some riders use thyroid pills in an attempt to quicken the body's metabolism, burning up more calories and allowing some riders to eat more without gaining weight. Because of the rapid heart rate often caused by this medication, the jockey may take another medication to slow their heart down.

If a rider allows himself the luxury of one solid meal a week, it's usually on Sunday night after the week's racing is concluded. With Monday and Tuesday being common dark days, they have a few extra days to reduce the extra pounds of the one quality meal they've enjoyed.

Some riders eat on a more regular schedule, however, and deal with implications in another way. Eating provides only momentary comfort for jockeys who utilize "flipping," or self-induced vomiting, as their means of managing their weight.

Jockeys who practice this morbid technique are known as "heavers." They often use a special area inside the jockeys' room restroom to take care of business. Nearly all jocks' rooms include a large stall with an oversized toilet bowel that resembles a floor mounted sink, known as a heaving bowl. Over time, frequent flippers become so accustomed to vomiting that they forego using their fingers as a trigger and learn to simply bend over the bowl and empty their bellies.

Flipping becomes compulsive. Once they start, it's nearly impossible to stop the practice. Some riders break down and gorge themselves with huge meals, sometimes inhaling 10,000 calories of mainly high-fat comfort foods in a single day. But the food rarely hits the digestive system, as they visit the restroom minutes later to flip it back up. They may repeat this ritual several times a day. Not only is this practice extremely unhealthy, it's also very expensive, as many flippers go through five or six huge meals a day.

Most heavers try to keep their bulimic activity secretive by flipping at home or in other private locations to protect their reputation and self-image. Riders are worried that if horsemen knew they were flipping, it could cost them business.

At 5'7" tall, Chris Herrell is a one of the taller jockeys. As a heaver for a dozen years, he tortures himself daily to make weight. Herrell, who ironically wants to be a Chef when his riding days are done, recalled the needed for guidance with weight control early in his career:

> When I first started riding and having trouble with weight, I asked a few older riders about reducing. They told me about how to use the hot box and about heaving. Now that I've been around awhile and have been heaving for a long time, young guys are asking *me* for advice. I show them how to do it, but I discourage them from it because it's such a horrible way to live.
>
> I'm thinking about food all day long, every day of the week. On a day that I'm not racing, I'll go the track and work horses in the morning. But as soon as it's done, I can't wait to get something to eat and I'll stop on my way home for fast food or something quick. My favorite is Waffle House. I'll have a big, greasy breakfast and then give it right back. A few hours later, I'm usually craving for something salty or spicy; just about anything that I know I can't have. Some of my favorites are Mexican, pizza, hot wings or just about anything deep fried. For dinner, I try and have something healthy, like steamed vegetables, but sometimes I'll end up having a pot of clam chowder or a plate of shrimp with butter and garlic over rice. I'm flipping right after I eat every meal, so I'm usually in the bathroom three or four times on a nonrace day.
>
> On the days I ride, I'll go to the jocks' room after I'm done at the track in the morning and hit the box, because I still have to pull more weight. The sauna really dries me out. I get so thirsty that I can't stand it and have something to drink. Then, I figure I might as well eat, because I'm going to have to give back the fluid anyway. So after heaving, I'm still dying of thirst, but can't drink or I'll be over [weight] again. In the summer, particularly, I get so dehydrated that I have to rinse my mouth out with water or my tongue sticks to the roof of my mouth. On days that I'm racing, I'll heave anywhere from four to eight times, depending on how often I eat.
>
> In order to flip, I have to have lots of food and fluid in my belly. I'll head to the toilet, or heaving bowl in the jocks' room, as soon as I've finished my last bite. I'll drink a coke on the way to be sure I have enough fluid inside. If I've had greasy food, I may need to drink warm water and heave a second time to be sure I've cleaned myself out good.
>
> Some guys use their fingers as a trigger to vomit, but I've been doing it so long now, I just bend over and it comes out on command. If I'm in a hurry, I can even control how fast it happens.
>
> I haven't had any major health problems with heaving yet, but my back teeth give me problems. I know to rinse my mouth out as soon as I'm done heaving to wash away the acid. Sometimes my stomach hurts from all the acid, and I might have a slice of toasted bread. It feels like it forms a ball in there and absorbs the acid. I'm not sure what the long-term effects of this are going to be, I haven't asked my doctor about it, and I'm afraid to find out.
>
> At the end of 2000, I had to quit riding because I just couldn't handle reducing and heaving any more. That's when I started at the culinary arts school and it's when I allowed myself to start eating again. I went from 110

pounds to 160 pounds in one trimester. As you can imagine, I couldn't even fit into my clothes any more.

It such a horrible way to live, but I have to do it to make weight. It's not what I want to do, but I have to do it.

I hope to keep riding long enough to graduate from school. I dropped out for awhile because I just couldn't ride and go to school at the same time. I hope to get back in and finish culinary school next year.

According to the National Eating Disorders Association, there are significant health risks of bulimia nervosa:

> The recurrent binge-and-purge cycles of bulimia can affect the entire digestive system and can lead to electrolyte and chemical imbalances in the body that affect the heart and other major organ functions. Electrolyte imbalances can lead to irregular heartbeats and possibly heart failure and death. The electrolyte imbalance is caused by dehydration and loss of potassium, sodium and chloride from the body as a result of purging behaviors.
>
> There is also the potential for gastric rupture during periods of bingeing and inflammation, and possible rupture, of the esophagus from frequent vomiting. Some may experience peptic ulcers and pancreatitis. For those that use laxatives, chronic and irregular bowel movements and constipation as a result of laxative abuse are common threats.

The stomach acids from flipping wears on tooth enamel, weakening teeth and leaving many jockeys with a mouth full of yellow, rotting teeth and gum problems. Depression is another concern commonly associated with the disease, an unhealthy complication for athletes already under great pressures and stress.

A sorrowful illustration of the terrifying physical risks of being a jockey and the tragic effects of abusing one's body and depriving it of vital nutrition over time is the sad tale of retired rider Randy Romero. Romero was a top jockey, winning over 4,200 races including a thrilling win aboard the undefeated Personal Ensign in the 1998 Breeder's Cup Distaff, beating Kentucky Derby winner Winning Colors in a spectacular stretch rally. His riding career spanned 27 years, but the trouble started early.

As a teenage rider at Louisiana's Delta Downs, veteran riders warned him that if he were going to stay in the game for long, he'd have to keep his weight down. He began flipping soon after. At first, flipping began with his fingers triggering the gag reflux process to empty his belly. After years of self-induced vomiting, his body no longer needing a starter button—he simply bent over and spilled the bucket. At the end of his career, Romero was flipping five or six times a day.

The constant battle against the scale took its toll. Over the years, thousands of diet pills, diuretics, laxatives and trips to the heaving bowl left him dehydrated, drained and constantly fatigued.

One riding injury after another plagued him throughout his tenure.

Too many broken bones to count, he went under the knife more than 20 times. Pain pills and anti-inflammatories became part of his daily routine.

In 1983, he nearly died in a freak "hot box," or sauna, accident at Oaklawn Park, located in Hot Springs, Arkansas. To induce maximum sweating for weight loss, he liberally covered his body with alcohol. He inadvertently brushed up against one of the hot-box bulbs and ignited. Before shocked friends could extinguish their burning comrade, serious damage was done. Over 60 percent of his body had suffered second and third degree burns. He withstood agonizingly painful skin grafts and cosmetic surgery for years.

Remorseful of all the self-inflicted abuse and accidents, Romero struggles on with hope: "I had lots of accidents over the years; they've added up, and I regret the things I did to keep riding. I took lots of anti-inflammatories, and they really hurt me a lot. When I had the explosion in the sauna, it didn't just burn me on the outside, it burned me on the inside, too. And I know the flipping for all those years hasn't helped me, either."

His body, unable to handle the years of overdone flipping, weight loss drugs and damage from the burns, broke down. He now suffers from kidney and liver damage. With drastically reduced kidney functionality, he requires weekly dialysis. He needs both vital organs transplanted, but was unable to obtain health insurance for a couple of years:

> Thankfully I'm on Medicare now. The doctors say 75 percent of my liver is gone, but before they'll do surgery, I've got to lose another 10 percent functionality. I'm on dialysis and just waiting for the OK for surgery. At least I'm not getting any worse.
>
> I don't know if my body could survive the surgery, though. I feel strong enough to go to the gym and workout, but then I come home and lay on the couch for a few hours because I'm so tired. The doctors are a little worried that the antirejection drugs might cause problems for me.

Like Romero, nearly all jockeys endure long sessions in the sauna. Jockey's rooms are typically equipped with two forms of saunas, or "hot boxes," to assist riders in reducing, or "pulling" weight. There is a wet, or steam, sauna, and a dry sauna with temperatures exceeding 180 degrees. Most riders are forced to hit the box daily to drop anywhere from a few pounds of water weight up to an astonishing ten pounds on race day.

Lenny Frazzitta, Jr., was one of the country's top apprentice riders in 1998. Today, like most riders, he hits the hot box in the jocks' room nearly every day before heading out to ride: "I start by taking a hot shower to get things started, then go into the sauna and sit at the top level for a few minutes to get a sweat going. Then I step out and put on baby oil to keep the sweat going."

Forced to reduce four or five pounds, he jumps right back into the box: "I'll do the first 10 minutes at the top level, which is 190 degrees. That's about as long as I can handle the high heat. My heart starts beating fast. I'll do another ten minutes at the middle level and then 10 on the floor level, which is a little cooler. Tiredly, I step out and weigh myself. I can usually drop two pounds in 30 minutes."

A few minutes later, he's back in for another round: "I may have to go in two or three rounds, depending on how I'm doing with weight. By this time, my mouth gets so dry it's overwhelming. I may have a freeze pop or two, but I only chew it up and spit it out. At least it's cold and flavorful. It defeats the purpose if I swallow the juice."

By the time he's done, Frazzitta is exhausted from the daily ritual: "You can't imagine how exhausted you get from hitting the box. To keep my energy level up, I take potassium pills and vitamins with a few sips of juice or Gatorade. On the days when I don't have to drop weight, I feel so much better and stronger."

After marathon sauna sessions, many riders are forced to lie down to regain their sense of balance and equilibrium before suiting up for their first race. Dehydration is a constant risk, yet taking in more than a few precious sips of fluid might put them overweight for their riding assignment.

No doubt, they feel weak after spending hours in the box. Many take to the track while suffering the effects of low-grade dehydration, riding while impaired with blurred vision and dizziness. Even veteran riders like Hall of Famer Gary Stevens, who fainted from dehydration after pulling weight in the box before taking on the day's races at Del Mar, need to be careful not to over do it.

Tragically, apprentice rider Emanuel Jose Sanchez, died earlier in 2005 a day after being admitted to the hospital with signs of dehydration. Sanchez, who was riding at Colonial Downs in Virginia, had spent time in the hot box to drop a few pounds and was sent to the hospital after acting strangely after his last race. He slipped into a coma that night and died the following day.

Clinical studies show that dehydration severely affects physical performance and creates serious health risks like hypokalemia, a shortage of potassium in the blood and a potentially life threatening condition. Clinical data suggests that a reduction of 5 percent or more in body weight due to sweating may result in serious ailments related to overheating.

Dehydration undoubtedly affects the jockey's strength, reactionary time and endurance. Riders who pull high levels of water weight are not capable of performing at their maximum. They're not only cheating themselves, but the people they work for and the general betting public, for that matter. But if they don't make weight, they're out of work. Many feel they have no choice.

Former rider Gary Lawless battled weight most of his eighteen-year career:

> I had a pretty lean diet, eating mostly fish and poultry, but I would hardly ever drink. It ballooned me up something terrible. As it was, I had to pull five or six pounds every day. It was so miserable that there were days I didn't even want to be there. You get so tired and drained that all you want to do is lay down and sleep.
>
> Once you hit the racetrack, though, adrenaline takes over and you're fine. But once you're done riding for the day, that last walk back to the jockeys' room reminds you how tired you are. I always slept real good at night after racing.

Most sports medicine experts agree that proper hydration is the single most important nutritional factor in promoting top athletic performance. If the jockey has deprived himself of fluid to the point of dehydration, the body may be unable to cool itself. As working muscles heat up from exercise, a dehydrated body may not be able to dissipate the heat, thus raising the body's core temperature, increasing the risk of heat stroke.

"Performance is directly and largely impacted by dehydration," Dr. Davis explained. "Although the jockeys' events are short timed, more like a sprinter than a long distance runner, the water imbalance caused by their extreme dehydration methods may limit their body's natural cooling down capacity. With extreme dehydration, it's like you're running with reduced blood volume, so your heart is working harder. It's similar to the experience of bleeding to death. It's very troubling."

If dieting, flipping and the hot box don't do the trick, riders may turn to medication for help in making weight. The two most common drugs used are Lasix, a form of diuretic, and laxatives.

Diuretics and various forms of "water pills" are used to pull retained water weight. Lasix, the drug of choice for most riders, causes them to urinate frequently. Repetitive use of diuretics may lead to multiple problems with the heart, kidney, liver, blurred vision, skin changes and sexual dysfunction. The most common problem riders experience from Lasix is severe cramps. Because the drug takes all the fluids, including vital nutrients, minerals and electrolytes from their body, riders suffer through stabbing cramps in their muscles and joints.

"Sometimes the cramps would be so bad that it felt like my hips and legs would lock up. It could be excruciating pain," said Lawless. "If you got into the starting gate and had cramps, that would be really bad because you don't have time or room to stretch out. Some guys got cramps in their arms and hands. Most of us would take potassium pills, which often helped, but you never knew when it would flare up again."

While Lasix aids riders in dropping water weight, it comes at a price:

> Diuretic medications cause the kidneys to dump water out of the body. This can cause a low blood pressure and increased heart rate [according to Dr. Davis]. The body has about five liters of fluid in the bloodstream at any one time. If you reduce the amount of water, the heart has to work that much harder to maintain the pressure. Not only are the higher heart rates detrimental to athletic performance, but the increased load on the kidneys can also be damaging. Electrolyte imbalances, combined with increased heart rates, can lead to serious heart rhythm disturbances, and even death. If the fluid is reduced to the point that the red blood cell count is increased, this can lead to sludging up the blood flow and an increased risk of stroke.

For graded stakes–winning jockey Ricky Frazier, overuse of the drugs nearly cost him more than just his riding career: "I've tried all the tricks to keep weight down over the year. Lasix really caused me problems, though. It nearly shut my liver down. The doc said I had something like only 12 percent liver function left and I was going to need a transplant."

Some riders chomp on Ex-Lax and other laxatives like they're candy. When used excessively, laxatives can lead to severe cramping, weakness, fatigue and, in extreme cases, cathartic colon, a condition where the bowel becomes dependent on drugs for normal function. Dr. Davis believes laxatives can put organs at risk: "Laxative abuse can lead to similar problems as the abuse of diuretic medications, but often not to the same degree. Life-threatening metabolic issues have still been reported. Most commonly, the constant use of laxatives will lead to a dependence on them just to have a regular bowel movement."

As a result of restricting food and fluid intake and using drugs to reduce weight, most jockeys suffer from some degree of fatigue and dehydration. If the jockey is also visiting the hot box for several hours a day, it's a prescription for serious trouble. Although most riders refuse to talk publicly about their problems for fear of losing reputation and business, industry estimates show that up to 85 percent of riders are practicing unhealthy methods of regulating their weight to meet riding assignments.

The combination of severe food restriction and fluid deprivation is a prescription for trouble for riders. When mixed with other extreme forms of weight reduction, such as drug-induced methods and lengthy sauna sessions, it can cause severe problems:

> If the jockeys combine two or more of these extreme measures, it increases their overall risk because so many body systems are being affected at one time [outlined Dr. Davis]. It's likely that the longer they practice these

methods, the more likely it is that they are going to get sick, potentially very sick.

Intentionally doing these things for their professional and monetary gain in a controlled fashion so that they can still compete, they probably become skilled at knowing how much of this they can physically tolerate at any one time, but they're probably not aware of what they're doing to their body's health.

Growing up near Santa Anita Race Track, Dr. David Baron, professor and chair of the Department of Psychiatry at Temple University School of Medicine, has some experience with the racing industry:

> I've been involved in Sports Medicine for a long time and have worked with college and professional athletes for many years. There are lots of commonalities between the ordeal jockeys go through and wrestlers, gymnasts and pairs figure skaters, but there are some significant variances, too.
>
> In most sports, there's a coach to help the athlete with all the aspects of training, educating them about things they should and shouldn't do to maximize performance, but that's not the case with jockeys. These jockeys will go to most any length to make weight so they can ride. Because they nearly all do it, it's almost like it's accepted as the price of admission into the sport. It must be addressed.
>
> Losing so much body fluid is a serious problem from a sports medicine aspect. There is a significant price paid with the risk of kidney and cardiac problems associated with the electrolyte imbalance. I'm afraid there is a misunderstanding of the significance of the health risks. The jockeys probably think they are invincible, but this is a serious problem.
>
> You can't rely on the jockeys themselves to solve the problem. It's doubtful they would risk their livelihood over it. They are very good athletes and people don't pay enough attention to this issue, but they should be. It's an important health issue and people seem more interested in horses and putting on the races than in promoting jockey health. I don't understand how the racing industry leadership structure works, but I think the jockeys probably need help from within the industry.

The racing industry has long struggled with the scale of weight issue, generally with jockeys crying for higher weights and horsemen concerned that more weight would lead to increased horse injuries. Many feel the owners and trainers care more about the horses than they do about the men and women who ride them.

While the scale has basically remained unchanged over the past century, some tracks have raised the bottom of the weight scale in the past few years, with minimums being raised by a couple of pounds at tracks sprinkled across the country.

Many in the jockey community feel the industry is unsympathetic to the jockeys' plight. Riders argue that raising the bottom of the scale would allow them to stop the vicious cycle of reducing to make weight.

They feel the jockey colony, in general, would be healthier, stronger and more durable.

"Many riders are cannibalizing their organs by riding at dangerously low weights," according to recently retired, outspoken jockey Shane Sellers.

> The Jockeys' Guild put a proposal in front of tracks that called for weights to be minimally raised and to begin testing riders for body fat ratios. In the proposal, if the jockey was under 5 percent body fat, he couldn't ride. Colorado recently adopted the rule and hopefully other states will now follow suit.
>
> This would cause many of today's riders problems, but we'd only be saving their lives. I know that I was under 5 percent most of my career but didn't realize it until recently. Now I'm worried about what the long-term effects of my lifestyle are going to be as I get older.

For the riders who don't have to reduce to make weights now, most are against the raising of weights. Apprentice rider Liz Morris rides the Hawthorne-Arlington circuit, where weights were recently raised

> For some reason, the weights are lighter at Hawthorne than they are at Arlington and you'd think they'd be the same. I've seen races written now at 124 at Arlington, which I think is the highest I've seen. I've seen that high for quarter horse races, but not thoroughbred. That same race would go at 122 at Hawthorne. You'd think it would be the same because it's basically the same people at both tracks.
>
> I don't think raising the weights too much is fair to horses or to the lighter riders. I think more horses are going to get hurt if the weight is too high. Most jockeys, though, want to change the scale, or they don't want to say anything negative about it because they're worried about upsetting other riders.

A veteran rider of 20-years, retired jockey Tom Chapman feels that the problems haven't changed much from when he was riding "I remember when they raised the weights a few pounds when I was riding, and it seems like the jockeys are having the same problems, so the change didn't seem to do much to help. The horses today don't seem to be able to carry the weight as well, either. I think some guys are just too big to ride."

Opponents are worried that if the scale were raised, the problem would only be extended out further. There are worries that jockeys would then have trouble making higher weights. Many light riders, like Pat Day, oppose the raise and worry about new riders being attracted by the higher weights. He's concerned that new problems would be created by luring in new riders, who might be tempted to try and make the higher weight, thus compounding the problem to a new generation of heavier riders.

One of the more outspoken horsemen against raising the scale is trainer D. Wayne Lukas, who feels jockeys are supposed to be light and that if they can't make weight, maybe they are in the wrong job. Lukas and others are concerned that the extra weight puts more strain on horses and will lead to increased equine injury.

Breeder's Cup winning trainer Todd Pletcher feels people need to look beyond old-school thinking on the issue: "I can sympathize with both sides. I think we need to make adjustments both ways. We need to raise the minimum weight jockeys carry, but without harming the horses. If they raise the bottom to something like 125, it's just going to increase the pool [of riders] that much more. I mean, I have exercise riders that are too heavy to race right now, but if the scale is raised too much, they might try and come down to that weight, and we'd still have problems."

Another concern horsemen have is that if weights are raised at some tracks, but not others, horses will be sent to the tracks where they can run with lighter-weight assignments. Jockeys, on the other hand, may be moving in the opposite direction, to locations where they may be able to ride a few pounds heavier. If so, this could create an unbalanced supply of quality riders, with more riders at the tracks with fewer horses.

A member of the management team at Santa Anita, retired Hall of Famer Chris McCarron has first hand experience with the scale: "It's been too long since the weights were adjusted. It should be raised across the board. We raised the weights here at Santa Anita at the end of the year about an average of four pounds. In cases where horses used to carry 114, they might now carry 118."

An initiative from the California Horse Racing Board in response to jockeys' pleas for higher weights led to a proposal recently to increase the minimum to 126, including the rider's tack. The only thing that's certain about the proposition is that it's certainly to heat up the argument on both sides of the issue.

No matter what industry representatives finally decide on the scale of weight issue, providing education and counseling programs for riders about nutrition and health maintenance would be a significant step in the right direction.

5

THEY'RE OFF!

The racing day begins and ends in the jockeys' room. It's home and headquarters for them. Inside, they find comfort, camaraderie and a host of support staff prepared to help them put on the pageantry and excitement of a day at the races.

The routine each rider takes to prepare for the day's work varies greatly. Some riders prepare quietly by themselves, while others can't sit still if their life depended on it. Most riders spend time reading the racing form, calculating how their races will be run. Not only do jockeys need to understand their own horse, they need to know what others are going to be doing. They predict where the speed will be coming from, who the closers are, which horses may cause racing trouble that they may need to watch for and try to come up with a variety of game plans to utilize once the running gets started.

Many riders read the racing form the night before and refresh themselves on each race's likely pace and racing scenario as race time approaches. Any scratches, changes in racing surface or other tactical dynamics that may be impacted must be considered. Off-track conditions often have an effect on the horse's abilities and require a fresh perspective on racing tactics.

Jockey Lonnie Meche is a believer in home study:

> I read the form the night before, usually 20 minutes on each race. To do it right, you've got to put your time into it. In order to comprehend everything, I don't like any disturbances. I'll look at everything, like who the speed horses are and how fast they'll be going; who the come-from-behind horses are and where they'll be coming from. I'll look back as far as the form goes to look at their races. I'll look at their workouts, how fast they've been working and who is training them. For example, Steve Asmussen doesn't work them fast, but they always come out fit and ready to the races.

I'll look to find the horse's best performance and try to figure out what he did that day. I'll try and ride him back to that race. If the track is muddy, I'll look at his previous races in the mud and his breeding.

My job is to try and figure out what I need to do to put the horse in the position to win. If I get him a good trip, keep him out of trouble and put him a position where he has a chance of winning, I've done my part. It all starts with planning ahead.

Most jocks' rooms are furnished with a large changing area that includes lockers, benches and storage areas for gear and personals. Other standards include some form of an exercise room, sauna area, kitchen, relaxation area and bathroom facilities. Higher-end rooms may include sleeping quarters, swimming pool and entertainment areas.

For many, getting prepared for the races means getting themselves physically ready. Whether it is stretching, massage, sauna or warming up on the Equicizer, jockeys all have their favorite routine. If any sore or aching rider needs stretching, massage or therapy, most tracks employ a sports-trained physical therapist to provide treatment. The racetrack physical therapist at Emerald Downs, Micky Marquez, is popular amongst the jockey colony: "I provide lots of pre-race stretching, massage, icing and wrapping. I may treat 30–50 percent of the riders every day. The jockeys get progressively more tired and sore as the racing week moves along. By Sunday, I'm really busy trying to keep up with everybody."

Racetracks maintain a first-aid room and employ a doctor to care for ill and injured jockeys, track personnel and racing patrons. Track physician Nina Spalek, MD, is responsible for clearing jockeys to ride at the start of the racing meet. When jockeys need to be taken off their mounts due to illness or injury, they must obtain the doctor's approval beforehand. As Dr. Spalek explains, jockeys are in a high-risk occupation: "I'm most cautious about head injuries and potential concussions. I see a lot of pulled muscles, sprains, strains and contusions. If a rider is hurt, sick or dehydrated and unable to ride, I have to report it to the stewards and other officials, even if the jockey wants to continue riding."

It's evident that a pecking order exists inside every jockeys' room, with top riders getting more respect, attention and preferred treatment. Because of the small confines of many jockeys' rooms, confrontation between riders is inevitable. Outbursts are usually short and rarely consist of more than a few mouthfuls of trash talk or scolding a young rider. If a rider has claimed a foul after racing, he's already talked with the stewards but will have to explain his case to an entirely different, and often unsympathetic, audience in the jocks' room.

There's an unwritten rule that riders offer a courtesy apology for race riding actions that may have affected the racing tactics of another rider.

While the excuse does little to cover up the obvious, everyone in the room is chasing the same prize and every one of them will do whatever they can to improve their chances of winning.

A rider in two Kentucky Derbies, Donnie Meche enjoys the camaraderie he finds in the jockeys' room:

> It's a great little world in there. We spend more time in the jocks' room with other riders than we do at home with our families. It's a friendly place and everyone gets to know everyone real well.
>
> Before the races start, I sit in the box to loosen up. After I get out, I'll stretch and relax until my first race. I psyche myself up and get in the zone for riding good races.

Jockeys try to learn everything they can about horses they will be up on, and much of the learning happens while in the jockeys' quarters. If they're riding a horse they don't know, they talk to other riders who've ridden the horse before, receiving tips and information on how to handle the new horse. The horse's trainer also provides valuable data on the horse.

Knowing about the horse's traits and habits in advance gives the jockey an opportunity to develop a plan to deal with the horse's tendencies. For example, some horses require soft handling and must be coaxed along, whereas a lazy horse might need a more hustled ride, shaking the horse up throughout the race to keep him focused on the task at hand. Some horses fight for control, and the jockey may need to compromise the little tussles to win the battle with his equine partner.

In between races, jockeys spend their time reading, playing pool, throwing darts, playing cards, watching TV, or whatever other pastime they enjoy. However, once the horses begin entering the starting gate, for riders in the jockeys' room without a ride, all eyes are glued to the race monitors throughout the area.

As Meche explained, there's no time to relax between consecutive races:

> If I'm riding two or more in a row, there's no downtime between the races. As soon as I get back into the room, I get my silks off and change for the next race. I'll wash my face and wipe down my boots and watch the replay of the race I just rode in. I might have a few minutes to sit down, read the form real quick to review the horses in the next race and wait for the clerk to call us out.
>
> If I have a break between races, I have time to relax on the bench and watch the next race. At most tracks, the jocks' room has Ping-Pong or pool tables if you want to play. In some places, there are TVs in the lounge or kitchen that shows races from other tracks, soap operas or whatever you want to do to stay relaxed.

Randy Meier, a graded stakes–winning rider and career leader at Hawthorne and Sportsman Park tracks, tries to learn as much as he can from watching the races:

In the jocks' room, I watch all the races and replays to see if there's a track bias for speed horses or closers and to see if the horses are winning from the fence or off the rail.

If there's a scratch, even if it's in the post parade or at the gate, it might change how the race will be run, so I have to adjust my plan. I need to know where people are going to be coming from. You want to know everyone's habits in advance. As far as doing your homework in advance, I guess you get out of it what you put into it.

For some of the bigger races, anxiety levels in the jockeys' room increase. Mark Guidry, a Grade I stakes–winning rider with 30 years experience, has learned to approach every race as though it's a big one:

> It doesn't matter if it's an $8,000 claimer or Grade I race, as a professional, you do your homework and get yourself ready. A win is a win, it's just that the payday is a lot bigger in a stakes race. For the big races, there's a little more tension and excitement in the room, for sure. I remember when I was young, I used to get butterflies when the stakes came up, but it's gotten easier with experience.
>
> Some guys might try to overanalyze the race, and sometimes being too smart hurts more than it helps. I try to relax and just go out and rely on my instincts. I try to just react naturally to whatever situation comes up in a race rather than planning it all out because it hardly ever unfolds the way you plan it.

Riders employ a valet to work for them in preparing their silks and racing equipment the jockeys' room. Each valet, grammatically pronounced "val let" by insiders, handles the jock room services for several riders at a time. The loyal and trusting relationship between valet and rider usually lasts for years. Thanks to the hard work of quality valets, rest assured we're not likely to see a "wardrobe malfunction" anytime soon.

Valet Dennis Snowden, who once had Hall of Famer Laffit Pincay as one his clients, explains that breaking into the ranks is difficult: "It used to be that in order to be a valet, you had to have been a jockey first. In fact, I rode about 100 races before I was able to work as a valet."

Valets gather and prepare the rider's silks, riding helmet, goggles, boots, saddle and whip. "They might call us butlers, because that's what we really are," the 33-year veteran explained. "Anything that the jockey needs or wants, it's my job to get it for him. If there's something I don't have, I'll go to the store and get it."

Racing silks are kept in the track's silks room, which is an oversized closet filled with racks of the horse owner's colorful silks, sorted by trainer. Silks are relatively all the same size and large enough to fit the taller jockeys. Jockeys secure the long sleeves by fixing a rubber band around their wrist at the desired length.

The valet escorts the rider to the paddock, which is typically located in close proximity to the jockeys' quarters, and meets him on the track after each race for unsaddling. Valets are allowed to assist the riders in weighing in and out from races. In some instances, tracks may employ "saddlers" to assist with this activity. After the rider returns to the jocks' room after racing, the valet gathers up the dirty laundry and gear, organizing and laying out the rider's clean equipment for the next race.

While employed by the racing associations, valets are paid an hourly wage and share in a "pool" of funds chipped in by the jockeys. In addition to these routine wages, valets typically receive a stake, or bonus, when their riders win.

Riders must report early to the jockeys' quarters before races, typically 30 minutes prior to the post time of their first riding assignment. They must disclose any overweight to the track's clerk of scales, the official in charge of weighing jockeys before and after races. Many clerks are former riders and also manage the jockey room activity.

As the Clerk of Scales in California, former jockey Paul Nicolo handles morning entries at the track, receives the scratches and sorts out the rider assignments and alternates. "In the afternoons, I check the riders out for their races on the scale in the jockeys' room before they head to the paddock. After the race, I weigh them back in out near the track. They have to come back from the race within a small allowance of the weight they left at."

The jockeys' official racing weight includes clothing, boots, saddle gear, whip, helmet, goggles and number cloth. Once the jockey passes the scale prior to the race, they are guaranteed the minimum jockey mount fee even if the horse gets scratched in the paddock or on the way to the gate, unless the jockey is somehow injured and requires a replacement.

Late in 2004, state investigators and police raided three New York racetracks, collecting entry sheets and jockey weight information, leading to the assumption that some jockeys may have raced carrying inappropriate weights.

One of the key documents in the research will be scale sheets, which are documents completed by the clerk of scales when jockeys weigh in for each racing event. It's likely that a comparison of the rider's assigned weight, the documented scale sheet weight and investigation of the jockeys' actual weight will be the focal point of the inquisition.

In the past, several such investigations found the clerk of scales allowing riders, often friends, to ride overweight, a violation of racing rules. If the investigation finds that weights were intentionally falsified, it would be a violation of state law.

If a jockey is unable to complete his riding obligation due to last-minute injury or illness, other jockeys who are without a horse in the race are eligible to pick up the opening. Oftentimes, the clerk of scales will ask the trainer who he wants to ride the horse, and the clerk will seek that rider out in the jocks' room. Jockeys can be fined for not fulfilling their riding assignments, unless they've been released by the track physician.

If the jockey and his gear don't make up the assigned weight, a weighted saddle pad is added to make up the difference. For example, if the rider is assigned 118 and weighs 114 with required gear, a four-pound saddle pad will be added to make weight.

In the jocks' room, and during the post parade, many riders try to memorize the silk colors of the other jockeys in the race, so they can identify where specific horses are during the running of the race and adjust their racing tactics accordingly.

Jockeys must enter the paddock with a positive attitude. It makes a difference, as horses seem to be able to sense the rider's frame of mind. When giving the jockey a leg up, most trainers will give the rider some form of instructions. Predictably, advice to break cleanly, get racing position, save ground and leave some horse for the finish is shared. Some trainers, like detail-focused Michael Dickinson, are known to give explicit instructions to their rider while others give the jockey freedom to do whatever he sees fit.

Midwest-based trainer Jere Smith, Jr., likes to keep it simple for his riders: "My advice is to keep the horse clear and moving. If it's the first time the jockey is riding the horse, I'll let the rider know the horse's tendencies. Maybe he lugs in or out, doesn't like the inside or likes to make his move on the outside. Some horses get a big heart on the lead or like to make one run."

Trainers may throw the rider a curveball and direct a different strategy than the jockey thought was their best game plan. Jockeys nearly always try to follow the trainer's directive, however, which may represent the owner's desires. Because the rider doesn't want to risk losing the ride, he'll follow the boss's directive.

Former jockey Jack Allen now trains horses from his base at Mountaineer Park in West Virginia. He feels he has an advantage over many trainers because of his riding experience and understanding of racing tactics: "I think I have a pretty good relationship with jockeys now. Because of my riding experience, I know that once you leave that gate, it's in the jockeys' hands, and my job is done. So, I let them pretty much ride their race. I offer very little instructions. I might tell him to lay close or let the horse settle into stride and make a late run, but other than that, it's up to them. I think they appreciate that."

Melody Brooks, a stakes-winning rider, wants full disclosure before she steps into irons:

Sometimes there's deceit between the trainer and jockey. I'd guess that 75 percent of trainers are honest and forward with what's really going on with their horse and don't put us jockeys in a dangerous position. It's easy for me to do my job when I know about the horse; it's uncomfortable when I don't know anything about the horse or barely know the trainer.

The trainers want us to try so hard to win, and I do, but if the horse has a problem and isn't fit or sound, or has a tendency to lug in or bolt on the turn, the trainer needs to be honest and tell me in advance. If he doesn't, then I can't do my job right, and it's unfair because it could be dangerous for me. We need to know everything about the horse to make good decisions about how to win the race.

Similarly, retired Grade I stakes–winning rider Shane Sellers feels he's been put in compromising positions too often:

I won the Florida Derby in 1998 aboard a horse named Cape Town when Lil's Lad was taken down after interfering with us. I was scheduled to breeze the horse and was told by one of the trainers assistants that the horse was sore and that I should just stay low and keep him in tight. He told me that a vet would ask me how the horse worked, and I should say he worked great. So, I worked the horse and he was pretty sore, trying to get out the whole time. After getting back to the barn, the doc asked me how he went, and I reluctantly told him he went good. Later, the horse eased in the Preakness and never ran again.

Jockey Jesse Campbell finds that some trainers are more difficult to ride for than others: "I've ridden for some guys who bet on their own horses. A trainer who gambles on his own horse brings too much emotion into it. You just learn to know which guys bet on their own horse and know that they can be more hot headed if the horse doesn't run well."

In the often close and crowded confines of the paddock, fractious and nervous horses can act up and cause jockeys and their handlers all kinds of problems. It's a dangerous situation when horses are rearing up, kicking out with their back legs or trying to run away from their handler's hold on the reins or lead shank.

Former jockey Gary Lawless, a stakes–winning rider himself, works as paddock judge in northern California and has seen his share of mishaps: "I'd say the worst accident I saw was when a horse flipped in the paddock and trapped the jockey, Brian Campbell, between him and the back of the stall. The horse landed on top him and pinned him there. I think he suffered a fractured pelvis. It was pretty nasty."

Lawless' role as paddock judge is to check the horses, make sure all racing equipment is in order and keep everyone running on time. With a call for "jockeys up," riders take a leg up into the saddle from the trainer and head for the track.

Along the way, the rider typically knots up the reins, chats with the lead pony rider and tries to keep the horse and himself relaxed. Because most thoroughbreds are high strung and anxious to race, most horses are attached by rope to a lead pony. Many jockeys take a sigh of relief when they finally get a bad-behaving horse out of the close confines of the paddock and onto the open air of the track. With the regal pomp and prestige of racing, the track bugler welcomes the horses as they enter the racing surface.

Amir Cedeno prepares for battle (photograph by Molly O'Brien).

The typical parade to post includes a ceremonial parade of the field in front of the grandstand, then a half-mile jog followed by a walk to the gate. The lead pony escorts the horse in the post parade and accompanies him in the warm-up process to help keep the race horse calmed.

When the fall and winter weather turns chilly, particularly in the Northeast, horses may be warmed up in the warmth and comfort of the trainer's barn and brought over to the paddock for saddling all ready to go. After an abbreviated parade to post, they'll head directly to the gate on a trot and be sent off and running in short order.

In the typical 10-minute post parade, riders need to settle their horses and get them to relax. Depending on the horse, they may need a little or a lot of warm-up to get properly loosened up and prepared for racing. Riders learn what each of their horses prefers, but if it's their first time and he doesn't know the horse needs a vigorous warm-up, his chances will be compromised.

Once they've left the paddock on the way to the gate, jockeys are not allowed to dismount their horse unless authorized by the starter in the event of an equipment problem, accident or some other delay.

Stakes–winning rider Justin Kravets learns the warm-up pattern of horses he frequently rides: "The trainer usually tells me what he'd like me to do in the warm-up with the horse. Certain horses need more time or a more rigorous warm-up if they're stiff. When you ride the same horse over and over again, you remember what they respond to. Some guys make notes about warm-ups and racing and refer back to their notes in the jocks' room before they head out."

Jockeys can often tell if the horse isn't interested in racing while jogging to the gate. It might be a change in his gait, swishing of the tail or some other clue, but the intuitive rider can sense the horse isn't primed for his best. Occasionally the rider will suspect something is wrong with the horse. But the jockey doesn't want to scratch the horse because it may lead to getting fired if the trainer or owner disapproves of his decision.

In cheap claiming races, where profits are hard to come by, the incentive is to keep the horse at the track and racing, at nearly any cost. However, higher-value horses and stakes-quality horseflesh are the stars of the show and handled with great care and patience. If a rider senses something isn't right in the pre-race gallop, he may pull trigger to get the horse scratched, while in a low-end claiming race, the grizzled veterans often go postward week after week with less regard for their long-term well-being. Approximately two-thirds of all races are claiming races, where horses figuratively run with a price tag on their head, meaning a qualified buyer may claim, or purchase, the horse for the price established in the conditions of the race.

In this scenario, if the trainer knows the horse is sore or injured and hasn't told his owner the horse is hurt, it puts him and the jockey in an awkward spot. While horses commonly race with an analgesic called bute, or phenylbutazone, to help with aches and pains, it doesn't prevent injury. Jockeys' don't like to get up on horses that are going to put them at risk.

Unfortunately, it's easier for the trainer to blame the jockey for scratching the horse than to tell the owner the truth and risk having the horse pulled out of the barn. If the horse ends up on the vet's list, the chances of getting the sore horse claimed in the near future go down, as sharp horsemen do their homework. Too often, it appears the jockey becomes the fall guy when less-than-honest trainers are scrambling to cover the trail.

While the track veterinarian usually takes a cursory look at the field during the post parade and at the gate, it usually takes an obvious limp, bleeding or a jockeys' worrisome comments to draw attention to an ailing horse. The vet inspects the horses as they load into the gate and may scratch an entrant at any point. Scratched horses may show up on the track's "vet list" and must have an official workout before being permitted to race again.

Jockey Rodney Prescott has scratched a few horses on the way to the gate:

> It happens once in a while. If the horse is sore for whatever reason, I can tell by the way he feels during the post parade. He might be limping or just feels off. I'll tell the vet, who'll ask me to jog the horse in front of him. If he agrees with me, the horse is scratched and if he disagrees, we go. If I feel the horse is really running just on three good legs, I can choose to take myself off by returning to the paddock for a jockey switch, but that's really rare.
>
> Most trainers are all right with jockeys scratching at the gate, but there are some that feel you're wrong because they didn't catch the horse's problem first. There are a few who don't care if the horse is three-legged; they just want him to race.

As the horses approach the starting gate, they line up in post-position order. The jockeys pull their goggles down and adjust the straps so that they don't overlap each other, to avoid pulling two down at a time when bringing down a dirty pair during the race.

The starting gate, or "iron monster," is a heavily constructed structure typically holding a dozen stalls with enough room for each horse and a small step for the handler, who holds the horse's head. The gate is pulled into position by an attached truck with a back-up truck or tractor available in the event of mechanical failure. While the posts, rails and stalls inside the gate are padded, they offer little protection for the rider.

The gate is a tight spot that many horses don't like. Horses don't take well to being stuffed inside a box. It's claustrophobic and threatening for many. While they may get used to the experience, apprehensive young horses place the rider on high alert.

The starting gate is the most dangerous part of the race because so many troubling things can happen. If the horse falls down in the gate, they can get stuck underneath it and thrash themselves something awful. They can hit their heads on the posts, scrape themselves getting inside the gate or rear up inside the stall and get hung up on the gate apparatus. Any of these acts can seriously injure horse and rider. Starting gate accidents are a major cause of racing injuries and deaths for riders.

As a veteran stakes-winning rider, Carl "CJ" Woodley knows all too well the dangers of fractious horses at the gate:

> Handling horses in the gate is one of the trickiest parts of racing. Horses are high-strung. They have their aches and pains and are often medicated. At the tracks where I usually ride, like Delta and Evangeline, we have some of the cheaper horses compared to bigger tracks. Sometimes the horses might not be as well schooled and professional around the starting gate, particularly the younger ones, so it's a little tougher on us jockeys.
>
> You can usually tell if you're going to have trouble with a horse if he's refusing to load. If he balks at the gate and they have to push him in, I try and just stay as relaxed and quiet as I can. The gate crewman will hold his head and get him pointed forward for me. Hopefully, we'll stand there just a few seconds and be off.
>
> If the horse rears up on his back legs, it can be serious trouble. Usually we get thrown off when the horse jumps up. Hopefully he throws you far enough that you'll clear the tailgate, or back of the stall. If you don't, you could get stuck between the horse and the heavy metal of the gate, or worse, you hit the ground. Now, the horse might either fall on top of you, kick you or swing around and be flashing his teeth at you, pawing and striking out with his front legs. It's really a very bad situation.

The race starter and gate crew, or assistant starters, are allies in providing jockey safety at the starting gate. The gate crewman steps into the stall first, leading the horse in. They step onto the side bars and lead the horse by shank or rein into the stall. The gateman will hold the horse's bridle, keeping his head pointed into the "V" of the two half-doors in front of him until the starting mechanism is triggered by the official starter.

Once inside the stall, the rider may back his horse against the rear doors to gain leverage at the break. Some nervous horses are temporarily tied up with a flipping rig, which is a leather strap placed around the horse's head and tied to the gate, so that he can't rear up in the gate. If the horse acts up in the gate, the handler is there to help see that jockeys don't get trapped between the horse and gate apparatus. Occasionally, jockeys jump off just in the nick of time, or get thrown out backwards into the waiting arms of the gate crewmen.

Jockeys learn to keep quiet and still on the horse in the gate. They must stay loose and avoid fidgeting around. They instruct the gate handler of what to do to help get their horse settled and relaxed prior to the start. Riders want their horses facing straight ahead with their hoofs flat on the ground and facing forward. Once horses start loading, if any of the horses isn't standing right, tossing his head or acting up in some way, the gate crew yells to the starter to wait on the start.

Both horse and rider experience an adrenaline rush in these final moments before the gate slams open. Any aches or pains disappear in anticipation of the raw power and thrill of racing that awaits. In these anxious moments, riders do a quick check of all systems. Do they have a good seat in the saddle? Do they have the reins and whip situated just right? Is the horse positioned correctly for a clean start?

Jockey Greta Kuntzweiler believes that getting settled in and waiting patiently help her horses get off to a good start:

> I keep focused on the doors in front of me and want to be sure my horse's head is pointed towards the "V." You can easily get caught off guard if you're not paying attention and looking forward. It we need to get straightened out, I'll tug on the reins or let the gate crew know. If I'm not ready, I'll be yelling good and loud so that we're not caught out of position. Once I'm in and situated just right, I just sit quiet and wait.
>
> Some horses move around and never stand just right in the gate but break good and clean anyway. Others stand well and break poorly to the right or left, so a lot of it depends on what he's thinking.

Riders incorporate various methods of positioning while awaiting the start. Their right hand typically holds the reins in a "cross," where both overlapped left and right side reins are held in one hand, and the rider's whip. As the last horse enters, they grab a swatch of mane with the right index finger high up on the horse's neck for leverage when the horse lunges forward at the break. With his left hand, the rider grabs another cross and a crop of mane lower on the horse's neck. The rider must allow enough slack in the reins for the horse to leap forward. Falling back into the reins, or "breaking the horse's mouth," stops them from breaking cleanly. If the rider lets out too much rein, he may have trouble regaining control of the horse.

Horses making their first start can pose riders a real challenge. Despite patient schooling and frequent rehearsals, the first time a young horse walks into a packed paddock, sees all the racegoers and hears the cheering crowd, it might send him over the edge. Jockeys try to keep their young steed settled down and relaxed. By the time they hit the starting gate, if the horse isn't a nervous wreck, the jock has done well. Even so, the first time a horse is loaded into the gate with a field of other excitable competitors, it can bring out the worst. Despite tender handling by the assistant starters, many first timers are rank and jumpy. Some get left flat footed when the gate snaps in front of them, getting off several lengths behind the field. Others come flying out of the gate like a rocket, scared to death and running as if their life depended on it. Learning from experience, jockeys find a horse's second trip out much more manageable and a better reflection of the horse's abilities.

Horses demonstrating serious trouble at the gate may be placed on the "starter's list" and must be approved from the gate before being allowed to race again. Official starter Mark Gibson explained that young horses must also be approved before making their first racing appearance: "Horses making their first start must have two official, published workouts with at least one of them coming from the starting gate within 90 days of the race. At least one workout must be within 45 days of the race. Many tracks require one gate work to be in company."

Having seen many injuries at the gate, Gibson explained his approach to getting the field loaded: "It's very dangerous for jockeys in that they can get thrown in the starting gate structure, dumped out the back or, worse yet, trapped between the horse and the gate. Our guys [gate handlers] try and help riders who get in to trouble. My goal is to get the field loaded quickly and sent off evenly from the gate without trouble."

In 2003, Gibson experienced the race starter's nightmare when he sent a field of fillies off with one horse still standing behind the gate: "Wouldn't you know it, and it was the biggest racing day of the year. It was a mile race, so the gate was set right in front of the stands. The horse was 9–5 and in the outside post position [furthest away from the starter's infield perch]. The gate crew was pretty quiet, and when I looked down the line, I thought everyone had loaded. But, they hadn't, and I sent the field off." With a packed house watching, Gibson may have been the only one in the house who didn't see the filly still standing behind the gate all dressed up with nowhere to go.

Occasionally riders are allowed to dismount at the gate if there's a delay in the start caused by a late scratch, injured rider or equipment trouble with one of the horses.

If the jockey is injured at the gate, the horse must be returned to the paddock or other designated area where the replacement jockey is allowed to mount the horse.

Anticipating the routine timing of the gate, many riders have a knack of judging the fraction of a second between the latch click of the mechanical gate hinges and the starter's bell when the gate doors pop open in front of him.

Among his many attributes, Randy Meier is known as a good gate rider, having a knack of getting horses out of the gate quickly:

5. They're Off!

I have a reputation as a good speed rider. The guy I first rode for told me that he bought horses for speed. He trained them for speed and he wanted me to ride them for speed, so that's what I did and I got hung with the reputation.

I try and relax in the gate, get nice and quiet and wait for the last horse to load. I pay attention to the starter's pattern. Maybe I have good ability to anticipate the break well, because when the bell rings, I'm usually right there.

Coming out of the gate, I might tap the horse with the whip on the shoulder and pick the bit up in the horse's mouth to help him get away quickly.

A few years ago, I used to ride a horse called Wilkies Lucky, who didn't like to load. He would either refuse to go in, rear up or fall over. We schooled him at the gate in the mornings and he'd be fine, but I guess he just had something about loading in race company. If you yanked on him or fought him, he behaved even worse. I'd try to help him calm down and not fight him, just going along with what he wanted. If the particular gate crew fella didn't know him, I'd tell him what to do with the horse. But once we got him in, he was a really nice horse, and he could really run.

At the break, most jockeys have one foot forward in the stirrups and the other one back in the saddle. In the event the horse takes a bad step leaving the gate, the jock can use the front or back leg as leverage to avoid tumbling over the top of the horse or falling off the rear if he takes a bad

In a stampede from the starting gate at Churchill Downs, jockeys rush their horses to gain early position (©Cris Forney Photography).

Moments out of the gate, jockeys may need to change their winning strategy on the fly (©Cris Forney Photography).

step. This common practice is not to be confused with "acey-deucy" stirrups, where the left stirrup is lower than the right. Popularized by Hall of Fame jockey Eddie Arcaro, this setup can aid riders in navigating turns.

As the starting bell clangs and the gates fly open, the field bursts out of the blocks in a stampede for the early lead. Riders push down on the horse's neck and often shout at their mounts to help them gain early momentum. Once he's out and running hard, which takes just a few strides, the jockey will take ahold of the reins to control direction and placing of the horse in the early stages of the race. The acceleration a horse displays when breaking from the gate to running at full speed is breathtaking. Within 25 feet, a thoroughbred racehorse goes from standing still to running at speeds exceeding 35 miles per hour.

It's important to break cleanly and avoid getting tangled up in the cavalry charge out of the gate, particularly with a speed horse that runs best on, or near, the lead. If on a horse who prefers to come from off the pace, the rider anticipates moving between or behind horses early in hopes of moving inside to save ground. Depending on what happens in those first few critical strides away from the gate, the entire race plan for the rider may be thrown out the window because of what's happened to him or to other horses.

One of the hottest young jockeys in the game today, and the leading rider by wins in 2004 is Rafael Bejarano. He was aboard the young filly sensation Angel Trumpet in Turfway Park's Gowell Stakes when he lost his foothold in both stirrups coming out of the gate, "The trainer told me that she was really fast and to try and go to the front right from the start. When the gates opened up, she jumped out real fast and I fell back in the saddle and lost both irons. Because I didn't want to take her back, I just sat in the saddle and reached down to grab the stirrups and hold them steady so I could get my feet in. It didn't seem to bother her at all, because she kept running strong." With the composure usually displayed by more experienced jockeys, the talented young rider masterfully regained control, got both boots in the irons before the filly had run a furlong and guided her to a three-length score.

If the horse doesn't leave the gate cleanly and head straight down the course, the jockey can be knocked off from slamming sideways into the gate on the way out, or lose a stirrup hold from brushing against the gate. If the horse stumbles in the opening stride, his head may drop, propelling the rider straight over the top of the animal, usually head first.

According to jockey Steve Hamilton, being patient after a slow start is the right move: "If we break slow, I'll just sit on him and let the race unfold in front of us. If you use your horse too much trying to get back into it, you won't have anything left in the stretch. Most horses have a good three-eighths run in them. If I'm on a speed horse and he breaks slow, I might let him run for an eighth to get position, but know that he won't be as strong later."

There are dozens of tangibles that affect the rider's strategy in the early part of the race—track dimensions, length of race, number of horses in the field, quality of competition, racing surface, track conditions and racing tactics to name a few.

Racetracks come in all different sizes and shapes, from tiny five-furlong tracks like Great Lakes Downs in Michigan to the mammoth 1½ mile oval at New York's Belmont Park. Depending on the distance of the race, the starting gate may be located close to the first turn or allow the riders a long run before hitting the bend. About 45 percent of American races are carded at the six-furlong, or three-quarter mile, distance and, at most tracks, include a three-eighths mile run before the turn.

Races typically include 7 to 10 entrants. It's much more common for the best horse to win in a small five-horse heat than it is in a full field of 12. With a dozen horses bursting out of the gate and fighting for racing position, so many things can go wrong. In smaller fields, there's simply less chance of racing trouble, and the rider's game plan is more likely to play out as projected.

Match races, where two horses go head-to-head, used to be the mainstay of racing in the 1800s. While there have been a handful of classic match races held in the past hundred years, they are virtually nonexistent in modern racing.

The great Man O'War crushed Triple Crown winner Sir Barton in Canada's most famous match race, held in 1920. In 1938, jockey George Woolf piloted Seabiscuit to the historic upset of Triple Crown winner War Admiral, with fellow Hall of Famer Charles Kurtsinger in the irons, in the Pimlico Special Stakes duel.

In 1955, the country's top two horses and riders combined for a high-profile, $100,000 winner-take-all showdown. Eddie Arcaro, aboard Preakness and Belmont victor Nashua, pulled the upset over favored Kentucky Derby winner Swaps, ridden by Willie Shoemaker.

The ill-fated 1975 "Battle of the Sexes" match race between Derby winner Foolish Pleasure and the grand filly Ruffian virtually ended the industry's interest in match races when the two-time champion filly broke down entering the first turn. She was later euthanized after struggling to recover from surgery.

Prior to the historic 1938 showdown with War Admiral, Woolf was aboard Seabiscuit in a match race against South American star Ligaroti, who

Jockey Mathieu Adam, seen here with mud flying all about him, drives for the finish at Keeneland (©Cris Forney Photography).

Jogging back after racing, this horse and rider are covered from head to hoof in mud, an occupational hazard in racing (©Cris Forney Photography).

was owned by Bing Crosby, in a memorable fight to the finish, literally. Seabiscuit and Ligaroti, with Noel Richardson up, battled side-by-side most of the way and were noses apart as they entered the stretch. Ligaroti, on the outside, drifted in and put the squeeze on the Biscuit along the rail. As the two horses thundered down the stretch virtually in unison, the two jockeys began battling each other. Reportedly, Richardson had grabbed ahold of Seabiscuit's saddlecloth and reins in an attempt to hold the horse back. Woolf retaliated by striking Richardson with his whip. The riders continued flogging away at each other down the stretch, and the horses raced under the wire together, with Seabiscuit getting the nod by a nostril. After the Del Mar stewards considered their options, they let the order of finish stand and suspended both riders for the rest of the meeting for their antics.

The condition of the racing surface is one of many factors jockeys must calibrate. Some horses take to sloppy tracks like fish take to water. In "off-track" racing conditions, many riders want to get out of trouble and get to the front, while others feel it's not really necessary. Sometimes it just tires the horse out more and sets it up for the closers. Many feel it's best to see how the previous races have been finishing before coming up with a strategy.

Riding on mucky racing surfaces creates yet another challenge for riders: "Riding in the slop is hard. There's stuff flying all over the place," according to jockey Billy Patin.

> You have to ride with caution because the racing surface gets really slippery. As a rider, you get more tired, too. There's mud going in your nose and mouth and it's hard to catch your breath. I try and catch a breather when there's a break, like when I get into the clear for a moment. Otherwise, I'm riding with my mouth shut or I'm going to be eating it.
>
> I usually go through four or five sets of goggles because they get covered so fast by the slop flying back at you. Even the reins get wet and slippery, so you really have to concentrate. It's so messy, but you get used to it.

With racing meets held all year long across the country, each track experiences unique challenges in keeping racing conditions safe for all parties involved. Stakes-winning jockey Paul Toscano has ridden all over the country and experienced racing extremes from the tropical weather in Florida to winter racing New York. "At Calder, the surface gets tight when it rains, not that it's bad when it's dry, just that it's one of the best tracks in the nation when it's wet. There are no lanes and the track surface is consistent from the rail to the outside fence. The only soft spot is along the rail on turn; it can get a bit splashy."

The track is well prepared for the unpredictable and ever-changing climate, which might be 95 degrees and sunny one minute, then pounding thunderstorms the next: "It might be a fast track for the first three [races] of the day, then it might storm and be sloppy for the next three, then dry up again for the last four."

In New York, racing goes on through the sleet and snow. "Heavy rains are the worst because the surface just can't handle all that moisture," Toscano said. "It gets so cold there sometimes, with really severe ice and cold. They treat the track with chemicals, but sometimes the weather is just too bad. The jocks might get together, walk the track and discuss the racing surface safety. Ice chunks can form in the surface, putting the horses and us at risk, and we just can't race because it's unsafe. Occasionally the races are cancelled for heavy snow, more so for fan safety than racing safety, as the horses are more than willing to run on just about any kind of surface."

Riding in the sometimes frigid weather of the winter meet at Turfway Park, Perry Ouzts does his best to stay warm;

> It can get pretty cold, let me tell you. It might be 15 degrees outside, but think about adding the wind chill factor to it from racing at 35 miles per hour. It must be below zero.
> We can't put a lot of clothes on because of the weight and still needing to be able to move around freely. We wear thin, lightweight stuff, like a neoprene undershirt, facemask and gloves. They help a bit, but it's still freezing out there.
> When you go out for your first race, it's the worst. It's bone-chilling cold, but at least we're not out too long. From the time we leave the jocks' quarters, take a leg up, jog to the gate, run the race and get back in, it's maybe only 10 minutes. After you've ridden one, you warm up a bit, and it isn't quite as miserable. I can't really complain, though; it is my chosen profession, although there are times I think about how nice it would be to have an indoors job.

Jockey Chris Herrell, who also rides the winter meet at Turfway, explained that snow and frozen rain create another hazard: "When it's snowing, the snow and dirt mix on the track and form these little ice pellets. When the horses run over that kind of surface, these ice balls come flying back at you like rocks, and they really sting. I try to position my horse up close behind others so the clods hit the horse in the chest and not in his face. If I can't get close enough, I have to go outside and out of the spray."

Riding in extreme heat and humidity creates a different challenge for horse and rider. Graded stakes–winning jockey Corey Lanerie recalled how the sweltering heat of Texas affected the jockey colony:

> One summer at Lone Star, we had a week or two where the temperature was well over 100 degrees. It was unbelievable heat. I was riding eight or nine races every day, and it was just miserable. It was so hot and humid that the

When one is shivering through the frigid weather of fall and winter racing, like jockey Juan Molina, Jr. (right), shown here with trainer Ernie Retamoza, bundling up in lightweight gear does little to help with the bitter cold (©Cris Forney Photography).

> track had bottles of Gatorade waiting for us at the finish line when we weighed back in. Usually we're very careful about how much fluids we take in, but I'd drink the whole bottle between races and not put on an ounce.
>
> Some guys who were still hitting the box before the races to make weight were getting so dehydrated with the extreme weather that they had to take their mounts off, or they would've passed out.

In rare cases, the track is ruled unsafe by the riders and track officials. As graded stakes winner John McKee explained, horse and rider safety is paramount:

> You just can't control Mother Nature. When the track condition is really bad, the jockeys and management usually meet to discuss the safety of the racing surface.
>
> One time in New York, it was raining so hard that you couldn't even see across the track. The jockeys were all dressed up and ready to go, but the rain

was so heavy that the track washed out in spots. It was just too dangerous for us to race, so they cancelled the card.

Regardless of track conditions, when jockeys take to the track, their riding style in the saddle is often a reflection of their personality. Whether they ride with an aggressive, opportunistic or patient style, every jockey follows some basic technical basics. The "rider's seat," or position in the saddle may look the same from a distance but varies greatly in style, body mechanics and technique.

Historically speaking, riders used to sit straight backed with legs stretched out long beneath them in the stirrups. In the 1890s, jockey James "Tod" Sloan found the advantage of short stirrups and a crouched riding position helped him win more races. In what journalists at the time called a "monkey seat," a new riding style was born. Sloan won an astonishing 46 percent of his races in 1898, including a five-or-five day in New York.

Playwright George M. Cohan adapted Sloan's story into the Broadway hit, *Little Johnny Jones*, which included the memorable hit songs "Yankee Doodle Dandy" and "Give My Regards to Broadway."

Today's riders don't actually sit in the saddle. Sharing many of the attributes of Sloan's style, with short stirrups, toes forward, ankles and knees gripping the horse's side, they ride crouched forward over the horse's shoulders in an aerodynamic pose. With lower limbs acting as shock absorbers, jockeys have legs of steel, balancing themselves on their toes and tugging at the reins in a dance of coordination, poise and strength.

With elbows tucked in tight, most riders hunch forward with their rump high in the air in the early stages of races and then lower themselves closer to the saddle when they hit the stretch. They move in rhythm with the horse's action, maintaining their hunched position and moving their arms in rhythm along the horse's neck. Riders try to sit still in the saddle, conserving both his energy and the horse's. Most American riders ride low in the saddle, only a few inches above the saddle and in an aerodynamic crouch over the horse's shoulders. In contrast, most European riders have a rather busy, mostly up-and-down motion and are in the saddle with elbows bent outwards on the upswing.

Having won titles at River Downs and Turfway Park, jockey Dean Sarvis described his version of an efficient rider's seat:

> It takes a few years to develop the seat the rider will use for the rest of his career. As a young rider, you adjust things like the length of your irons, position on the horse and your riding style. It just takes time to find what's most comfortable and efficient for you.
>
> As far as my personal style goes, I like to get as low as I can and still be able to push strongly on the horse with my arms fully extended. You need to

be able to comfortably switch sticks, pump his neck and still stay behind the horse's head. You want to be tucked down low and level with the horse's back and not bouncing around or rocking back and forth. All that movement takes away from the horse's momentum. It's important to be strong down the lane. From the eighth pole home is where it counts the most.

Angel Cordero had the best seat of any rider I've seen. I had the chance to ride against him when we were both a lot younger, and I learned a lot from just watching him. I tried to model my style after his. No one else was as fluid as he was. He was low and aerodynamic and had flawless technique. When he was in an all-out drive on the horse, he was so smooth that it looked like he was painted on the horse.

Sitting chilly in the saddle, riders should be calm and patiently poised to pounce when the right opportunity presents itself. Most jockeys can tell which rider is up on various horses in the race just from the style they ride with. They are so used to seeing each other ride in races and replays that they can pick out other riders from their technique alone.

Riders must have strong hands to direct and guide their horse. Former wrestler Mick Ruis has plenty of muscle to get the job done but acknowledges many horses need a softer touch:

> Some horses have what we call a light move, which means they have a sensitive mouth and can't handle the pressure of the bit being moved around in their mouth. If you yank around on the bit, they might throw their head around or run erratically.
>
> With a horse like that, I use my body weight to help guide the horse. By shifting my body to the left as we enter the turn, the horse will usually follow my lead and angle left. It's similar to riding a bike or motorcycle. It's something Alex Solis taught me when I was first starting out, and it's really helped with that kind of horse.
>
> When you're racing and you see that you're going to need to move inside or outside, you need to plan ahead. If we're approaching the stretch, for example, I need to be looking in front and around me to figure out if I'm going to be moving by the time we hit the three-eighths pole. If the horses are going too fast in front of me, I figure they'll get tired and start backing up, so I want to get clear and outside of them. If I'm running behind a horse who seems to be picking up speed and capable of running on, I might tuck in behind him and follow him through a hole. The key thing is that you have to make a commitment early to go inside or outside of other horses; you can't hesitate because you might get trapped or lose ground changing course.

Regardless of riding style, jockeys must be prepared for anything once the horses are off and running. Horses are unpredictable, and some simply run erratically, no matter how much time the trainer spends schooling them. Young horses, in particular, are known to duck and dive from a reflection off the rail, shadows on the track, loud noises or unanticipated movement alongside the racetrack.

"I was up on a young horse at Aqueduct one day," jockey Dennis Carr, an 18-year riding veteran, explained.

> I was also young, and I think it was only my third race. The race started down in the chute, and I was on the rail. As soon as we hit the gap, the horse veered left and made a hard left-hand turn. He tried to jump over the temporary rail but hit it instead and shattered the rail. He tripped over it, throwing me over the top, then he fell on top of me.
>
> I got tested really early to see if I could handle this line of work. Although I fractured my left wrist in the accident, I was only 18 and bounced right back. I learned that young horses and inexperienced riders are a bad combination.

Jockeys may need to be aggressive on some horses to get them involved in the race early, while other horses relax into stride early, and the jockey can sit still and be patient until the right moment. Generally speaking, riders find geldings, or male horses who've been castrated, to be the most dependable ride. Colts have tendencies toward aggressiveness, and fillies can be extremely skittish or reliably hard-headed. Some horses run smoothly and gracefully, while others "ride as rough as an old washing machine," according to jockey Rosemary Homeister, Jr.

Some horses are well behaved and will always run true and straight for the rider, while others couldn't run straight if their life depended on it. They require the full concentration of the rider and demand every ounce of energy to keep him on track. Some horses are easily distracted and let their eyes, and legs, wander. Trainers may try blinkers or shadow rolls to help keep the horse focused on the track lying in front of him. Blinkers, which are basically a hood that fits over the horse's head and includes plastic cup-shaped blinders, restrict the horse's side vision and help him stay focused on racing straight ahead. Adding blinkers typically helps the horse show more speed during the early stages of the race.

Young horses making their first start are so scared that they often just run as fast as they can for as long as they can, paying no attention to their pleading rider. The babies are often just reacting; they don't understand the instructions the rider is sending them. They're racing as hard as they can to get their nose in front, sometimes forgetting the basic lessons of training, like handling turns. Sometimes jockeys have to pull left as strongly as they can to get youngsters angled into the turn. With time and experience, most catch on quickly.

Racing at "bullring" tracks, those small tracks with mostly turns, requires a different kind of strategy. Jockey Lenny Frazzitta, who has ridden all over the East Coast, shared that getting position is critical: "Because the turns are right there after the start, getting off quickly is important. The turns are so much tighter that you need to use some horse early to get near the front. It's so much harder to come from behind on a short bullring track than regular track. If you break slow, you have to just let your horse get himself together and hope things back up to you. If you rush him early, you'll just use his energy up."

Prior to entering turns, jockeys must think ahead to get their horse well positioned. Gaining racing position and saving ground are fundamentals of racing strategy. Getting into the right spot can't be done at the cost of using too much of the horse's energy early. It won't do any good to sprint to the front of the pack, save ground and hit the stretch on a horse with rubber legs. Albeit, breaking from an outside post position and getting pushed wide into the "clubhouse," or first turn, often costs the horse several lengths that may be insurmountable.

Most riders feel the toughest race to ride is the longer, two-turn race, which requires more thinking and planning. Longer races require more strategy and decision making. The rider can't just jump out in front and hope to last. Riders want their horses to switch leads twice. Horses must change leads, meaning they change from running with the right leg forward on the straightaways and switch to the left leg lead around turns. Failure to switch leads tires a horse out prematurely. If the horse doesn't change leads on his own, the rider may prompt the horse with a quick tug on the reins to turn his head and tap him on the shoulder a few times.

Jockey Aaron Gryder uses a helpful analogy to describe the benefit of a horse changing leads: "It's like if you try to carry a heavy bucket of water to the end of your street in one hand. You might make it the whole way, but your arm is going to be really tired. If you'd switched hands halfway down the street, you'd be sharing the load between arms and likely make the walk faster."

Depending on how long the run is to the first turn, the jockey may need to be thinking about position right out of the gate. If it's a short distance to the first turn and a large field of horses, it's a prescription for trouble. Even with careful planning and clever riding, jockeys often find themselves pinched back or hung out wide. For retired jockey Sara Jones, a crowded first turn sent her tumbling:

> When you go into the first turn, you've got to have your horse's nose in the pack or at the shoulder of the horse to the outside of you. If not, you've got to get out of there and back off, because horses are going to be coming over to the inside when they hit the turn.
>
> I can remember one time when this horse was outside of me entering the turn and starting coming over on me. Although I had inside position, I guess I wasn't far enough up. The outside horse just dropped in on me, and my horse pulled back, but we clipped heels anyway and fell. My horse did a somersault and threw me off. Somehow the horses behind me avoided stepping on me as they went by.

On some turf tracks, which are typically located inside of the dirt tracks with much tighter turns than dirt tracks, short runs to the first turn are common. At Del Mar, for example, long distance races typically include a quick dash to the first turn. It's vitally important for the rider to gain position early, without using too much of the horse's energy up. If the rider gets packed wide on the first turn, or gets shuffled back into the crowd, it's very hard to make up the lost ground against the usually tough competition. Oftentimes, it's the horse who gets the best trip that wins this kind of race.

Jockey Joe Judice, a 25-year riding veteran and winner of more than 3,000 races, explained turf races require a different mindset: "Turf racing is easier and kinder on horses. The grass and slower pace early aren't as exhausting on the horses. But it always seems like there's a bottleneck around the first turn, so it's very important to get good position early and then just hope for the best down the stretch."

Some turf tracks include a dirt crossover at some point along the way, where the turf track is offset and interrupted by a patch of the dirt racing surface. For some horses for the first running over the dirt that slices through the grass, they aren't quite sure what to make of it and jump onto it, giving their rider a hiccup in their stride.

Knowing one's horse and what he's capable of is a significant advantage to cagey riders. Riders may try to intimidate other horses by forcing them to race in tight quarters. Some horses will do it and seem to relish the competitiveness, digging in and trying even harder. Others shy away from it in obvious displeasure. Knowing your horse's temperament and limits in advance pays dividends when managed wisely.

Horses seem able to perceive the confidence riders have in them, responding to kindness, praise and affection. They love the attention of stroking, petting and talking with them. Some jockeys are gifted with horse sense and always seem to get the most out of their mounts. Some horses and jockeys seem to click with each other, winning when partnered.

Racing tactics are the game within the game. Jockeys are well aware of where all the horses in a race should be. Good riders are opportunistic, saving ground and gaining advantageous racing position every chance they get. He must be able to make decisions. He must have a willing nerve; hesitating will cause riders to miss winning opportunities. He must decide if he should take the inside route or go wide around horses to move up and secure racing position immediately. Any hesitancy may see the hole in front of him instantly evaporate. When a rider loses his nerve, they will choose the safe route every time, taking their horses wide around others rather than slicing through the holes that often lead to victory.

Grade I stakes–winning jockey and 2000 Eclipse Award–winning apprentice Tyler Baze isn't afraid to put his horse wherever he thinks he has the best chance of winning:

> Sometimes horses will be afraid to run in tight quarters and the jockey has to stay strong in the saddle to keep him in there. If you don't, most horses would prefer to get out of the crowd and will drop back out of it. If you hang in there and wait for a hole to open up, once the horse sees daylight, his heart gets bigger, and he explodes through it.
>
> As a rider, you don't even think about it, race riding strategy just comes naturally. I'd rather be the one intimidating others than to be intimidated. A rider intimidates others by putting pressure on them, putting them in bad racing spots by closing down a hole, squeezing them closer to the rail or boxing them in. Jockeys will do whatever they can to win a race. It's all done safely, but if I can make it more difficult for someone else to win, it only helps my chances.

In most cases, pace makes the race. Getting horses into the position that allow them the best chance of winning is what separates the men from the boys. Many races are won by horses leading from start to finish, or "wire-to-wire." Making the lead and keeping it is like playing cat and mouse with the field. In some races, it's simply "catch me if you can," while in most cases the rider must measure the horse's pace throughout, saving enough energy to go "coast-to-coast."

Stakes-winning jockey Dyn Panell wins plenty of races on the front end:

> If you have to fight for the early lead, it tires the horse out because you're usually going too fast. If I can make the lead without having to fight for it, I'll take ahold of my horse with a short rein, talk to him and try to get him to relax. I try and judge how fast I'm going by how hard my horse is working. On small horses, sometimes you think they're working hard because they have shorter strides, and on bigger horses with longer strides, they can fool you by going too fast. I'll be as still as possible on the horse and just make sure he's on the correct lead as we go into and out of the turn.
>
> I'll take a look around to see if anybody is coming. If nobody is there, I'll wait as long as possible to send my horse. I can usually tell how much horse I have left at the quarter pole, but some horses get a big heart when they're running on the lead, and the longer they run without pressure, the bigger their heart gets. If the horse hasn't been pressured early, he'll be tough to run down.

With an intuitive sense of timing, some riders have more skill and ability with nursing front-runners along. While every good jockey has the ability to adapt and must be able to win on all sorts of horses, some jockeys are reputably better on these "speed" horses and are more often hired for their hustling abilities.

Through repetition, jockeys learn to judge pacing. In a split second, he must calculate how fast he's going. Some riders actually count in their head, although by the time they hit the first quarter mile pole, it might be too late to do much about it. While many can tell the difference between a horse running a quarter-mile in :21 and :22, it's usually how hard the horse is working under the rider that tells him how quickly he's traveling. If he's working too hard early, the rider knows he's going to be toasted when the stretch drive arrives.

Some horses don't like running in front and will look around for other horses to run with, or worse yet, wait for someone to engage them in racing. It doesn't matter how much urging the rider provides, some horses follow the herd instinct that draws them in. For the most part, horses are creatures of habit. They run how they're trained. They'll repeat the behaviors they've learned in the mornings when they race in the afternoons. Some horses known as "morning glories" train brilliantly in the morning workouts and disappoint in the afternoon races, greatly frustrating their handlers.

Some horses do their best running from just off the pace. These "stalkers" often give the rider the favorable advantage of being able to use a little speed to get position early or tuck in behind a hot pace and pounce when the time is right. Stakes-winning rider Ryan Barber likes having that flexibility:

> If I'm riding a stalker, I want to break well and let the horse find his stride. There's no reason to rush, so we just bide our time. I'll make my move when I think the time is right. If the pace is slow, I might go after them early. If they're running fast up front, I know I can run them down late. Most jockeys have a mental clock in the their heads to judge the pace. It just comes naturally with experience.
>
> If my horse isn't balking from the dirt hitting its head, I can stay in behind other horses and try and save ground. But if he doesn't like it, I'll swing outside for a clear path. Sometimes the inside is slower, anyway. At somewhere like Philadelphia or Mountaineer, you want to be outside and not on the rail.
>
> When we come to the turn, I'd prefer to save ground, but usually have to go outside of horses to have a clear run. They say that if you circle the field, it costs you five lengths, but if you're on the best horse it doesn't matter. From there, it's race riding and hoping you get to the wire first.

While it's exciting to see, jockeys who bring their horse streaking from far back in a flying finish must have luck on their side. If on one of these "deep closers," it's more of a momentum-building run and gradual buildup of the horse's speed than an all-out sprint for the finish. Most hard runs start about three-eighths of a mile from the finish. When the rally falls short, it's often not an error in the jockeys' sense of timing, but the gradual slowing down of horses in front of him just isn't happening fast enough.

Over the past two years, no one has won more races than Ramon Dominguez. With 836 wins in that period, he certainly knows how to win on any type of horse. The thrill of bringing a deep closer home first starts with the rider allowing his horse to find his comfort zone:

> Once we leave the gate, I want to get him relaxed and just take it as easy as possible. I try to be patient, listen to the horse and let him go wherever he wants to go. If he wants to be last early, we'll be last. If the pace is very slow, I'll try and stay in touch with the field without rushing my horse.
>
> I'll try and stay out of trouble and try to save as much ground as possible, particularly if it's a two-turn race. If we're wide on the first turn, I'll try to take the inside lane or slice through a hole later to make up ground. I like to go around other horses on the last turn to assure I have a clear path down the stretch.
>
> You pretty much have a good feel of how much horse you have left at the half-mile pole. If the horse is grabbing the bit, you know they're going to finish up pretty well. I can tell how well we're going to finish up by looking at how the horses around us are running, although I get fooled once in awhile. Depending on how the race is developing, I'll start going after them at the half-mile or three-eighths pole.
>
> When it's time to go, I ask them for run, and they respond for me. Down the stretch, I try not to do anything that's going to hurt the horse. If he's giving me everything he's got, I'm just helping him stay in rhythm and hope we get there first.

Horses typically run their fastest early in the race and run slower as the race progresses. A front runner may run a 22-second opening quarter mile, followed by a 23-second quarter and then come the last quarter in :25 to complete six furlongs in 1:10. The come-from-behind horse may run the opening fraction in 24 seconds, pick the pace up between the half-mile and three-eighths poles and clock a 23-second quarter and then finish up in 24 seconds to accomplish a 1:10.

A rider's judgment about when and where to go during the race somewhat depends on his confidence in the horse. He may need to adjust his race based on where he is and where he thinks he should be. If he rushes the horse to gain position early, it may leave him flat later. He needs to know before he makes the move. If the jockey feels the pace is moving too slowly, he may ask his horse for more run early. It's all about the internal clock every jockey has in his head.

Seven-time Eclipse Award–winning rider Jerry Bailey is a master of judging pace:

> I suppose it comes with experience. Some guys have a real knack for judging the pace. I think you just learn it from experience and from repetition. It's like learning how fast you're driving your car without looking at the speedometer; over time you just get a feel for it.

In the early stages of this turf race, jockeys focus on securing advantageous racing position (©Cris Forney Photography).

One of the basic principles in judging pace is to never ask your horse for more than he is capable of. In a nutshell, if you use too much gas early, you'll have an empty tank when you need it in the stretch. On some speed horses, they just need to go as fast as they can for as long as they can, but on others that can tolerate being pulled back, you can back off if the pace is too hot. You're not going to be able to out-muscle a 1,000-pound animal, but if the horse is workable, you can put him where you want him, and he should respond when you call on him in the stretch.

Jockeys always want to be as close to the rail as possible, unless the inside lane is deep and slow. Saving a length or two along the way makes a difference at the finish. Anything that forces the horse out and away from the rail works against him in the race. Sometimes a horse will drift away from the rail on his own if he's fighting against the bit in his mouth or if he's suffering some type of leg pain. More often, the jockey will move the horse wide to run around or between horses or in anticipation of horses slowing down in front of him.

If another horse cuts over in front of him, the jockey may need to check, or rapidly slow his horse down. By temporarily hitting the brakes on his horse, he should avoid clipping heels with other horses, which often leads to the rear horse loosing his footing and falling. Other times, a horse may want to run off, or accelerate rapidly, into a wall of horses in front of him. Again, the rider may be forced to check or literally risk running into trouble. In either case, it's difficult to get most horses motivated and energized to collect themselves and get running again. In the optimum trip, all the momentum is forward.

While going through a hole along the rail saves a lot of ground, not everybody is willing to do it. It's a dangerous spot, as the hole can close quickly, leaving the rider the choice of stopping suddenly, or worse yet, crashing into other horses or going over the rail.

Successful riders are able to get horses to relax for them. If he fights the animal too much, he may break his heart and the race will be lost. He needs to compromise with the horse, so as to not drain the horse's reserves, yet keeping him in the chase.

Jockey Michael Baze, a young stakes-winning rider, learned the virtues of getting horses to settle in the race early: "I was on this really fast horse back East, and there was another horse in the race that was just as quick. I didn't want to go head-and-head with him because I was worried it would take too much out of my horse. So, after we broke out of the gate, I took a real strong hold of him, leaned back and pulled him back to sit off the hip of the other speed. I got him to relax, and when we hit the stretch, he just blew by the other horse."

Getting horses to relax is something Hall of Fame jockey Kent Desormeaux knows a few things about:

> Getting them to relax is kind of a give-and-take relationship. My job is to get the horse to run as fast as he can without burning up all of his energy. I need to help him carry himself as quickly as possible and still save something for the stretch.
>
> On some horses, I drop the reins a bit to help them get settled, and others I pull tight on the reins, then release on the reins and try to help the horse find his best stride. Many horses do their best when they run up close behind other horses. They still have that herd instinct in them, and they relax better for me when they can follow others.

Jockeys will do whatever it takes to win. Given the opportunity to make things more difficult for one of the other horses, there's not a moment's hesitation for "race riding." If it means cutting off other horses that are charging up from behind, or forcing horses wide or intimidating other horses by running in tight quarters, they'll do it instinctively. Putting the favorite into a tight spot is no-brainer for every rider. While they don't want to hurt their horse's chances of winning, they will set the trap for another contender if they feel it's their best chance to pull the upset.

If up on the "chalk," or heavy favorite, the jockey is more likely to take the safe route, running around horses rather than gambling with an inside trip or waiting behind a wall of horses in hopes that a hole opens up later. Riders feel the pressure of higher expectations when riding the public's choice. When things don't work out as hoped, they feel remorseful.

"If you're up on a big favorite, it's almost a relief to get the job done and win," according to jockey Mike Luzzi. "If I'm up on the heavy favorite and we get beat, I question myself first to try and figure out if I did something that caused him to lose. I want to ride the horse the way he wants to be ridden, meaning the way he runs with the best chance of winning. If the chalk runs badly, maybe there's fitness or health problems we didn't know about before the race. Sometimes the favorite simply isn't the best horse, though."

Sometimes horses win "just for fun" in effortless fashion and draw away to win by 5, 10 sometimes even 15 lengths. "It's fun and easy when a horse wins so effortlessly," said veteran jockey Danny Sorenson.

> Sometimes they're just that much better than the others, or maybe they're on the improve and the other horses just don't run well.
>
> When it's that easy, the rider just has to be sure that someone isn't flying up late. I try and to keep the horse focused on the task by chirping at him, tapping him on the shoulder or showing him the whip. You just want to be sure no one is sneaking up on you.

Some horses will try to run right over horses in front of them, although most sense the tightness and will back off on their own. Some horses who have trouble rating are intentionally directed behind a wall of horses, forcing them to slow their pace down in hopes of saving more energy for the stretch drive.

Getting trapped behind a wall of tiring horses is one of the worst places for riders to get stuck. If there's a horse on their immediate outside, they can get trapped inside a three-sided box and the only way out is dropping back, or "stopped," and you don't win races by going backwards.

If there's a gap between horses in front of them, the jockey must instantly decide if the hole is big enough to get through, if there's enough time to get through the hole and what lies in front of them if they make it through the gap.

Sometimes jockeys' friendships carry over to the racetrack. For example, if two riders are buddies and one is aboard a horse who is faltering in front of him, his friend may slide out to open up the inside lane for his pal. If it were any other rider, however, he'd stick to that rail like he was glued to it and force others to beat him the long way around.

Jockeys can gain an advantage by running in the best part of the track, avoiding the deep or slow footing. On fast tracks, the racing surface is evenly balanced and consistent from the inner rail to the outer. After raining, however, pockets and lanes of faster racing surfaces commonly form.

Most riders will try and move towards the part of the track where the tractor has been. The dirt is more likely to be tighter there. The risk is that if he doesn't hit the groove where the tractor has been, he'll get caught in the thicker and softer spots, where the tractor wheels pushed the soil to the side of the tracks. Horses frequently slip when they hit these spots, momentarily losing their footing. The jockey feels the bobble, as the horse may alter his stride and lower his head. Jockeys will watch other races and talk with other riders in attempt to find where the best footing is.

While riders may holler in the gate or shout at the break, they're mostly quiet during races. Other than chirping or coaxing their horse along during the race, the only other time they get vocal is when there's trouble brewing on the track. If someone is getting pinched off, having their clear running path violated or getting squeezed out, they're not hesitant to scream out about it. Riders can tell someone is in serious trouble by the severity and urgency in their fellow rider's voice and will do what they can to avoid putting anyone in danger of falling.

Some riders, however, do enjoy race chatter, trash talking and poking fun at each other during the running of races. Jockey Joe Bravo recalled a recent incident with Jerry Bailey:

> We were in the post parade at Gulfstream and a fan yelled to Jerry, "You need to win this one, Jerry." Quick to respond, Bailey yelled back to the guy, "I don't *need* to win any race, but I'd like to."
>
> So as the race unfolds, I'm in front by two lengths at the eighth pole, but I felt this shadow closing in on me. It was Bailey, of course. He caught me late, and as he went by, he hollered "This one is for that fan who *needed* to win."

As the horses in front thunder down the backstretch, dirt from their hooves is shot backwards, spray-painting everything behind them, including horse and rider. A horse catching dirt in the face can get discouraged and quit trying, particularly the first time it happens to them. If able, the jockey will try to position his horse close up behind other horses so that flying dirt hits his mount in the legs and chest and not in the head. Too close, however, leaves him no room to maneuver if the leading horses start to slow down.

Jockeys' faces get coated from brow to neck, with only the goggle-covered eyes spared. As the race progresses, jockeys pull down the top, dirty set of goggles, dropping them below their chin to expose the fresh set below. Through repetition, they learn to make the switch so quickly, you have to be watching for it or you'll miss it. Jockey Justin Kravets explained, "I'm right-handed, so I hold the reins and whip in my right hand and change the goggles with my left hand when they get muddied up. It really only takes a second to change them, and after riding awhile, it comes so naturally that I don't even think about it."

How many sets of goggles the jockey uses depends on the distance of the race and conditions of the racing surface. If running behind other horses, dirt and mud flies back and covers horse and rider. In a six-furlong race on dirt, three sets of goggles, stacked one on top of another, are sufficient. As the goggles get dirty, riders drop the top set below their chin to expose the next clean set beneath. If the track is sloppy, an extra pair or two is required. If the race is longer, another set of goggles may be added. Seldom does a rider race with more than six sets in place.

Graded stakes-winning rider Danny Sorenson learned a trick years ago from a veteran rider, Larry Pierce, about goggles that's helped him assure he always has a clear view of the racing:

> The visibility when racing in the slop is really bad. Unlike a car with its windshield wipers, we can't clear our goggles when racing, we have to pull down the dirty set to expose the clean pair underneath.
>
> When I was younger, Larry showed me a technique he used where you pull the top pair down only on one side, so that you're seeing out of one side. When that side gets dirty, you drop down the other side, and you're clear on that side. This way, the goggles last twice as long, and I never have to worry about running out.

Flying dirt isn't the only obstacle facing riders. Occasionally racing shoes fly off, posing a more serious threat. Jockey Joe Steiner is lucky he didn't have more serious injuries when he was hit by a flying shoe several years ago: "I was at the half-mile pole when I saw this horseshoe coming straight back at me. It was like it was in slow motion, but I didn't have time to react. It struck me square in the nose, and I blacked out for just a moment. I'm surprised it didn't knock me clean off the horse, but somehow, I managed to hang on and get back into the race and actually finished third, with blood gushing everywhere."

Sometimes unusual circumstances put riders at danger. When racing one night in California, jockey Chris Lamance unexpectedly raced in complete darkness: "We were running down the backstretch one night, and then all of a sudden, the track lights just went out. It was totally unexpected. I was afraid to slow down, afraid to drift out, so I just sat still and let the horse do the running and held my ground. Thankfully, the horses kept running as though unaffected by the darkness. I could barely see a silhouette of the horses around me. Thank God the lights came back on a few seconds later, or I don't know what would've happened."

When racing one evening many years ago at Turfway Park, Grade I stakes-winning jockey Brian Peck had an unexpected bump in the night:

> I picked up a horse in the fourth race when one of the other riders didn't show up for his mount. I was 18-years-old at the time and just getting

started, so I was thrilled to get on anything, let alone a 4–1 shot with a good shot of winning.

It was the first long race of the night and I made the lead real easy and had a clear lead as we hit the backstretch. I guess the starting bells spooked two deer who were drinking at the lake behind the track's toteboard. They took off running across the infield towards the woods behind the track.

Unaware of the eminent danger, Peck was taking measure of the field when the deer bolted out of the darkness.

The first deer jumped out onto the track in front of me at the five-eighths pole and scampered across the track. I looked back and yelled something to the other riders about it. When I turned around, there was a second deer who ducked under the rail right in front of me and hit my horse square on in the front legs. It was like when you're on a bike and something goes into the spokes of the front wheel and the rear end comes over, my horse's back end came up and I was catapulted 40 feet forward in the air.

I hit the ground near the rail, but was disoriented enough that I couldn't crawl under the rail fast enough to get out of the way. Two horses ran over me and busted up my arm pretty good. I went in to the hospital and thought they'd patch me up and send me home, but they ended up doing surgery. I needed two metal plates and screws to keep it all together. I was in a cast for 10 months.

Luckily for Peck, he healed from his injuries and successfully returned to riding. For Peck and other riders, when it's time to pick up the pace of the race, usually at the far turn, or three-eighths pole, there are several techniques employed to set the horse into full stride. The jockey may chirp at his horse, snap the reins to shake him up, reset the bit in his mouth or pull out the whip and give the horse a few taps on the shoulder or rump. Horses respond to chirping and smooching during races, taking the communication as encouragement to pick up the pace. If the jockey needs to send a more direct message, he may re-set the bit inside the horse's mouth by throwing the reins forward and then pulling them back again, so that the horse gets a new hold on the bit, often resulting in a new burst of speed.

Jockeys use a racing whip, also known as a "stick" or "bat," as a form of communication with the horse, instructing him it is time for maximum effort. It is impossible to predict how a horse will react to being hit with the whip the first time. While they may be exposed to shoulder and hindquarter tapping in the morning workouts, when they hit the racetrack with a full field of competitors flying around them, anything can happen. If hit on the left side, the horse may spook and dart to the right in attempt to run away from the whip. This was the case in the 2005 Preakness, when runner-up Scrappy T veered sharply into the path of eventual winner Afleet Alex. With one solid whack from jockey Ramon Dominguez, Scrappy T dove directly into the path of the hard-charging winner, causing the horses to clip heels. Afleet Alex went nearly to his knees, and it's a miracle he was able to rebound, regroup and continue on, let alone gather himself up and draw away from the field.

Grade I stakes-winning rider Aaron Gryder recognizes every horse responds differently to the whip:

> Fillies can be more finicky than colts or geldings, so you learn to adjust to whatever a particular horse likes. If you reach back and they don't respond, hitting him every stride won't make him go any faster. You can feel it if the horse responds or resents being hit. If the horse swishes his tail after being hit, he probably doesn't like it. Some just need one whack, and they're on go for the whole stretch, but most seem to need a reminder every few strides.
>
> When I'm passing horses on the outside, I use my left hand a lot, even though I'm right-handed. I figure I'd rather have the horse drift out than risk him coming inside if I hit him on the right.

The point of the whip is to make the horse run away from it, as if to scare them with it. Sometimes just showing the whip to the horse as he's running will get him going. Switching the stick from one side to the other helps remind them that it's there.

Brutal use of whips is strictly prohibited. Jockeys can be penalized through fines or suspensions for improper, or excessive, use of the whip. The whip is used as a signal to horses, encouraging them that it's time for an all-out effort. Once the horse has been hit, it doesn't matter how many times they hit the horse; he's not likely to run any faster. If the jockey persists on swinging away at the horse needlessly, the stewards won't take kindly to it.

Occasionally a horse is so soundly beaten that he is "eased," or coasted, by the rider. Easing a horse occurs when the jockey pulls the horse out of the race because he is no longer competitive. Each jockey is responsible for assuring his horse is ridden out in every race, meaning he may not be eased up without proper cause, such as injury or being hopelessly beaten. If ever caught "stopping" a horse, the jockey would lose respect of not only their peers, but also trainers and owners, which would severely cut into their business and put their license at risk with the stewards. Jockeys are responsible for giving their horse the best effort to win and must be ridden with that intent.

One of the nicest guys in racing, jockey Donnie Meche, was suspended from racing in 2003 for a year when, according to the Louisiana State Racing Commission, his horse, Cleaning House, was not given a fair chance to win. The horse stumbled out of the gate, was wide on the turn and finished fast. Meche, who said the horse wasn't striding well, appealed the decision to no avail. Worried about regaining his reputation, he worked hard for his comeback in 2004 and enjoyed a fast start in 2005, among the leading riders in the "races won" category.

Jockeys who ride carelessly and allow their horse to impede or hinder another horse may be found guilty of interference. While they are allowed to ride their horse in the part of the track they choose, they are not allowed to guide their horse into the path of another. They are also not allowed to unnecessarily force their horse to shorten his stride to feint suffering a foul. If the stewards feel the jockey intentionally caused a foul or put other riders at risk of injury, they are certain to issue a severe penalty to the offender.

As if there aren't enough ways for a horse and rider to get into trouble during a race, unpredictable setbacks, like a slipped saddle, snapped stirrup or broken rein could wipe them out. "I remember that some of the bridles used to connect the reins with screw connectors," explained Joe Steiner. "I had a rein come loose and completely fall off coming out of the gate. All I had was the outside rein. Thank goodness it was an older horse and he knew what to do. I just sat chilly, and he took care of himself on the turn and down the lane. After we finished the race and were jogging out, I yelled to the outrider that I needed some help, otherwise I don't know when he would've stopped. I was lucky to make it through."

While jockeys won't push a horse if he's laboring, it's important that they be able to distinguish between a lazy horse who needs a vigorous ride and a real trier who is beaten and faltering. Kenny Tohill, stakes-winning rider, tries to keep his tiring horses running well by finding their button: "With a 1,200-pound animal, the best you can do is to manipulate them into giving you a little bit more when they're getting tired. You don't want to hinder the horse in any way, meaning you should have no motion that goes against the horse. Everything should be in rhythm with the horse. Every horse has a button, or way, that gives them a little boost; the trick is finding out what the button is on different horses. I might try tapping him lightly with the whip, whipping hard, hollering at the horse or really pushing him hard; whatever it takes to get them to extend themselves for you."

The rider likes to wait until the horse hits the stretch and switches leads before asking him for his full on run. The jockey will "push the button," or send his horse when he can't wait any longer. He hopes the horse will re-break, or rapidly accelerate, and take off again. He will listen for approaching horses and through peripheral vision can see them coming from behind. He may take a peek with a quick turn to the side, under his arm or under his rump. When another horse threatens to pass, the jock calls on all the reserves the horse has. If the horse "spits the bit out," or quits pulling aggressively against the reins, the rider will quickly try to get him re-engaged.

When the horses hit the "top of the lane," or homestretch, the jockey calls upon the horse to give his best. The rider will lower himself in the saddle, twirl his whip around into position and begin riding hard, pumping the horse's neck in rhythm with his quickening stride. Hopefully the

In the heat of battle, one horse savages his competitor (photograph courtesy of New York Racing Association. Adam Coglianese, photo contributor).

rider has found a favorable position around the turn and is positioned with a clear path in front of him. The shortest distance from the head of the stretch to the finish is a straight line. Changing lanes and maneuvering around horses eat up valuable time in the all-out sprint to the wire. As the horse lays his ears back and digs in, the rider pulls out the whip as he drives down the lane toward the finish.

The thrill and excitement of a hard-fought stretch duel is certainly one of racing's highlights. As the horses labor to inch their nose in front, the jockeys are fully engaged in the battle, doing everything they can to get his horse home first. If it's a close call at the wire, the jockey must push down on the horse's neck as they hit the line, hoping to gain an inch or two for the photo.

As the leading money-winning rider in the country last year, 2004 Eclipse Award–winning jockey John Velazquez knows how to hit the line first: "When it gets close to the wire, that's when you really get down and ride your hardest. You're already using the whip by now and you push on the horse in good rhythm with him, driving on him real hard to try and get to the wire first, asking him to give you that extra little bit. You want to ride hard all the way past the wire so you don't lose any momentum."

Kent Desormeaux practices a few techniques to help squeeze a few extra inches out at the wire to win the photo finishes: "Some people call it throwing a cross or shortening the hold on the reins, but I twirl the reins in my hands a bit, which screws the bit into the horse's mouth. By grinding it in there a bit, the horse grabs ahold and it helps him strain for the last few strides at the finish. Right at the line, I might use my riding crop to tap him on the ear or under his chin to encourage him to stretch his head out for me."

In the years before photo finishes and before video cameras were installed at racetracks, races weren't always won by the fastest horse. Jockeys were known to grab horses' tails in front of them, hold onto another rider's silks, intentionally knock another rider's boot out of his stirrups or throw his horse directly into the path of another if it helped his chances of crossing the finish first.

In the 1933 Kentucky Derby, known as the "Fighting Finish Derby," jockeys Herb Fisher and Don Meade became engaged in hand-to-hand combat as their horses, Head Play and Broker's Tip, respectively, raced nose-to-nose down the famed Churchill Downs stretch. In the upper stretch, Head Play was on the lead when Fisher moved him inside to put the squeeze on hard-charging Broker's Tip. Meade grabbed Head Play's saddlecloth, worried he was going to get knocked out of position. Fisher responded by hitting his counterpart on the head with his whip. As they grappled towards the wire, each rider trying to out grab the other to gain

Top: Splashing their way down the stretch, horse and rider push hard for the wire. *Bottom:* As horses battle down the lane, notice the jockey on the first horse changing muddy goggles to get a clear view (both photographs ©Cris Forney Photography).

an advantage, the horses were inseparable. Because photo-finish technology hadn't yet been invented, the stewards mulled over what to do with the scuffling riders, who carried their fight over into the jockeys' room, and blanket finish. In the end, the stewards awarded the narrow victory to the maiden Broker's Tip and issued long suspensions to both jockeys.

In many races, the winner is virtually decided long before the finish, when he dominates his competition, receives a dream trip or takes advantage of a favorable pace scenario. In some cases, however, certain victory somehow eludes the leader. Devon Loch, ridden by jockey Richard "Dick" Francis, three-time Edgar Allan Poe Award–winning mystery author after his retirement, offered us one of these great, true racing mysteries.

In the 1956 Grand National, Francis was up on Devon Loch, who was owned by the Queen Mother. The Grand National is a 4½ mile steeplechase marathon covering 30 jumps. The favorite, Must, fell at the first jump. Prior National winner Early Mist also made an early exit after tumbling. Francis pulled hard early to keep his mount reserved and out of trouble. As the race wore on, it was evident he had a big chance to win the English classic, moving up and into contention as the race wore on.

Rewarded for his patience and well-measured ride, Francis was first over the last hurdle and had clear sailing ahead. Devon Loch took off with a full head of steam for the wire. With the screams of the British crowd cheering the royal favorite home, he opened up daylight on the field, and imminent victory was surely at hand. Unbelievably, fifty yards from the finish, Devon Loch simply belly flopped!

With no forewarning and while in full stride, the horse appeared to slightly jump. His hind legs stopped, and he skidded on the turf before collapsing onto his stomach. The horse shockingly came to a sprawling rest, with his front legs spread out in a V-shape and his hind legs nearly straight out behind him.

The horse struggled to his feet moments later, but the race was lost. What really happened to Devon Loch on that dreadful day remains, ironically for Francis, a mystery. Did the horse experience some type of cardiac event? Did he attempt to jump a phantom fence or water jump? Was it a muscle cramp? We'll never know. To this day, Devon Loch's name is synonymous with irrational falls in Europe, and the legend lives on. Unfortunately for Francis, he isn't remembered in racing circles for the championships he won, but the disastrous one that slipped away.

Once horses cross the finish line, they are eased up and jog out before returning for unsaddling. Riders simply stand up in the irons, and most horses slow down on their own, while strong-willed horses may require hard-pulling slow up. Most pull ups are noneventful, although jockey Corey Nakatani once knocked Ryan Barber, an apprentice at the time, off his mount while pulling up after a race by throwing him a forearm. Barber's horse had lugged in on Nakatani during the race, squeezing him off and forcing him to pull up suddenly. Nakatani was suspended for the balance of the Del Mar meet and placed on probation for a year.

Shaun Bridgmohan, 1998 Eclipse Award–winning apprentice rider, occasionally receives instructions from his trainer to put a little extra "air" into his horses during the post-race jog out:

> The trainer may tell me to gallop out strongly for an extra eighth or quarter, trying to leg up the horse for going longer. The extra work helps the horse build up the air for the stretch out.
>
> I usually jog my horse out to the backstretch, stop and let him stand for awhile and look around, then turn and jog back to the groom for unsaddling. It's important to always keep your horse on a straight path when jogging out just in case something happens. By the time the horses hit the wire, they're pretty tired, so I try and keep his head up so he doesn't stumble. I remember a horse not long ago falling after a race, and the horse behind him fell over him. No one got hurt that time, but it just shows that it can still be dangerous.

Usually somewhere around the quarter-mile pole past the finish line along the jog-out trail, a walkie-talkie-equipped outrider waits for any riders who may elect to claim a foul of interference. If so, the outrider contacts the stewards, who often begin looking at the film even before the jockeys return for unsaddling and questioning. At some tracks, they still use an older version of the "all clear" verification by asking riders to wave their whips to the steward's box or post their objection with the clerk of scales.

Jockey Chris Emigh explained how the process worked for him recently,

> There was a horse in front of me to the inside, and I was drawing up on his outside. Another horse came closing from behind me on the outside, and it felt like he was coming in on me. He kept coming in, and I got shut out and had to pull up hard in midstretch, practically standing up at the eighth pole.
>
> So as we jogged out, I found the outrider and told him what happened. When I got back to unsaddle, the clerk of scales handed me the phone, and I talked with the stewards: They asked me what I thought happened, and I told them I got squeezed out and I thought it was the outside horse, who eventually went on to win. So they looked at the film and found that it wasn't the outside horse coming in, but actually the inside horse, the one on the lead, who came out. I guess because I couldn't see the fence because of the horse inside me, so I didn't realized he drifted out. The one outside me had kept running straight.
>
> The stewards took the inside horse down, and I moved up to second, which was right. They put all of us on the film list, and we had to watch the

replay with the stewards the next morning. After we watch the movie, we discuss what happened and what we could've done different. Sometimes we might be issued days or get fined, but in this case there wasn't any punishment.

Lots of trainers ask why we don't claim foul more often, and it's because if we claim every frivolous foul, the stewards might not take me seriously when there's really a foul they need to deal with.

After review by the stewards, a horse may be disqualified. If the horse's number gets taken down, the disqualified horse is placed behind the horse that he interfered with. So, if a horse finishing second, but disqualified for bothering a horse finishing fourth, the disqualified horse would be placed behind that one, moving the original third- and fourth-place finishers up a spot. In cases where the horse interferes with the majority of the field, he may be placed last.

The rider is likely to be placed on the film list, meaning he must appear before the stewards the next day to review the video replay of the race. They may choose to suspend the rider, although a fine is more likely because tracks like to keep riders racing. The call on suspensions is entirely up to the stewards, and it's based on severity, intention and the jockeys' attempt to avoid the incident. Fines typically increase with occurrence. Suspensions vary from a few days up to a month for serious, deliberate actions that place others in danger.

Occasionally, horses unfairly impede with another's opportunities, leading to disqualification. Graded stakes-winning rider Casey Fusilier had his number taken down after winning when his horse brushed into another:

> I was laying third of fourth on the turn for home and racing about three lengths behind the leader. I angled out so that I could have a straight path to the finish and asked my horse to go. He responded and made a run for the lead. As we passed the last horse, who was outside of me, we brushed him. I didn't even notice it at the time, because it happened so fast, but the back end of my horse hit the other horse on the shoulder and the other jock had to take up for just a second.
>
> I really didn't know anything had happened until I was jogging back to the winner's circle and I saw the "Inquiry" sign up on the board. So I had to talk with the stewards on the phone and tell them what happened. Then you just wait and wait until they make a decision. In this case, they took my number down. The horse I brushed ended up running third, beaten a nose for second. I guess the stewards felt that the interference cost the horse second.

One of the top jockeys of his era, Walter Blum is a Hall of Fame rider and former president of the Jockeys' Guild. After a spectacular 25-year career in the saddle, Blum worked as a Florida racing steward for another 25 years and retired at the end of 2004. Well versed in the laws of the sport, Blum explained the basic role of stewards: "In general, we uphold the rules

5. They're Off!   137

of thoroughbred horse racing and the state laws and statutes regarding racing. We're the officials in charge of the race meeting and all the licensees involved with racing at the track. With jockeys in particular, we're looking for clean, honest and fair race riding."

Over the years, he's seen sweeping changes in jockey colonies and riding styles:

> When I was riding back in the 1950s and 60s, 90 percent of the jockeys were American kids. Toward the 1970s, the influence of Hispanic jockeys started really increasing. I'd say 95 percent of today's jockeys at Calder are from outside the country. Many of the riders who come outside the United States now, like riders from Panama or Puerto Rico, for example, are taught to not let anyone run inside of them. So, when they come over and race here, there might be a five-yard opening along the fence, which is plenty of room for a horse, and someone tries to get through, they'll ease in and shut the rider off.
>
> They may ride for pennies in their country and they come here because they can make thousands a week if they're good. When I rode, I only got 10 percent of winning rides purse and I had to get my money from the trainer

There appears to be no holds barred in this battle to the finish (photograph courtesy of New York Racing Association, Adam Coglianese, photo contributor).

and he had to get it from the owner first. It's not like that anymore. These young guys can make a lot of money.

We'll call a "Stewards Inquiry" if we see something we want to look at. An "objection" can be filed by an owner, trainer or jockey. Either way, we'll watch the race replay, talk with the affected riders and make a decision.

Let's say there's a 10-horse field and the outside horse swerves inside at the break and interferes with half the field. We're probably going to disqualify the horse.

If the horses are racing down the stretch with everyone trying to get to the wire first, let's say there's a horse along the rail and the jockey is hitting him left handed and he's drifting out. If the jockey never corrects his horse, and he interferes with the horse outside of him, we may take his number down and put him behind those he bothered.

The next day, we'll show the movies to the riders and school them on what they did wrong. They're just race riding the way they were taught, and we'll tell them to ride straight down the course. They realize pretty quickly that they have to straighten up. They're all honest guys, but they're competitive and sometimes get careless. Most of the time, it's the horse's fault. If the jockey tries to correct his horse's action, we probably won't suspend the rider.

After an uneventfully run race is completed, jockeys are weighed out at a designated area alongside the track immediately after unsaddling. They are most typically required to return within a two-pound variance of their weigh out number. The wiggle room is allowed to accommodate for weight gained or lost due to sweating or gained from rain, dirt or mud. Rarely does a rider come back in excess of the allowance. Calder Race Course clerk of scales Victor Sanchez has not seen a disqualification due to weight in his 20 years at the track.

Jockey Ricky Frazier is one of few riders to experience such trouble after unsaddling. Several years ago in the Final Fourteen Championship at Bay Meadows, he came back three pounds light after winning the $250,000 race by a nose aboard Allijeba: "I think the saddle chammy [material that stops the saddle from slipping] was changed from the one I weighed out with to the one the trainer had. It must've been heavier, because I didn't have any contact with the saddle from the time I weighed out in the jocks' room to the time I dismounted and the valet took the saddle. The investigation went on for weeks. In addition to losing the purse, it was the embarrassment that bothered me the most."

He weighted out on the scale at 123, three pounds lighter than the horse was supposed to carry. Originally suspended for six months by the stewards, he took the case to court, and the sentence was reduced to probation.

Even after the post-race jog-out is completed, strange things can happen. Recently, jockey Sandi Gann was thrown from her mount as she waited

Avelino Gomez demonstrates the flying dismount after taking down the 1963 Futurity at Belmont aboard Bupers (photograph courtesy of New York Racing Association. Adam Coglianese, photo contributor).

to enter the winner's circle at Turf Paradise. Apparently the horse, Sky Hoof Hearted, was startled having his blinkers removed prior to stepping in for the photo and threw the veteran rider, who suffered a broken leg in the fall.

Entering the winner's circle, jockeys enjoy celebrating in a variety of ways. Some make the sign of the cross in praise to God; some give thumbs up or flash the "V" for victory sign. Jockey Rosemary Homeister blows a kiss to the camera, in honor of her grandfather, while jockey Lanfranco "Frankie" Dettori leaps high in the air with a flying dismount to jump off his winners.

One of the old traditions occurs when jockeys approaching the winner's enclosure wave their whip upwards toward the sky before tossing it to their valet. What looks to be a thanks sent to the heavens used to be the practice of notifying the track officials high atop the grandstands that all is good with the race, there are no objections and a wave of acknowledgment to the track announcer.

Retuning from a losing effort, jockey Ben Russell prepares to dismount (photograph by Molly O'Brien).

Nearly all trainers, or their assistants, will review the race briefly with the rider after unsaddling. Trainers want to hear how the horse traveled, what kind of trip the horse had and what suggestions the jockey might have for next time out. The opportunity exists for the rider to sell himself if he wants another try on the horse. It's a good time to build trust and relations with the trainer, and owner, if the race didn't go well. Apologizing for a misjudged timing or unfortunate racing usually help his chances in picking up the mount next time out.

With a wave of the whip upstairs, rising star John McKee celebrates another victory (©Cris Forney Photography).

Kentucky-based trainer Joan Scott appreciates a rider who can provide something constructive after the race: "I work too hard with my horses for some guy to come back and shrug his shoulders. I like the guys who have been around awhile and can tell you something when they come back after the race, not some canned bull. 'He didn't like the track' may be the truth, but maybe he's a hog that needs to be dropped is more like the truth. Give me an honest response, but I expect a knowledgeable response also."

Likewise, trainer Kenny McPeek wants his riders to be honest with him about his racing stock: "The worst thing a rider can do is sugarcoat things for me. I want him to tell me if the horse can't run. He's not doing me any favors if he makes up excuses."

When horses run poorly, it's easy to blame the jockey for a bad ride, but most often that's not the case. Trainer William "Buff" Bradley is forgiving when things haven't gone quite according to plan: "A jockey that comes back and admits when he made a mistake will most likely get to ride my horse back. I usually don't fire a jockey unless he doesn't follow instructions or has a bad attitude towards the horse."

From the jockeys' perspective, Aaron Gryder feels honesty is the best approach when reviewing the race with the horse's trainer:

Martin Pedroza on his way back to the Jockey's room at Hollywood Park (photograph by Debra Gruender).

I'll explain what happened during the race and tell him about any situation that came up. Maybe we broke slow, stumbled or got bumped around. I don't make up any excuses or a story just so I have something to say. I'll tell him, honestly, if I think the horse needs to be dropped a notch or two. If I lose my job because I'm honest, that's OK. I'm going to win for some other guy because of it.

The stories are always shorter if you win, of course. But even then, sometimes there's something you need to tell the trainer. I won one today, for example, and jumped off after the photo and told the trainer that the horse had been crossfiring, which means the horse changed leads up front around the turn, but didn't switch in the back. It didn't hurt this one, but it could tire the horse out more or cause him to hit hooves or nick himself up.

While some trainers have high expectations and can be quite critical, they can also help a rider improve his game. For jockey Corey Lanerie, working with record-setting trainer Steve Asmussen was both challenging and rewarding:

> I used to ride a lot for Steve. He worked real hard and everyone that worked for him worked hard. He had a barn full of really good horses, so there was always lots of pressure to perform. He expected to win all the time, which put the pressure on me. If I didn't win, he would want a very detailed explanation of what happened. He knows his stuff and would tell me what I missed in my description of the race. He would tell me what I did wrong, like if I could've saved ground here, or ran into the hole there. He really drilled into me sometimes about mistakes I made. After a while, it beat down on my confidence, but at the same time, I praise him for helping me become a better rider.

Sometimes a timely suggestion from the jockey after the race can help the trainer improve the horse's performance next time out. Such was the case for jockey Shaun Bridgmohan: "I remember riding a really nice filly for Pat Kelly named Pelham Bay. She'd broken her maiden first time out, pretty easily. She continued to run good for awhile, then fell off form a bit. I think she finished fifth in a stake, and I told Pat that I thought blinkers might help her be more focused and keep her mind on business. He put blinkers on, and she came back to win the Maid of the Mist Stakes at Belmont next time out by five lengths, so it worked out good that time."

Jockey John McKee found his suggestion of sending a filly over a route of ground paid dividends: "I used to ride this filly that showed a good kick every time she ran short. She demonstrated good stamina, finished fast and always galloped out strongly. I told the trainer that I thought she'd probably route well, and sure enough, he sent her long and she improved a ton. I got to stay on her, and she ended up being a real good allowance horse and proved to be much better going two turns."

On the walk back to the jockeys' room, many riders enjoy the chatter, jeers and mild heckling with race fans. Most riders acquire a small following of fans and are always well supported when they bring home a winner, earning instant accolades from new admirers with winning tickets in hand. On the flip side, however, there always seems to be some loudmouth with a losing $2 ticket who thinks he was robbed and can't wait to dump his troubles on the beaten jockey.

Kenny Tohill remembers a heckler incident that shook him up several years ago after a big race disappointment:

> I was up on odds-on favorite Bedside Promise in a stakes race. He'd just been shipped to the track and had a bad van ride. He wasn't at his best and ran horribly for me, finishing up the track. As I was walking back to the jocks' room, this guy was screaming at me about the race, saying I cost him money and then he threw his beer on me. Obviously I got really upset, but the older riders explained to me that part of what we do is putting on the show of racing, and people are going to get upset and yell at you sometimes. They told me that it's not the end of the world, to forget about it and just get ready for the next race. It changed my outlook, and I never really get upset any more when somebody goes off on me.

As jockeys tread in and out of the jockeys' room all day long, the glamour of racing fades with muddied silks, sweat and bruises, but dawns anew every day, as racing never sleeps.

6

THOSE ARE THE BREAKS

Around the turn, jockey Ralph "the Portuguese Pepperpot" Neves, aboard Finnikins, had a wall of four horses right in front of him. With nowhere to go, the fearless 19-year-old rider was just biding his time when the outside horse broke a leg and went down, setting off a chain-reaction accident that dropped all four horses directly in his path. Finnikins screeched to a halt, sending Neves flying over the top. Finnikins couldn't make it over the fallen horses, stumbled, fell and landed directly on top of Neves.

Jockeys, track attendants and medical personnel rushed to his aid. Jockeys were seen yanking the horse by her tail off the limp and lifeless rider. They tried reviving him on the track, but he showed no signs of life. He was removed from the track in a pick-up truck because the track didn't have an ambulance on site. In the track's first-aid room, the doctor's attempts to revive him failed. Shortly afterwards, he was pronounced dead at the scene. The track announcer told the somber Bay Meadows audience that the jockey had died and requested a moment of silence.

Neves was taken to the hospital, where he was covered in a white sheet, toe tagged and sent to the morgue. In a long-shot attempt, a physician injected a shot of adrenaline directly into Neves's heart. While there was no immediate response, shortly later Neves miraculously awoke from the dead. As the story does, the startled medical officials wanted to keep him for observation, but Neves was vehemently opposed, insistent on completing his riding assignments for the day. He snuck out a hospital window, hailed a cab outside and rushed back to the track.

As the jockeys were taking up a collection for his wife, Neves flew into the jockeys' room, demanding to ride his next mount. Jockeys and racing officials were shocked. His wife fainted at his sight. In his own remembrances, Neves claims that he was chased by racetrack officials in the front of the stunned grandstand when he insisted on riding his remaining horses. He was battling the legendary Johnny Longden for the riding crown, which included a $500 bonus and a gold watch from Bing Crosby. Neves was allowed to ride the next day and won the meet's jockey title. Even as a young lad, he knew he'd be lucky someday because his last name was "seven" spelled backwards.

This story has most certainly been embellished over time as it's been retold, including a version in which Neves came back to win five races the following day, and it's impossible to know exactly what happened to Ralph Neves on May 8, 1936. What we do know is that he became much more than a racing legend. Despite his hot temper, and a daredevil riding style that often put him in the steward's doghouse, Neves rode to racing brilliance and is honored in racing's Hall of Fame.

While jockey deaths are rare, averaging about one a year, Neves's story illustrates two points—horse racing is a very dangerous sport, and jockeys are extremely tough and stubbornly durable.

Hitting the ground at 40 miles per hour, crashing into the rail, being crushed against the gate or being trampled by thundering hooves can cause serious injury. Racing and training injuries range from simple contusions, to damaging of internal organs and catastrophic injuries leading to paralysis or death.

Industry estimates are as high as 30 racing accidents per week, nationally. Most accidents lead to some form of injury for one or more riders. According to the Jockeys' Guild, an average of five jockeys are injured every day in racing across America.

Jockeys accept pulled muscles, bruises and broken bones as occupational hazards. Career-ending injuries—severe head injury, paralyzing injury to spinal cord, organ damage and severely broken bones—are less common but a constant danger for riders every time they saddle up. The most common injuries to riders involve contusions and fractures to ribs, hips, collarbone, arms and legs.

Veteran rider Gary Baze has had so many serious injuries, he can't remember them all:

> My first serious injury was a broken collarbone in 1976. Later that year, I broke my left cheekbone. Two years later I broke my left ankle and tibia. I also broke three vertebrae in 1978. I wasn't really hurt again until 1985. In February, I took a bad fall when my horse went down. An artery leading to my kidney was damaged, and I was bleeding internally before getting to the hospital. It was touch and go for awhile. I lost 70% kidney functionality and also suffered spleen damage from the accident.
>
> In 1989, I broke seven ribs. I missed six months of racing following a

compound right leg fracture in 1992. I broke my ankle and tibia again in 2002. And somewhere along the way, I don't remember when, I broke another four vertebrae in my back.

Despite all the setbacks and a five-year stint as the Jockeys' Guild West Coast manager, Baze just keeps coming back for more: "I've never found anything else that keeps my interest. I just love racing. I love the horses. I love the horsemen. I love the game."

For a jockeys' spouse, seeing them suffer through these physical and emotional tortures can be torturous. While most appear calm on the surface, the sorrowful look of fear in their eyes when their loved one is down on the turf is a grim reminder of how violently dangerous the sport can be.

As a former trainer and current agent for her husband, Paul, Kathy Melancon has seen her share of riders go down on the track:

> Your stomach falls out from underneath you when someone you love goes down. I remember one time Paul went down right in front of me. I ponied the race, and the horses had just broken from the gate. They might have gone a $\frac{1}{16}$ of a mile from the gate when he went down. It's nerve wracking until you know he's going to be all right. This time, he hurt his shoulder and was sore for awhile, but otherwise okay. Every time he hits the ground, it makes you think about how much is at risk out there. We talk about what could happen, and it scares us.

Despite the risks, riders are internally driven to their calling. As jockey Kevin Mangold explained, it's a matter of perspective: "I take risks all the time. But once you've ridden in a race, I don't think it's possible to sit out. If your health permits, it's just too much fun. Don't get me wrong, the business is tough, dangerous and hours of hard work, but for that brief 20 seconds when you're coming down the stretch in front, it's truly unbelievable. It's worth the risk."

According to the Jockeys' Guild, 144 jockeys have died riding since 1940, when records were first kept. Most recently, jockey Michael Rowland died February 9, 2004, five days after falling at Turfway Park. Rowland was thrown from his horse when it broke down while racing on the lead and collided with two other horses. Rowland was trampled by the horses running behind him. He underwent brain surgery at University Hospital in Cincinnati, but remained in a coma until his death.

Rowland won 3,996 races in his 24-year career and had won numerous riding titles. He'd just moved his tack to Turfway Park for the winter meet so he could be with his wife, a trainer there.

Jockey Chris Quinn died a year after sustaining serious injuries from a racing fall on July 19, 2003, at Fairmount Park in Illinois. Quinn was thrown from his mount, Wiley Hunt, when it clipped heels with another horse, sending Quinn to the ground. He was trampled by a trailing horse.

He sustained massive head injuries in the accident and spent six weeks in a hospital before moving to a rehabilitation facility, where he remained until his death. While he didn't break any bones in the accident, he was partially paralyzed and unable to speak.

In 2001, apprentice jockey Arnold Ruiz died after suffering massive head injuries in a fall at Beulah Park. Ruiz was aboard Winds of Sonora when the filly stumbled and went down in mid-stretch, sending the young rider to the ground. He was run over by two horses behind him, with one of them kicking him in the back of the head.

Jose Carlos "JC" Gonzalez died from a fall when his horse broke down on the lead at Fairplex Park in Pomona on opening day in 1999. Gonzalez was catapulted off his mount, Wolfhunt, hit the ground headfirst and was run over by the horses running behind. Gonzales died of massive head injuries before he made it to the hospital.

Many riders become temporarily disabled from riding injuries, and several have become permanently disabled in accidents. More than 50 of the Jockeys' Guild members are permanently disabled from paralyzing riding injuries, including Hall of Famer Ron Turcotte, regular rider of the immortal Secretariat. Turcotte was paralyzed in a 1978 racing accident.

A kind-hearted man, jockey Rudy Baez didn't think twice about picking up an open horse at Rockingham Park on August 6, 1999. He had no idea that his mount, Gaitor Bait, was to be his last:

> Away from the gate, my horse was getting intimidated by the other horses. He was running like he was scared. I tried slowing him down, but he was shying away and heading towards the fence. He brushed into the rail, tripped and sent me flying. I landed head first, breaking my spinal cord. I've been in a wheelchair ever since.
>
> At first, I was depressed and just sat around the house feeling sorry for myself. But with time, I realized how lucky I am that God gave me another chance. So I started doing simple things and realized that the more I did, the better I felt. I'm convinced He kept me alive to help others. I've learned that every day is a gift to be shared with others.
>
> Most people have no idea how dangerous horse racing is. One minute you're out there just doing your job, then this 1,200 pound horse makes up his mind he's going to go somewhere, and there's nothing you can do to stop him. He might rear in the gate, jump the rail, make a U-turn or stumble. Sometimes you know you're going to fall, and you can bail out before you crash into the rail or other horses, but at 40 miles per hour, it all happens so quick that you can't do anything about it. Before I broke my back, I probably had 15 or 20 serious accidents. I'd broken bones all over my body—hands, arms, shoulder, ribs, legs, feet, you name it.

Baez, who won over 4,000 races and numerous riding titles at Suffolk Downs and Rockingham Park, speaks to other spinal cord injury patients at local hospitals and works with the Jockeys' Guild in raising funds for the disabled jockeys. Last year he returned to the racetrack as the clerk of scales at Suffolk Downs.

No two racing accidents are identical. Many racing falls occur when a horse takes a bad step, clips heels or breaks down in front of other horses. Riders can be thrown, or unseated, when their horse trips, falls, rears up, swerves or bumps another horse. In many cases, these accidents propel the rider forwards over the stumbling horse, sending him flying head first into the ground and directly into the path of oncoming traffic. If the jockey isn't knocked unconscious by the fall, he instinctively curls up into a ball or rolls under the inside rail to avoid being trampled.

Grade I stakes–winning rider Frank Lovato, Jr., has fallen too many times to count in his long career. As he described, accidents happen so fast, there's no time to brace for impact:

> When a horse clips heels, breaks down or trips, everything happens in a fraction of a second. While it feels like slow motion in your head, it's over before you know it. Your reflexes take over because there's no time to respond.
>
> Going that fast, when you change direction or stop, the rider just gets flung from the horse. It's so brutal and fast that sometimes you can't get your limbs tucked in, you can't turn your head or anything.
>
> One time I went down so hard, I didn't remember anything about the fall. The horse I was riding broke a leg and I went flying. Next thing I know, I'm laying on the ground with the wind knocked out me holding the horse's reins, bridle, blinkers and my whip still in my hands. From the speed of the fall, I'd taken all the horse's equipment with me. The horse was standing along the outside fence with only his saddle on.
>
> If you take a fall and have enough consciousness and enough mind control to react, you roll up into a ball and just stay there. In your mind, you're praying there isn't a horse ready to crash into you. You count the seconds that seem like hours until the last horse has run by.

Jockeys don't actually sit on a horse when racing; they're perched above the horse's shoulder, balanced on their toes in the saddle stirrups and gripping the horse with their legs. Because of this, they are at high risk of being thrown off when the horse stops or suddenly changes directions.

Jockey Michael Baze took a double hit in a nasty fall in New York last year:

> I was racing in tight quarters when my horse clipped heels with the horse in front of us. I was crouched forward in the saddle when he took the bad step, and his head came straight back and slammed me in the face. He hit me so hard that it shattered my nose. I ended up in the hospital for a week and had reconstructive facial surgery to put a plate in there to support my eye socket.

The blow knocked me off right away, and I hit the ground rolling. One of the horses running behind us ran over me, but I escaped without a scratch, other than having a bloody face. When I talked with Aaron Gryder, rider of the horse that went over me, he told me that they hit me so hard he thought it would've killed me. I guess I was lucky that time.

At such high speeds, it's difficult for the trailing horses to avoid the spill. Horses may dart to the side or attempt to jump the fallen horse or rider, unseating their rider with the sudden change of direction. Falling horses often generate a domino effect on the horses running behind them, often taking several down with them. However, some of the worst looking falls leave horse and rider injury free.

While all racing accidents are dangerous, according to the report "Jockey Injuries in the United States" by Anna Waller, ScD, Department of Emergency Medicine and Injury Prevention Research Center at the University of North Carolina at Chapel Hill, about one-third of jockey injuries occur when horses are entering, within or leaving the starting gate.

Dr. Waller's report, published in the Journal of the American Medical Association, was a comprehensive study of over 6,500 jockey injuries covering a four-year period. The report cites an injury rate of 606 incidents per 1000 jockey-years. As Dr. Waller explains, the numbers are quite startling:

> The injury rate means that for the population of licensed jockeys in one year, for every 1000 jockeys, we found 606 injuries reported in our data. Since these were all medically treated injuries, that is an extremely high injury rate. Because the denominator of jockeys may have included inactive jockeys and our data required a rather lengthy injury report form to be completed, this is probably a conservative estimate of the true injury rate for this population.
>
> We were only allowed access to very limited information. I was very impressed by the Jockeys' Guild and their commitment to the jockeys. They seemed genuinely committed to trying to make the lives of jockeys better and healthier. There is very little literature about the health of jockeys. Frankly, there is probably more written about the health of the race horses than the health of jockeys. I would love to see a more detailed study of jockeys, perhaps looking into their health issues in general, not just injury, but I'm not sure there is the political buy-in from the racing community to do this.
>
> Most public focus is on a select few of extremely successful athletes, while most people in the profession have a very hard life. Like other professional athletes, jockeys rely on their bodies for their living. When you mix in the whole "making weight" issue and the fact that many young jockeys will forego their education to pursue this career, this is a sport that carries many, many risks for participants.

The report showed that 30 percent of all head injuries, 40 percent of arm and hand injuries, and 52 percent of leg and foot injuries occur at the starting gate. Riders can easily be thrown or pinned against the starting gate walls or posts when the horse enters the gate or rears up or falls over once inside the gate.

Jockey Ricky Frazier suffered a serious leg injury in a gate accident at Golden Gate Fields when his horse became agitated: "My horse flipped in the gate and my leg got trapped between the gate and the horse. It crushed my tibia. My leg was broken in seven places. I was told I'd never ride again and would be lucky if I was able to walk. Like most of us, though, I fought through it and was back in a year."

Similarly, jockey Joe Steiner was injured when his mount acted up in the gate:

> My horse reared up and flipped over backwards in the gate, and I got pinned in the back of the stall. I was hanging upside down outside the back of the gate with the fallen horse trapping my legs between him and the back door, just kind of stuck there. The gate crew were really fast in getting in there, though, and virtually lifted the horse off me.
>
> My leg really hurt and I knew something was wrong with it, but I rode anyway, actually bringing in three winners after the accident. I was really hurting, though, and went to the hospital after the races. They told me I had cracked a bone in my leg and not to ride again until it healed. But I went back to the track the next morning to work some horses and broke it for good when a lead pony slammed into me.

On January 18, 1975, jockey Alvaro Pineda was killed in a starting gate accident at Santa Anita. Pineda's horse reared in the gate and flipped over backwards, crushing Pineda's head against the gate's steel frame. He was killed instantly.

About 44 percent of injuries occur when jockeys are thrown or fall from the horse when racing. Fallen jockeys are vulnerable to out-of-control horses scrambling to avoid the accident. Many riders are stepped on or kicked by horses while fallen, oftentimes leading to broken bones and sometimes serious head injuries.

T. D. Houghton, sixth-leading rider in the country by number of wins last year, suffered a serious head injury in 2002 and was lucky to survive. He fought his way back through rehabilitation to return to racing 16 months later. "My horse clipped heels and went down. The rider on the horse behind us tried to avoid me, but couldn't, and the horse struck me in the back of the head. I was in bad shape for quite some time. I had contusions on the front and back of my brain. I was in the hospital for a week getting around-the-clock care. They were watching for hemorrhaging and seizures because I had some bleeding on the brain. For a while afterwards, I had no peripheral vision or short-term memory."

Houghton went through months of speech, memory and motor skill therapy:

I had to re-learn things all over again. I couldn't remember names or places. Once I was told, it came right back, but I just couldn't remember simple things. I remember taking my kids to the zoo, and I would recognize the animals, but couldn't think of what they were called. A peacock ran in front of us, and I couldn't think of the name. At the polar bear exhibit, I drew a blank. It's hard to explain to my children.

At first, after the accident all I wanted to do was get better and be able to take care of my kids and someday live on my own again. I didn't even think about racing. As I started to get physically better, the occupational therapy people told me that it would be hard for me to learn new things, so how could I go back to school and get trained for another job? I knew I had to be able support my kids, and riding is all I really know how to do. I didn't have too much of a choice, really. Lucky enough, I got my health back.

On May 9, 2004, Rick Wilson was flipped head over heels when his mount, first-time starter Advance to Go, tripped leaving the starting gate. Wilson, who ranks 20th on the all-time win list with 4,939 victories, suffered serious head and neck injuries.

While Wilson doesn't remember anything about the race, or that day, his agent later told him what happened: "He said the horse stumbled coming out of the gate and popped me off over the top. I kind of landed on all fours, and she tried to jump over me, but kicked me in the head as she went over."

As he lay face down and motionless on the Pimlico track, the gate crew rushed to his aid while the field continued racing. As the horses came back around the turn, the track outriders waved to the riders, signaling them to pull up their horses and veer away from the fallen rider as they raced towards the turn.

Wilson was immediately airlifted from the track to the University of Maryland Shock Trauma Center, where he underwent life-saving surgery: "I had bleeding in the brain. They ended up putting a plate in the right side of my head. Now I have a horseshoe shaped scar there to show for it. The doctors tell me it will be a year or two before everything heals up. I broke my eardrum and still have some equilibrium trouble. They said I'll probably have to go back for surgery to fix that up sometime."

He's made significant progress, but is frustrated at times with the process: "I'd say my recovery is slow, but steady. At first, I couldn't remember anything and my short-term memory was really bad. I've been seeing a Physical Therapist, Occupational Therapist and Psychologist to help me regain my memory and help get my brain working good again. Right after the accident, I couldn't think long enough to do anything, but they've had me reading and working problems, and I'm doing better now."

Fortunately for Wilson, he's had the full support of his family in the recovery process: "My kids and wife have been a godsend. I wouldn't have made it without them. They've pretty much put their lives on hold for me."

A hot button in the racing industry, many riders are unable to obtain health and accident insurance. As independent contractors, jockeys don't work for the racetracks or the racing associations; they work for themselves. Like other self-employed individuals, they are responsible for their own accident, health and life insurance. Racetracks provide a $100,000 policy for racing accidents but nothing beyond that. Wilson is fortunate to have purchased a few health policies on his own and was able to benefit from Maryland's Workmen's Compensation program, one of a handful of states currently covering riders under that program.

After jockey Gary Birzer became paralyzed from the waist down after a racing accident on July 20, 2004, at Mountaineer Race Track, it became evident the industry had a serious problem on its hands as Birzer, and hundreds of other jockeys, are riding without the benefit of additional catastrophic insurance.

"If you have a bad accident, you can be in real trouble," explained veteran rider and Jockeys' Guild member Brian Peck. "The tracks provide a $100,000 policy for injuries, but that could be gone in a few days at the hospital. After that, the jockey is at risk of losing any money he might have saved. Any equity in their house or car could be gone. He could lose it all. We're at risk every time we walk out to ride."

Peck and 14 other riders walked away from racing at Churchill Downs in November 2004 in protest of the industry not offering adequate accident insurance for the jockeys. The jockeys, in turn, were banned for refusing to ride because of the safety and insurance concerns. Jockey Shane Sellers was escorted off the track property in handcuffs: "It took brave riders to step forward and take a stand. Track Management told us 'If you don't like it, grab your tack and get out of here.' I just went in to pick up my tack, and they handcuffed me and hauled me off."

Rider Scott Saito, one of the Jockeys' Guild "delegates" who represents riders at the local track level, attended the Guild's annual assembly last year to learn more about the insurance issue: "It's really become quite a big stink over the insurance issue. From what I understand, the Guild is asking tracks to provide a million dollars in catastrophic insurance for us. The Guild used to provide a supplemental policy but no longer does. They feel it's the track's responsibility to provide us with insurance, but the tracks feel that because we're self-employed, we should have to pay for it."

In March 2005, Churchill filed a lawsuit against the Guild in hopes of preventing future walkouts. The Guild has denied they organized the boycotts, countering that Churchill is trying to break down the unity demonstrated by the jockeys.

The Guild formerly provided an additional $1 million coverage for jockeys hurt on the track; however, the policy was allowed to lapse in 2002. The Guild cited the cost of the program had become too expensive. Many riders claim they were not aware the additional insurance had lapsed and were riding with the assumption they had the catastrophic coverage. Racetracks contribute over $2 million annually to the Guild, and in past years, the Guild has used a portion of its funds to supplement riders with accident insurance and disability income for injured riders.

Currently, only five states currently cover jockeys in their workers' compensation programs, with the bulk of the funding coming from within the industry. It's likely that number will increase in coming years once the industry and governments figure out how to pay for it. In the meantime, some racetracks are stepping up to the plate while waiting for the Jockeys' Guild, the NTRA (National Thoroughbred Racing Association) and other industry organizations to figure out a compromise. Gulfstream Park boosted its insurance to $500,000 after jockey Gary Boulanger was critically injured in a stakes race. Churchill Downs, Inc., recently announced that it will provide $1 million coverage at six of the company's tracks.

While the racing industry considers jockeys to be independent contractors, in many regards, much of what they do is regulated and restricted. On the other hand, some feel riders waffle between being self-employed or employees of racing associations, depending on what works best for them on any particular issue.

In an attempt to solve the puzzle of who pays for the additional insurance everyone agrees that the jockeys need, NTRA formed a work group, the Jockey's Medical Insurance Panel, to address the issues. The panel includes leaders throughout the racing industry, such as jockeys Jerry Bailey and Pat Day, retired rider Donna Brothers and Jockeys' Guild member representative, Darrell Haire, a former jockey and Grade I stakes-winner. Recommendations from the high-powered panel, and other like-type groups lobbying for fair and equitable insurance coverage for jockeys, are finally starting to make headway in improving the equation for riders, although they are unlikely to achieve industry-wide agreement.

According to Haire, the Guild is lobbying for the protection the riders deserve: "The jockey profession is very dangerous and riders at risk every time they ride. The Guild feels the tracks should pay for the insurance to cover the jockeys when they race at their tracks. We feel the tracks should assume the risk for the dangers jockeys face every day. The tracks want the jockeys to pay. Many of the riders are only making $35 on a losing ride and that's before they pay their agent and valet. If they had to pay another $5 or $6 per mount for insurance, they wouldn't be making anything at all. It's getting ridiculous."

6. Those Are the Breaks

The conflict over the insurance issue has led some riders to relocate from their favorite tracks or racing circuits close to home to other parts of the country where they may be covered by the state's workers' compensation programs. The lack of adequate insurance was the primary reason behind legendary Gary Stevens' refusal to ride in the 2004 Breeder's Cup races. In the case of Shane Sellers, a former Breeder's Cup winning rider with over 4,000 victories in the bank, the risk of riding without sufficient insurance forced him into retirement:

> It was an easy decision, really. I was left with no choice.
>
> I was always thinking in the back of my mind that it's not worth risking my life, and my family's future, over this. I talked it over with my wife, and we agreed that it was in our best interest for me to step down.
>
> I've ridden in Kentucky, Florida and Louisiana most of my career and they have no workmen's comp in those states. The $100,000 insurance tracks pay doesn't come close to offering enough protection. When Gary Birzer went down in West Virginia, the insurance didn't even make a dent in his medical bills. Last time I heard, the bills were almost a million dollars and climbing.
>
> When things blew up with Churchill over the insurance issue, it was very frustrating. The tracks are making tons of money but aren't willing to take care of the jockeys. They spent over $100 million in renovations at Churchill, but it cost me $950 to ride in the 2004 Derby on The Cliff's Edge. It cost me $250 a ticket for my wife and kids just to come watch me ride. I earned $55 by finishing fifth.
>
> I've ridden in 13 Derbies and it's probably cost me $10,000 and that's just not right. It doesn't cost Kobe Bryant any money to play in the NBA playoffs. How can a jockey be losing money when he's riding in one of the premier events in all sports?
>
> More than $80 million was wagered on the race, and there were more 30 paying sponsors for the Derby. Tracks are making a ton of money off the riders. We've tried numerous times to negotiate with tracks, but they refuse to come to the table. They treat us like slaves. It's ludicrous.
>
> Riders need to stand up and fight for what they deserve. I don't think the industry will respond unless we do. I've pretty much cost myself a Hall of Fame career because I'm willing to stand up for myself and fight for what's right. I've cost myself a lot of riding opportunities and a lot of big wins because of it. If all 1,300 riders in the Jockeys' Guild took the same stand and walked out, it would shut the industry down. Without riders, there is no horse racing, period.

Prior to the formation of the Jockeys' Guild in the 1940s, riders were often mistreated and taken advantage of. There were no support systems in place to help fallen riders. Led by a handful of jockeys, including Eddie Arcaro, John Longden, Charlie Kurtsinger, John Pollard and Sam Renick, jockeys came together for their common good.

To raise funds, the jockeys relied on their public recognition and celebrity status as they hosted dances, shows, dinners and sporting events. Over the years, Guild members worked to improve rider safety and health insurance for riders.

According to the published mission statement on the Jockeys' Guild website, the nonprofit organization professionally lobbies for jockeys' rights and entitlements; "Our mission is to promote, protect and serve the welfare and prestige of the American professional jockey community with integrity, equity and justice."

Today, there are some 2,000 licensed jockeys in the country, and 1,300 of them belong to the Guild. According to Darrell Haire, member representative for the Guild, about 95 percent of the riders in today's races are Guild members.

Tomey Jean Swan, an active rider who used to race at bush tracks before women were allowed to race in 1969, is a former chairman of the Board at the Guild and currently resides as the vice-chair:

> The Board is the ruling part of the Guild. Dr. G [L. Wayne Gertmenian] and the rest of the administrative team work for us. The new management team has been such an asset to our organization. They've really gone above and beyond what we'd hoped they'd be able to do.
>
> For years, jockeys have been walked all over. They're not often recognized as professional athletes and often treated like second-class citizens. We're hoping to change people's opinions and get these great athletes the recognition and treatment they deserve. We try to take care of our own, too. For example, we try to take care of the disabled riders as much as we can, but it's not enough. We need the industry's help.

Brian Peck is an active member of the Guild's Board of Directors: "The Board is a group of nine jockeys, nominated and elected by a vote of our peers. We work with the Guild leadership in the best interest of the jockeys as a group. Before the Guild's new management team came in, there were only a few guys making decisions for the rest of us. Jockeys didn't have much of a voice, but now things are well organized and jockeys play a much bigger role in decision making."

The Guild has come under fire recently from several industry groups, and many of its own members, for questionable financial decisions. After a late filing, it was reported that the Guild revenues had dropped 31 percent in 2003. After several months of ambiguity, the Guild agreed to allow the California Horse Racing Board, which contributes nearly $1 million a year to the Guild to manage insurance claims for jockeys in the state, to look at their books. This came after a request from over one hundred riders, in the form of a signed petition, was denied.

Even Guild president Dr. L. Wayne Gertmenian has come under the microscope of scrutiny recently, as his credentials included claims that he served in several important positions in the Nixon and Ford administrations. It was reported that archivists at the presidential libraries were unable to verify his declarations, although he insists the resume is valid. Gertmenian and his company, Matrix Capital Associates, took over management of the Guild in 2001. Despite all the conflict and uncertainty facing the Guild, members gave the president a vote of confidence by renewing his contract through 2008.

Out of sheer frustration with the Guild, a group of jockeys from California formed their own nonprofit organization, the California Jockeys Guild. The group, led by veteran rider Ron Warren, Jr., is seeking to secure health benefits for jockeys.

When a rider becomes injured at the track, they are usually sent or taken to the track's first-aid station. Racetracks employee an emergency medical services crew in the event an injured rider requires life-saving care or emergency ambulance transport to a local hospital.

Head and neck injuries are a major concern with accidents. Concussions, either suffered directly as a result of the fall or from being hit or kicked by the hooves of horses, are the most common head injury. While jockeys wear riding helmets for safety, they help but don't eliminate serious head trauma in violent accidents. The helmets are made of rigid material and are designed to offer protection against crushing.

A racing helmet may have saved the life of Ricky Frazier after his horse went down: "On Thanksgiving Day at the Fair Grounds in 1984, I broke my neck in five places. My horse fell, and I went down. Two other horses went over the top and one of them stepped on my helmet and crushed it. I was lucky it didn't kill me. Thank God for helmets. I was able to bounce back and was riding five months later wearing a neck collar."

Twenty-two-year-old jockey Desiree Hamilton is on the long road to recovery from a serious accident she had two years ago. On September 21, 2002, she was working a horse, Pawns and Kings, from the gate at Retama Park when things went horribly wrong:

> Shortly after we came out of the gate, he had a heart attack and went down. I fell and he somehow landed right on top of my head, cracking my helmet all the way around, but it saved my life.
>
> The ambulance took me to the hospital, where I was treated for a fractured skull. I was in the hospital for six weeks. I underwent neurological surgery for ruptured arteries in my head and had therapy for a long time afterwards. I really don't remember anything about the accident, but people told me it was really bad, and things were touch and go for awhile.

Thanks to the track's insurance policy and her own personal insurance, the majority of her $600,000 medical expenses were covered.

As a young female rider still riding with the bug, Hamilton has had a difficult time acquiring mounts: "Coming off an accident like that, and being a girl, I guess people don't put much faith in me yet. I'm working my butt off in the mornings, galloping and breezing every horse I can, but only getting one or two horses a week in the afternoons, and they're usually not very good ones. I can't make a bad horse run good."

Despite her remarkable medical recovery, it appears horsemen don't trust that she's physically ready for racing: "My eye was messed up in the accident, and I have permanent discoloration in one eye but no trouble with my vision. I have to put in eye drops for dry eyes after I ride, but I see just fine. I've passed all my physicals and eye checks, but you know how rumors are. People are worried that I'm not the same, or that as a girl, I'm just not strong enough."

Riders wear a padded safety vest under their silks, which softens blows but has little effect on reducing injuries to ribs and back. Stakes-winning rider Russell Woolsey was spared from serious injury by his safety vest a few years ago at Atlantic City Race Course: "I was coming around the turn for home, and my horse bobbled. I went off and landed flat on my back. Before I could move, the horse behind me stepped directly and squarely onto the middle of my chest. The horse hit me so hard that it left a hoof print on the vest, just like it had been written on a chalkboard. The blow even ripped the silks, but the vest saved me. It might have killed me, otherwise."

The next morning after recovering from a fall, the rider is likely to feel like they were run over by a truck. Likely still pumped up from racing and traumatized from the fall, many don't even realize the significance of their injuries until they wake up with missing skin, bruised muscles or cracked bones.

Veteran stakes–winning rider Joy Scott has taken more than her fair share number of falls: "I've been dumped so many times I don't keep count any more. You usually know if you're hurt bad because you can't get up or your head is spinning. When that happens, the first thing you're thinking about is hoping that everything still works, like your arms and legs. Sometimes you get broken up pretty bad, but you're glad just to be alive."

Jockeys have a very hard time of it if they are unable to ride due to injury. They feel left out and isolated when watching out others racing. They'll rush back from injuries as quickly as they can.

For a jockey, ignoring the body's signals of pain is something they get used to early in their career. Working through pain is required if they want to maximize riding opportunities, for a day out of the office means someone else has the opportunity of stealing their rides away. Retired jockey Tom Chapman explained the rationale behind riding through the aches and pains: "You know that when you're gone from the track, someone else is going to pick up your horses. If they win on the horse, or do well on him, they're going to get the future rides, too. It goes both ways, but when it's you that's hurt and unable to ride, it feels unfair. So, if you're able to ride through the injury, you do, so you avoid someone else taking your business away."

Like most riders, Chance Rollins has ridden through pain so he could keep his business intact: "It's something we all do. I remember one time I got thrown off a horse in the morning and just landed wrong. I broke a few ribs, but I had to keep going. I just had to bear the pain and ride through it. As a jockey, you don't really take time off unless there's no way you can ride."

Dealing with the anxiety of returning to riding after serious injury was the most difficult part of Hall of Famer Chris McCarron's career:

> The first few times you fall, you figure it just comes with the territory and you get over it. But after you've had a serious injury, like when I broke my leg in four places, you really stop and think about what you're doing. When I was healing, I contemplated whether or not I wanted to do this [be a jockey] forever, knowing the dangers of the sport. Was it something I was willing to risk? It's an exciting and exhilarating experience to ride these great animals, but I had to weigh the risks out. Going through that anxiety was really tricky, and it sure builds character.

Jockeys are driven to prove themselves all over again when coming back from injury. Many worry that owners and trainers will doubt their abilities to regain their courage and nerve after a bad fall. While jockeys clearly understand the perilous dangers of their chosen profession, they'll risk their lives as long as they can physically get up in the saddle. Like the horses they ride, racing is in their blood.

As a former rider, trainer Dawn Harrison admits she'd still be riding if her body could handle it: "I transitioned from being a jockey to becoming a trainer in 1996 due to one of numerous injuries. You can understand it was not my first choice. I would still be riding, but I'm running out of limbs to fracture. I miss the action as a jockey. I could ride 15 in the mornings and 7 in the afternoon, whereas now as a trainer, I might race one or two a day."

The industry is grossly understudied in terms of preventing jockey injuries and protecting rider safety. General equestrian studies have been done, but too little has been done to investigate jockey accidents, injury prevention and safety. Because of the relatively small number of athletes in the jockey profession compared to other pro sports, manufacturers appear reluctant to pursue research and development of improved safety products. In order to significantly improve rider safety, the industry will undoubtedly need safer equipment.

Gary Wadler, MD, earned the International Olympic Committee's President's Prize and frequently serves as an expert for the government on matters involving medicine in sports. He is also the personal physician for a Hall of Fame jockey and believes that fitness and preparation can help riders survive the dangers of their rigorous profession:

> I've treated a lot of elite athletes over the years. Certainly, jockeys have unique issues. They compete in a dangerous, life-threatening sport.
>
> They are terrific athletes. They must have a certain level of toughness, determination and courage that is quite unique. The jockey I cared for was in incredible physical condition when he was riding. He ate right, worked out all the time and dedicated his life to his profession. I'm sure that's why he was the superstar that he was.

More education to riders about injury prevention and the benefits of stretching, physical therapy strengthening and proper nutrition may help alleviate some overuse injuries. Adding more padding inside the gate would certainly help minimize injuries to horse and rider.

Some racetracks continue to use outdated and dangerous pipe rails with exposed gooseneck supporting posts adjacent to the racing surfaces. If the rider falls or is thrown from his mount and collides with the rail or supporting post at the forty-mile-per-hour racing speed, it's a prescription for disaster.

While some tracks have added padding to existing rails, it does little to improve horse or rider safety. Since jockey Roy May was impaled by the railing in a racing accident at now-defunct Prescott Down's twenty-five years ago, many tracks have upgraded to improved railing. When May was thrown from his horse, the wooden rail broke into pieces, skewering the rider through his midsection. "The track was real small, and when the horses hit the turn, one of the horses inside Roy pushed his horse towards the outside fence," explained his widowed wife Sherry Simpson:

> As the horse crashed into the rail, Roy tried to jump off, but one of the boards broke, and he was impaled by it, right through the stomach.
>
> He had a four-foot section of board sticking out on one side and eleven feet on the other. They rushed him to the hospital with the ambulance doors open because they couldn't get them shut. He was in surgery for a long time. The board just missed his heart, but broke his sternum and they had to remove some of his ribs in order to get the board out.

Several years later, May died prematurely as a result of the internal injuries he suffered in the devastating accident.

Tomey Jean Swan, stakes-winning rider of quarter horses and thoroughbreds and active member of the Jockeys' Guild board of directors, suffered serious injuries in a rail accident at New Mexico's San Juan Downs. In 1992, Swan and fellow riders were concerned about the safety of the dangerous rail at the track: "I was telling the other riders to be careful and stay away from the rail because it could kill somebody. Next thing you know, I'm riding in a futurity trial, and my horse bolts for the rail. I jumped off just in time and my horse crashed into the rail. The rail broke apart and pierced the chest of my horse and killed her. I landed wrong and busted my knee and leg. I couldn't walk for over two years and spent time in a wheelchair and crutches. It took five surgeries and a good doctor to finally get me back on my feet."

In November 2004, a number of jockeys walked out in a dispute over accident insurance and what they felt was an unsafe rail at Hoosier Park, forcing the cancellation of the day's racing card.

Many tracks now utilize a patented Fontana Safety Rail. According to Fontana Products President Rich Fontana, about 75 percent of the tracks in the country use his Safety Rail on their dirt or turf tracks. Made of aluminum, the rail has gone a long way in improving horse and rider safety: "We started in 1980 and installed the first product at Del Mar. Based on what we've heard from outriders, jockeys and horsemen, I'd guess we've saved the lives of maybe 200 horses and jockeys so far. Jockeys like Chris McCarron, Mike Smith and Laffit Pincay tell us it's saved their lives and saved countless numbers of horses.

The rail system includes some unique features that drastically improved upon the pipe-based rail systems. "Our product comes in 8 foot sections and is installed with no welds. The gooseneck supports include two 45-degree angles, which helps with the flexibility. The rail will give and absorb some of the energy from impact, protecting the horse and jockey. Because there's a protective cover over the rail and the gooseneck, if the horse or jockey falls onto the rail, they roll off rather than slamming into exposed railing," said Fontana.

The Safety Rail system saved veteran rider Chance Rollins from further injury when he took a spill at Golden Gate: "About three jumps out of the gate, my horse broke down and I pulled her up as quickly as I could. She was heading right for the rail and then the saddle slipped, so I stepped off onto the rail covering and slid off without a scratch. If it wouldn't have had the covering, I could have been hurt bad."

As a race horse owner and breeder, Fontana is passionate about horse and rider safety:

> I worked on the California Horse Racing Board and have worked on racing safety issues for more than twenty years. In addition to working on the Safety Rail, I've been concerned about racing surfaces for a long time. They compress the surface so much now, then put a sealer over it. I think it's dangerous for the horses. More and more horses are breaking down all the time. It's disappointing that we've really learned nothing about safety in this sport.

> For example, what we call the rider's safety helmet is really nothing more than a skull cap. It's not a protective helmet. Guys are still getting hurt all the time.

If a rider becomes seriously injured and unable to ride, temporarily or permanently, there are a few support systems in the industry available for them, depending on their unique situation. An initiative of the Jockeys' Guild, the Disabled Jockey's Fund provides benefits for temporarily and permanently disabled jockeys. The Fund offers riders vocational training, physical rehabilitation, assistance with special equipment, vehicles and housing for the disabled. According to Disabled Jockey Endowment Board chairman David Woodcock, "We are attempting to raise arbitrarily $10 million in funds, so that the interest on the investment vehicle would be sufficient to fund the program. Eventually, when we met our financial goal, the dividends derived from the investment would be transferred to the Jockeys' Guild and paid out through the Disabled Jockey's Fund. Because all the Board members serve voluntarily, there are no operational expenses to the Endowment. Everything goes to the injured riders."

According the Guild, there are more than 50 riders who are permanently disabled resulting from riding injuries and another one hundred on short-term disability at any given time.

Through membership dues and option payments, the Guild offers group medical and dental insurance to its members. A life insurance benefit is also provided. In the future, the Guild hopes to offer some form of educational programs to help support riders.

In 1987, Judy McCarron, jockey Chris McCarron's wife, and actor Tim Conway formed the Don MacBeth Memorial Jockey Fund. The fund was named after the late rider, Don MacBeth, who died from cancer earlier that year, 10 days after receiving the George Woolf Memorial Award. MacBeth, a well-respected rider, gave much of his own time to help those less fortunate than himself.

The fund helps jockeys and exercise riders who may be struggling while recovering from injuries to make ends meet, according to the Fund's Vice President Chris McCarron:

> It was born out of the need for financial assistance and emotional support to the riders who were injured in racing. Since its inception, we've helped over 1,600 riders and raised over $2.5 million in funds.
>
> The typical case is an injured rider who was unable to put enough money away when he was racing to take care of expenses in the event of a career-ending injury. We help them stay afloat by helping them with the basic staples, like car payments, house or rent payments, tuition expenses and such. We try to help as many riders as we can and help them from falling through the cracks.

According to the Fund's executive director, Tony DeFranco, most of the program's funding comes from donations and fundraisers:

> We have about 50 tracks across the country participating in Jockeys Across America, which is our biggest fundraiser. We usually get started the first Saturday in July with many tracks doing some type of program during the summer.
>
> Most tracks form some type of committee with jockeys, spouses and track officials putting together their events. I'd say Canterbury Downs does the best job of putting together their program. They have a jockey foot race, silent auction, a pheasant feed, raffles and they sell racing memorabilia. They brought in around $45,000 last year.
>
> We were able to help about 100 jockeys and exercise riders last year and we paid out about $240,000. The recipients, who are sometimes really struggling, are so appreciative of our help.

Formed in 1943, the Jockey Club Foundation provides financial relief and assistance to needy members of the racing industry. A charitable trust, the Foundation follows a philosophy of providing a safety net to program recipients and has provided over $10 million in support since 1985, according to Robert Curran, Jr., vice president of communications. Originating from the Jockey Club, the program helps racetrack personnel from all walks of life: "We're a guardian angel to many people who don't even know we exist before they are directed our way."

Benefits include monthly assistance or lump sum payments, depending on the beneficiary's circumstances. Nancy Kelly, executive director of the Foundation, said that approximately $600,000 was paid out in benefits last year: "If people aren't able to get help from the Jockeys' Guild or Don MacBeth Fund, they may be able to find help with us."

While there is some overlap in these benevolence programs, each offers a unique service, and they work together in the best interest of jockeys and other racetrack workers. Working with local racetrack programs, the nationwide Chaplaincy program and the Jockeys' Guild, the industry is now providing good support for the hard-working jockeys who've put their life on the lines for decades with a dire shortage of advocacy or aid available when things suddenly go bad.

7

BEST OF THE BEST

The racing industry has several awards honoring top horses and the people who own, breed, train and ride them. Among that group, there are four major awards given annually to jockeys—the George Woolf Memorial Award, the Isaac Murphy Award, the Mike Venezia Memorial Award and the Eclipse Awards for the top apprentice rider and top overall jockey.

The George Woolf Memorial Award, named in honor of the great rider known as "the Iceman," was instituted in 1950. The Canadian-born Woolf was known for his calm demeanor and ice-cold nerves of steel when racing. In a short 18-year career, he was twice the nation's leading money-winning rider, despite only picking up 263 mounts in 1942 and 227 rides in 1944 when he won the titles, often weakened by diabetes and unable to ride. He won 19 percent of his career mounts.

He was known to have often demanded $1,000 in advance of stakes races, plus 10 percent of the purse money, during the Depression Era. Among the great horses he rode are the legendary Seabiscuit and Horses of the Year Challedon and Whirlaway.

Woolf died in 1946, the day after suffering massive head injuries after landing head first from a fall at Santa Anita. He was enshrined in racing's Hall of Fame in 1955 and the Canadian Hall of Fame in 1976. A bronze statue of Woolf graces the walking ring at Santa Anita racetrack.

The George Woolf Memorial Award is given annually in recognition

The number of career victories for a listed jockey reflects his/her official record earned at North American racetracks as compiled by Equibase Company LLC and may include foreign races from other sources. Neither Equibase Company LLC nor The Jockey Club Information Systems, Inc. verify jockey records for races run in foreign jurisdictions, with the exception of the World Series of Racing and the Dubai World Cup events. Jockey and trainer leader lists, displayed either in North American-only statistics or including the selected international races, are always available at www.equibase.com.

of a jockey whose distinguished career has reflected credit on themselves and the sport of thoroughbred racing. The recipient is selected from nominations made by the Jockeys' Guild and Santa Anita Park, sponsor of the award. Final voting for this prestigious award is made by jockeys across the country.

The Isaac Murphy Award memorializes the great 19th-century jockey who won 44 percent of his career mounts, including three Kentucky Derbies. Sponsored by the National Turf Writers Association, the jockey with the highest winning percentage for the year, with a minimum of 500 mounts, captures the award.

Begun in 1995, the Isaac Murphy Award has gone to Russell Baze, the king of northern California racing, after every season except for 2004 when it was awarded to Ramon Dominguez. Dominguez, the second-leading rider in the country by wins in 2004, won 28.3 percent of his races. Baze narrowly missed repeating yet again, with 27.1 percent of his horses winning.

The Mike Venezia Memorial Award honors jockeys who exemplify extraordinary sportsmanship and citizenship. Venezia, known as a devoted family man, was killed in a racing accident at Belmont Park in 1988 when his horse, Mr. Walter K, broke down and threw the rider off. Venezia was trampled by a trailing horse and died on the racetrack. Respected as a skilled rider, he was active in the community and a proponent for jockey safety.

Created by the New York Racing Association, the winner of this award is selected by voting of fans, turf writers and jockeys. This annual honor began in 1989, when the first award was given posthumously to Venezia.

Racing's first official champions were recognized by the Daily Racing Form, beginning in 1936. Today, Eclipse Award winners are selected in partnership between with the National Thoroughbred Racing Association, National Turf Writers Association and Daily Racing Form in voting for official year-end honors of horses and humans in several categories. Since 1971, Eclipse Awards have been given to the country's top jockey and top apprentice, as well as top horses and owners, breeders and trainers. The prestigious awards serve as the pinnacle of racing achievements.

The Award honors Eclipse, the great 18th-century racehorse and sire. Unbeaten in 18 starts, Eclipse shows up in the pedigree lines of 85 percent of today's racehorses as one of the greatest breeding influences on the thoroughbred breed.

The National Museum of Racing and Hall of Fame, located in Saratoga Springs, New York, honors the achievements of those horses, jockeys and trainers whose records and reputations have withstood the test of time. Currently, jockeys become eligible for induction after twenty years from first obtaining their license. Many riders feel that entrance into the Hall of Fame is the pinnacle of their career. One of the all-time greats, Angel Cordero cherishes the day he was inducted: "Being honored in the Hall of Fame was the ultimate reward for me. I'll never die there. People will be coming in long after I'm gone and will still be hearing about me."

Who is the greatest rider of all time? It's tough enough to compare jockeys of the same era, let alone equitably compare riders of yesteryear with modern-day marvels. It's also nearly impossible to fairly compare riders from outside the United States to stateside riders because they simply don't square off against each other often enough. Hence, the following pages provide a brief retrospective of arguably the most influential riders over the past 50 years of American racing history.

Johnny Longden

Born in Wakefield, England, Longden's family migrated to Canada while he was a young boy. After working with pack mules in the mining industry as a young man, he performed "Roman riding," where the jockey rode with one foot on the back of two different horses ... and raced.

So it seems only natural that the small, fearless man wasted little time making a big name for himself. He rode his first winner, Hugo K Asher, at Salt Lake City racetrack in Utah on October 4, 1927. In 1943, he rode Citation into the records book, winning the Triple Crown, including a smashing 25-length win in the Belmont.

As the best rider of his generation, he led the country in purses earned twice and three times the leading rider by wins. In 1956, he passed Sir Gordon Richards as the winningest rider. When Longden hung up his tack for good after 39 years of riding, he was the all-time leader with 6,032 victories, winning almost 19 percent of his races.

Nicknamed "the Pumper" for his ability to push horses to their best, he rode the best horses of his time, including Horses of the Year Whirlaway, Swaps and Busher.

With his friends Eddie Arcaro and Sam Renick, he helped form the Jockeys' Guild in 1940. In 1952, he was honored with the George Woolf Memorial Award. He entered racing's Hall of Fame in 1958 and entered the Canadian Hall of Fame in 1976. In 1994, he was recognized with the Eclipse Special Award.

In a fairy-tale ending to his remarkable career, Longden entered the 1966 San Juan Capistrano stakes as an aging rider, well past his prime. He'd won the race the previous year aboard George Royal, whom he was partnered with again in this final ride of his grand career. Only this time,

George Royal was on a long losing streak and had been crushed in his most recent start.

Bet down to 6–1 purely for sentimental reasons, the long shot George Royal woke up under Longden's masterful handling. Turning for home, Longden's horse was engaged by hard-charging Plaque. While Bobby Ussery was all out on his mount to squeeze every inch out of George Royal's lead, the legendary Longden simply pushed his horse with a confident hand ride to the wire, hanging on to win by a head in one of racing's most dramatic moments.

After retiring from riding, Longden turned to training, where he continued his racing success. His first training winner was ridden by fellow Hall of Famer Bill Shoemaker. Longden trained Majestic Prince, near winner of the 1969 Triple Crown. He remains the only rider in history to both ride and train a Kentucky Derby winner.

Johnny Longden passed away on his 96th birthday, Valentine's Day 2003.

G. Edward "Eddie" Arcaro

"The Master," as they called him, was truly that. Arcaro was undoubtedly the best rider of his time. Born February 19, 1916, in Cincinnati, Arcaro left school at 14 to become an exercise rider. The following year, he rode his first race. Although it took him a long time to break through, nine months to be exact, he broke his maiden south of the border on January 14, 1932, at Mexico's Agua Caliente Race Track.

From humble beginnings, Arcaro blossomed into one of the top riders of all time. He is one of only two jockeys listed on ESPN's top one hundred North American athletes of the 20th century list. Sports Illustrated once deemed him "as the most famous man to ride a horse since Paul Revere."

Arcaro was as smart on a horse as he was strong. He had great hands and sat chilly in the saddle, timing his finishes superbly, winning most of the photo finishes he was involved in. He is the only jockey to ride two horses to Triple Crown glory, with Whirlaway in 1941 and Citation two years later. He won five Kentucky Derbies, taking the 1938 edition on Lawrin, winning with Hoop, Jr., in 1945 and again with Hill Gail in 1952. In total, he won 17 Triple Crown races. In the 1959 Belmont, his mount, Black Hills, went down and another horse ran over the fallen rider. If not for his riding helmet, he may have been killed. As it was, he was pushed face down and unconscious into a puddle on the racing surface and could've drowned.

He rode all the best horses of his time, including nine that were honored with Horse of the Year acclaim. In addition to his Triple Crown winners, he was aboard Horses of the Year Assault, Hill Prince, Nashua and Sword Dancer; two-time Horses of the Year Challedon and Native Dancer and five-time Horse of the Year Kelso.

In his 30-year career, including his one-year suspension in 1942 for reckless riding, he won 4,779 races, winning on nearly 20 percent of his mounts. At the time he retired, he was the top money-winning rider of all time and led the country in purse earnings six times. He was the top big race jockey of his generation, winning 549 stakes races. In 1994, he was awarded an Eclipse Special Award. His accomplishments were recognized with the George Woolf Memorial Award in 1953, and he was enshrined into the racing Hall of Fame in 1958.

Unlike so many professional athletes who stay in the game too long, Arcaro left racing on top, retiring in 1961 at the top of his game. In addition to providing racing commentary on television, he was the cofounder of the Jockeys' Guild and served as president for twelve years. Arcaro passed away in 1997.

Bill Shoemaker

At birth, Shoemaker was so small, at one pound three ounces, that even his doctor wasn't sure he'd survive. As the story goes, his grandmother put him in a shoebox in the stove with the door left open, as a crude incubator, to help him make it through the first night.

Born in Fabens, Texas, he was a natural athlete, a champion wrestler and competitive boxer as he grew up. He began exercising horses at Hollywood in 1948 and rode his first race the following year, joining the winner's club on April 20, guiding Shafter V home first at Golden Gate Fields. Like most young riders just starting out, he had it rough at the beginning and often slept in tack rooms.

The strong-handed Shoemaker broke Johnny Longden's all-time win record in 1970. He was nation's leading rider by wins five times, winning 22 percent of his tries, and retired as the all time leader with 8,833 victories in 1990. His record has since been surpassed by fellow Hall of Fame jockeys Laffit Pincay and Russell Baze. A tribute to his durability, he won races in six decades.

With soft hands, smart head and a large heart, he always seemed to get the most out of his horses. He had a knack of putting his horses in right spot at the right time. In 1985, he became the first jockey to win $100 million in purses and led the country in earnings a remarkable ten times.

"The Shoe" rode in 26 Kentucky Derbies, the first of 16 straight in 1952, and won aboard Swaps in 1955. He won again three years later with

Tommy Lee and again with Lucky Debonair in 1965. In 1986, at the age of 54, he won the Kentucky Derby aboard 18–1 oversight Ferdinand, masterfully threading him through a small hole along the rail in the upper stretch to take command of the race. Eighteen months later, he performed magic again, winning the 1987 Breeder's Cup Classic on him. In total, he won 11 Triple Crown races.

The Kentucky Derby that Shoemaker might be best known for isn't a race he won, but should have. The 1957 Derby field was one of the strongest fields of all time with racing stars Bold Ruler and Round Table in the lineup.

Shoemaker was aboard Gallant Man. Racing towards the rear, Shoemaker skillfully guided his colt between horses to move within striking distance turning for home. Down the stretch, he engaged Iron Liege, with Bill Hartack up, for the lead. As the horses raced side-by-side in a classic stretch duel, Gallant Man looked the stronger of the two and began inching away. As they thundered past the roaring crowd, Shoemaker mistook the sixteenth pole as the finish marker and stood up in the irons. In that split second, Iron Liege stormed back in front. Shoemaker immediately realized his mistake and jumped back into the fray. He got Gallant Man back into full stride and rallied but fell a nose short of collaring Iron Liege at the wire.

In a remarkable twist, Gallant Man's owner, Ralph Lowe, had dreamt his jockey stood up early. The loss may have crushed most riders, but the classy Shoemaker acknowledged his blunder and bounced right back. Gallant Man and Shoemaker returned to turn the tables on the field in the Belmont, drawing away to win by eight lengths.

At a scant 4'10" tall, in the public's eye he was a racing giant. His loyal following grew even bigger the next year with a horse named Silky Sullivan. With a come-from-behind style unlike any other, Silky became a folk hero and captured the heart and imagination of American culture like few horses have.

A handsome colt, Silky wasn't making headlines with his brilliant times or smashing victories; it was the way he did it that took your breath away. His rallies from the clouds, flying by horses like they were standing still, skyrocketed him to stardom.

Silky nearly always broke last from the gate, and it was only a matter of strides before all Shoemaker could see in front of him were heels and rumps of the horses racing away from him. In some races, he fell to the rear so quickly it looked as if he might have missed the start, but that was just his way. His cantering gait seemed to be telling everyone he was in no hurry to get moving, and Shoemaker eventually learned to be patient and let the big chestnut run his race.

On February 25, 1958, Silky faced eight other three-year-olds at Santa Anita in a 6½ furlong allowance race. In typical fashion, he went right to the back, falling a remarkable 41 lengths back. In racing, that's lights out and game over, but not on this historical day. Shoemaker pushed the button around the turn, and Silky exploded with a rally that defies the believable. He blazed down the stretch, scorching the final half-mile in just over 44 seconds to win by a half-length. Silky Sullivan truly was greased lightning.

Generating Hollywood-like celebrity status, fans cheered him at every opportunity. Media-hype snowballed as Silky quickly become a national equine hero. His reputation preceded him to Kentucky that year. He was so popular that he had his own ghostwritten newspaper column and TV show. A week before the Derby, he graced the cover of Sports Illustrated and Time magazines.

Silky and Shoemaker went off as one of the favorites in the 1958 Kentucky Derby and were clearly the sentimental choice of racegoers. For the first time, CBS used a split TV screen to show the full field. With Silky spotting the field 32 lengths, it was the only way to keep him in the frame. Gallantly trying to close the gap on the best three-year-olds in the country, "Silky" was outclassed and well-beaten. Even in defeat, the racetrack announcer called his name more times during the running of the race than winner Tim Tam. Never has there been a more celebrated 12th place finisher than Silky Sullivan and his champion rider.

As the winner of over 1,000 stakes in his 42-year career, he rode the top horses of his generation, including Horses of the Year Ack, Damascus, Forego, John Henry, Round Table, Spectacular Bid and Swaps.

About a year after hanging up his tack, Shoemaker was paralyzed after a car accident. He'd been drinking prior to the tragedy. Returning to the racetrack as a trainer, his friends rallied around him and supported his new venture.

Shoemaker was president of the Jockeys' Guild for 15 years. He won the George Woolf Memorial Award in 1951 and the 1990 Mike Venezia Memorial. The winner of three Eclipse Awards, Shoemaker was selected as one of ESPN's top 100 North American athletes of the 20th century. He was inducted into racing's Hall of Fame in 1958.

Bill Shoemaker, perhaps the greatest rider the sport has even seen, passed away October 12, 2003.

William "Bill" Hartack, Jr.

Bill Hartack was born in Edensburg, Pennsylvania, and grew up on a farm. At age 20, he brought home his first winner at Waterford Park in West Virginia.

It didn't take long for the intelligent rider to make a big splash, as he was the country's leading rider by number of races won in his third season. He led the nation in wins three years straight, 1955–1957, and added a fourth in 1960. He won aboard 20 percent of his mounts and retired with 4,272 wins. As the hottest rider in the country, he was the top money earner in 1956 and 1957.

In 1964, he nearly won the Triple Crown, winning the Derby and Preakness aboard the legendary Northern Dancer before finishing third in the Belmont. Five years later, he brushed with Triple Crown glory again, winning the Derby and Preakness aboard the gallant Majestic Prince before losing the Belmont. In all, Hartack won five Kentucky Derbies, capturing the classic in 1957 with Iron Liege, Venetian Way in 1960 and aboard Decidedly in 1962. He shares the record for most Derby wins with fellow Hall of Famer Eddie Arcaro. In total, Hartack won nine Triple Crown races.

The gifted rider was aboard several top horses of that era, including five time Horses of the Year Kelso and Round Table along with champions Tim Tam and Carry Back. He was recognized as not only the top rider of his day but one of the top professional athletes in all of sports, gracing the covers of Sports Illustrated and Time Magazine, despite his reputed dislike for the media.

Near the end of his career, Hartack moved his tack to Hong Kong, where jockeys are allowed to ride with heavier weights. After two years there, he retired from racing in 1981. For the past several years, he's worked as a racing official and currently works at Louisiana as a steward.

Hartack entered the Racing Hall of Fame in 1959.

Braulio Baeza

Baeza grew up in a racing family, with both his father and grandfather being jockeys in his native Panama. He grew up living across the street from Hipodromo Juan Franco Race Track, where he rode his first race in 1955.

In 1960, while on vacation in the United States, he was noticed by powerful owner Fred Hooper while he was exercising a few horses and was offered a riding contract. Unable to speak English at the time, Baeza signed on and shortly booted home his first American winner, Foolish Youth.

Over the years, the stone-cold-faced Baeza climbed the ladder of success, winning stakes all over the country. He had a classic riding style, from his straight back and poised post parade manor to his graceful seat in the racing saddle; he was as smooth as silk.

The winner of three Belmont Stakes and a Kentucky Derby aboard

Chateaugay in 1963, he totaled 3,140 wins at an 18 percent win rate in his 16 years of American racing. He was the country's leading money-winning rider five times.

He regularly rode aboard two dozen champions, including five Horses of the Year. In 1968, he was aboard the brilliant Horse of the Year Dr. Fager when he scorched a world-record mile in 1:32⅕, surpassing the record he'd set two years prior aboard Buckpasser, the 1966 Horse of the Year. He had the call on Horse of the Year Arts and Letters, whom he guided to victory in the 1969 Belmont, denying Majestic Prince the Triple Crown. Two other Horses of the Year, Ack Ack and Damascus, also benefited from Baeza's masterful skill of pace and timing. The list of champions he piloted to stakes wins include legendary names Affectionately, Foolish Pleasure, Gallant Bloom, Roberto, Shuvee and Susan's Girl.

In 1968, he was recognized with the George Woolf Memorial Award. He won the Eclipse Award as the country's top jockey in 1972 and 1975. The National Racing Museum inducted him into the Hall of Fame in 1976, the year he retired.

Baeza now works as a clerk of scales.

Angel Cordero, Jr.

The son of a jockey, Cordero was born in Santurce, Puerto Rico. He rode his first winner at El Comandante Race Track in his native land in 1960 and came to the United States two years later and went on to become one of the country's all time greats.

By 1968, he was the country's leading rides by races won. A clever rider with a knack for speed horses, the fierce competitor finished his career with 7,057 victories, good for 7th place on the all-time list. He won aboard 18 percent of his mounts. At one point, he won 11 consecutive riding titles at Saratoga.

The winner of six Triple Crown races, he won three Kentucky Derbies, scoring aboard Cannonade in 1974, the 1976 running with Bold Forbes and the 1985 classic on Spend A Buck. He also won four Breeder's Cup races.

As a young rider, unaware of the stardom he was to be blessed with, Cordero had modest ambitions when he first set foot on the racetrack: "As a young rider, I had steps or goals I wanted to accomplish in my career. To start with, it was to ride my first winner. After I did that, I wanted to win a stakes race. Then I came to the U.S. and it started all over again. Of course, every jockeys' dream is to ride in the Kentucky Derby. I was lucky enough to win three of them."

Known for his prowess with front runners, he was the nation's leading money winning rider three times and retired with $164 million in earnings.

Cordero was as energetic as he was animated, flashing his big smile after winning big stakes races across the country. He rode on many of the best horses of his generation, including Triple Crown winner Seattle Slew, Horse of the Year All Along and champions Chief's Crown, Gulch, Life's Magic and Slew O' Gold.

Cordero was honored with the George Woolf Memorial Award in 1972, won the Mike Venezia Memorial in 1992 and won back-to-back Eclipse Awards in 1982 and 1983. He entered Racing's Hall of Fame in 1988.

Cordero currently works as a jockeys' agent, handling book for John Velazquez (the leading money winner in 2004), and still manages to find time to exercise horses most mornings.

Ron Turcotte

Born in Drummond, located in New Brunswick, Canada, Turcotte left school when he was 14 to help his father in the lumber business. Working with horses hauling logs out of the timber country, he learned about horsemanship and patience with the animals. Four years later, he went to Woodbine racetrack looking for work and caught on walking horses. He won his first race in 1962 aboard a horse named Pheasant Lane at Ontario's Fort Erie.

He's best known for his smashing 1973 Triple Crown performance aboard Secretariat. After a record setting performance in the Kentucky Derby, where Turcotte brought "Big Red" from last to first, he cleverly moved early on a slower Preakness pace to what should have been another record, if not for a malfunction with the track's timing mechanism.

The 1973 Belmont Stakes lives in the history of racing as one of the most powerful displays of sheer power, stamina and dominance ever. Allowing Secretariat to blaze through early fractions often seen in sprint races, Turcotte and his mount put away Sham, Derby and Preakness runner up, after scorching six furlongs in 1:09.8. Secretariat simply ran away from the field and blazed down the stretch by himself, pulling further away with every stride. In deep stretch, Turcotte, unable to avoid a tempting peek over his left shoulder, found the field far, far back. As they crossed the wire, he had put an incredible 31 lengths between Secretariat and the rest of the field, covering the grueling 1½ miles in a record 2:24.

In addition to his Triple Crown, Turcotte won the 1972 Derby and Belmont aboard Riva Ridge and the 1965 Preakness on Tom Rolfe.

While Turcotte never led the annual standings for wins or earnings, he consistently rode atop the best horses in the country, including Horses of the Year Arts and Letters, Damascus and Fort Marcy. He guided Northern Dancer, Kentucky Derby and Canadian Horse of the Year, to his maiden victory. Turcotte finished his career with 3,032 victories.

He won honors as the top Canadian jockey in 1962 and 1963. He entered the Canadian Racing Hall of Fame in 1980 and was the first jockey ever appointed the prestigious Order of Canada. Turcotte won the George Woolf Memorial Award in 1979 and was inducted into the National Museum of Racing's Hall of Fame the same year.

His riding career came to a sudden halt when he became paralyzed from the waist down after a riding accident at Belmont Park in 1978.

Laffit Pincay, Jr.

Born the son of a great rider, Pincay rode in Panama before coming to the United States at age 17. On July 1, 1966, he won his first race stateside aboard Teacher's Art at Arlington. He won his first stakes race the next day.

A physically strong and aggressive rider, Pincay won many of his races using his muscle to get horses rolling early or outmuscle the competition down the stretch. He was the dominant jockey of his generation, leading the nation in earnings six times. He retired with $237 million in purse earnings, fourth all time.

On December 10, 1999, he guided Irish Nip home first to pass Bill Shoemaker as the winningest rider of all time. Riding against kids young enough to be his grandchildren, he seemed to only get better as he got older, winning 200-plus races each of his last three years riding, a feat he hadn't done in the previous nine years. When he retired in 2003 at the age of 56, "The Pirate" had set the new record with 9,530 wins, capturing 20 percent of his races.

He won four Triple Crown races, including three Belmonts in a row, with Conquistador Cielo in 1982, aboard Caveat in 1983 and on Swale in 1984, whom he'd also won the Derby with. In 1986, he captured the Breeder's Cup Classic on Skywalker and pulled back-to-back doubles in 1989 and 1990 with Bayakoa. In total, he won seven Breeder's Cup races.

Pincay was known as a classy individual, respected by fellow jockeys and horsemen for his professionalism and generosity. He rode the country's best horses, including Horse of the Year John Henry and Spend a Buck, champions Gamely, Susan's Girl, Desert Vixen, Kentucky Derby–winning filly Genuine Risk and Triple Crown winner Affirmed, who never lost with Pincay in the irons.

In his 39 years of racing, he reportedly broke his collarbone 11 times, broke 10 ribs, twice broke his back, punctured lungs and broke his thumb. He also battled weight problems all his life and possessed the muscled physique that belied his age.

He was honored with the George Woolf Memorial Award in 1970 and the Mike Venezia Memorial in 1996. When the Eclipse Awards were initially established in 1971, he was the first winner as the nation's top jockey. He won it four more times, including his finale fourteen years later. He entered racing's Hall of Fame in 1975.

Eddie Delahoussaye

Born in New Iberia, Louisiana, "Steady Eddie" comes from a family of racing, as his father owned horses and his uncles trained at nearby tracks. By the time Eddie was 11 years old, he was riding quarter horses in match races.

Although he began riding thoroughbreds at the Fair Grounds in 1967, he didn't break through until the following year at Evangeline Downs, winning aboard Brown Shill in June.

Delahoussaye is known as a smart and patient rider, exceptional with come-from-behind horses. A winner in 16 percent of his tries, he won 6,085 races, good for 10th place on the all-time win list. In 1978, he led the country in number of races won.

Consistently in the top 10 for yearly earnings, Delahoussaye's mounts earned $195 million, which ranks sixth all time. He won a total of five Triple Crown races, including a magnificent rally aboard Gato Del Sol in 1982 Kentucky Derby followed by the gate-to-wire win on Sunny's Halo the following year. He won a total seven Breeder's Cup races including the 1992 Breeder's Cup Classic aboard Horse of the Year AP Indy.

He rode aboard many of the nation's top horses including champions Cardmania, Hollywood Wildcat, Princess Rooney and Risen Star.

The easy-going Cajun is known as an honest man of high integrity. Like many, he battled against weight and the bottle through his 34 year career. He retired in 2003 after suffering career-ending neck and back injuries in a Del Mar fall in 2002 summer racing at Del Mar.

He was recognized with the George Woolf Memorial Award in 1981 and entered racing's Hall of Fame in 1993.

Sandy Hawley

Sandford "Sandy" Hawley was born in Oshawa, Ontario, and is simply the greatest Canadian rider of all time.

Growing up like many young Canadian boys, Hawley had dreams of becoming an ice hockey star. He began hotwalking horses at 17, promoted to groom and worked as an exercise rider before obtaining his jockeys' license. He won his first race at Woodbine Racetrack on October 14, 1968, aboard Fly Alone. Hawley went on to have unprecedented success at the Ontario oval, winning 18 titles there.

The following year, he was North America's top apprentice rider with 230 victories. In 1973, he became the first rider to win 500 races in a season. He was the leading rider in the country by races won four times. He finished his 31-year career with 6,449 wins, 9th on the all-time list, winning 21 percent of his tries. In 1976, he won the Eclipse Award as the nation's top rider.

A true gentleman who always carried himself as a professional, Hawley possessed a superb judge of pace. Although he didn't win an American classic, he won major stakes in Canada and the United States aboard great horses like Canadian Horse of the Year L'Enjoleur, Desert Waves, Golden Act, Highland Vixen, Kennedy Road, Kiridashi, Smart Strike and Youth.

As the leading rider in Canada a record nine times, he was twice chosen for the Lou Marsh Award as Canada's top athlete and twice won the Sovereign Award as the country's top jockey. He was recognized for his contributions to Canadian racing with the 1976 Order of Canada, a prestigious award given to Canadian citizens for truly outstanding individual accomplishments. He entered the Canadian Racing Hall of Fame in 1986.

He had a nasty fall in the post parade at Woodbine in 1995, suffering broken ribs, fractured pelvis and internal injuries that twice required surgery. He retired from racing in 1998. However, his injuries pale in comparison to his courageous battle with cancer. At one point, doctors didn't expect him to survive more than a few months, but through treatment, a rigid diet and sheer determination, Hawley beat the odds.

Hawley was recognized with the George Woolf Memorial Award in 1976 and entered the National Museum of Racing Hall of Fame in 1992. He retired in 1998, working in the racing industry since hanging up his saddle.

Pat Day

Pat Day grew up on a farm in Eagle, Colorado, and always wanted to be a rodeo star. Despite his diminutive 4'11" frame, he lasted two years on the rodeo circuit before moving to the racetrack.

He won his first race at Prescott Downs in Arizona on a horse named Forblunged in 1973. Within a few years, Day's reputation as a highly skilled rider began building, and in 1982, he battled legendary Angel Cordero for the country's top riding honor, winning the crown by two wins.

As Day climbed the ladder of success to reach the top, he nearly ruined it all in a battle with booze and cocaine. Winning led to arrogance, wild parties and denial. Unable to find inner peace and contentment, his racing success was unfulfilling. He was heading for big trouble.

In a Miami hotel room in 1984, he had a spiritual experience that changed his life forever; "I was watching TV evangelist Jimmy Swaggart on television before I went to sleep. I turned the TV and lights off and fell asleep. It felt like I'd been sleeping for hours when I woke up refreshed and turned the TV back on. But only a few minutes had passed. The evangelist was still on and people were streaming towards the alter. I felt as though God was calling to me. I committed myself to Christ that night and it saved my life."

The event was so profound that he thought God might have been calling him out of racing and into ministry. Ironically, his own words came back as the career guidance he was seeking: "In interviews I'd been doing prior to this, I'd be asked how I was able to get horses to relax so well or how I kept tired horses running hard, and I'd always tell them it was a God-given talent. It was then I realized that my calling was through racing, not outside of racing."

Day's career skyrocketed, as he captured the inaugural Breeder's Cup Classic aboard a 31–1 oversight Wild Again and won the first of his four Eclipse Awards that year. On September 13, 1989, he won a record eight of nine races in one day at Arlington Park. Two years later, he won a record 60 stakes races.

Nicknamed "Pay Day," he's been one of the most consistent big stakes riders in the country, picking up rides on top horses all across the country. He is the country's all-time leading money-winning rider with purse earnings exceeding $297 million, adding another $10 million last year. He has over 1,000 stakes wins to his credit, including 25 worth a million dollars or more.

Day led the nation in wins six times. With 8,803 wins, he sits fourth on the all-time list. He won an impressive 22 percent of his races and was in the top three 54 percent of the time. The fifty-one year-old Day retired in 2005, ending a brilliant riding career while still at the top of his game. Not only will he be missed as one of the sport's best riders, but as one of its best people.

Chris McCarron

McCarron was born in Dorchester, Massachusets, and wanted to be a hockey star when he was growing up. He was later introduced to racing through his older brother, jockey Gregg, whom he credits as being a major influence in his life.

He first came to the racetrack in 1971 as a hotwalker. He rode his first winner on February 9, 1974, aboard Erezev at Maryland's Bowie racetrack. That season, he rode a record 546 winners and earned the first of his two Eclipse Awards as the country's top apprentice rider.

In 1988, McCarron became the first rider to win $5 million in purses in one year. In the same year, at 33-years-old, he became the youngest jockey to surpass $100 million in lifetime earnings. A master of pace and tactics, he led the country in purse earnings four times and finished his career with nearly $264 million is purses, tops at that time, and currently ranks third all time in that category.

One of the smartest riders to put on silks, he was the country's leading rider by races won three times and retired with 7,141 victories, sixth on the all time list, winning 21 percent of his races and hitting the board more than half the time.

In 1987, he won the Kentucky Derby aboard Alysheba and took the 1994 "Run for the Roses" aboard Go for Gin. In total, he won six Triple Crown races. Among his nine Breeder's Cup victories are the 1988 Breeder's Cup Classic with Alysheba, the next year on Sunday Silence, the 1996 running with Alphabet Soup and back-to-back scores in the Classic with Tiznow in 2000 and 2001.

The list of horses he rode in his brilliant career include Horses of the Year Criminal Type, John Henry, Lady's Secret, and champions Bayakoa, Flawlessly, Forty Niner, Glorious Song, Lehmi Gold, Paseana, Precisionist and Turkoman.

Fittingly, he won his final ride aboard a horse named Came Home in the 2002 Affirmed Handicap at Hollywood on June 23, 2002.

He was honored with the George Wool Memorial Award in 1980, the Mike Venezia Memorial in 1991 and the ESPN ESPY Award in 1995. He won his second Eclipse Award, as a journeyman, in 1980. McCarron entered the racing Hall of Fame in 1989.

Actively involved in the Don MacBeth Disabled Rider's Fund program, McCarron has given much of his own time to the industry. He played a key role in the movie Seabiscuit, helping design the racing scenes and playing the part of Hall of Famer Charlie Kurtsigner, War Admiral's jockey.

McCarron joined the management team at Santa Anita racetrack after retiring and is now reportedly preparing to open a jockey training school in Kentucky.

Jerry Bailey

Born in Dallas, Bailey is one classy Texan. The son of a dentist, his flashy smile, good looks and incredible talent have made him the icon among modern-day riders.

By the time he was 12, Bailey was riding quarter horses. His racing career started at Sunland Park in New Mexico in 1974. He won in his first try race aboard a horse named Fetch.

Bailey is a real student of the game and takes to the track well prepared every time out. He's known as an exceptional turf rider with an impeccable sense of timing. He always seems to be in the right place at the right time, particularly in stakes races, with a 21 percent winning rate. He's won nearly 40 races with purses of $1,000,000 or more.

His magic hands of gold have escorted horses to the winner's circle more than 5,800 times, winning about 20 percent of his races. He's won handfuls of riding titles across the country, and led the nation in earnings six times. Last year, his mounts earned over $15 million, fourth in the country, averaging $24,460 per start. His career total, at more than $287 million, ranks second all time.

In 2003, he posted a record 70 stakes wins, including 55 graded stakes wins, including his thrilling come-from-behind win in the Belmont Stakes on Empire Maker to deny Funny Cide the Triple Crown. He has nearly 1,000 stakes wins behind him.

In total, Bailey has won two Kentucky Derbies, with Sea Hero in 1993 and Grindstone in 1996, among his six Triple Crown scores. He's won a record 14 Breeder's Cup races, including the 1993 Breeder's Cup Classic aboard 133–1 shocker Arcangues, whom he'd never seen before taking a leg, setting off the largest win payoff in Breeder's Cup history. He repeated with wins in the 1994 Classic aboard Concern and 1995 with Cigar.

He's ridden the best of horses in his primarily injury-free career, including the brilliant Horse of the Year Cigar. Twice voted Horse of the Year, Cigar won 16-straight races and retired as America's all-time money winner with almost $10 million in earnings with Bailey in the irons most of the time.

He was recognized with the George Woolf Memorial Award in 1992 and the Mike Venezia Memorial the following year. He twice was chosen for the ESPN ESPY Award as the year's top jockey, capturing the award in 1996 and 1997. Bailey entered into racing's Hall of Fame in 1995. Of all the public recognition he's received, none is more remarkable than wining the record seven Eclipse Awards. He won his first in 1995, and other than 1998, he's won every year since then, until being upstaged in 2004.

Bailey served as the Jockeys' Guild President from 1990 to1997, was instrumental in pushing for improved jockey safety and led the movement to require the wearing of safety vests.

Russell Baze

Russell "the Muscle" Baze hails from a large racing family. His father, Joe was a jockey; brothers Dale and Gary are also riders; even his cousin, the fine young rider Tyler Baze, joined in the family tradition.

The Canadian-born Baze began riding at 15 and won his first race aboard Oregon Warrior in 1974 at Yakima Meadows in Washington state. Today, Baze virtually owns the mid-level tracks in northern California, having won 27 consecutive riding titles at Bay Meadows and 24 straight at Golden Gate Fields until his streak was broken due to injury.

Year after year, he's compiled 400-win seasons, a phenomenal accomplishment in any year, let alone repeating the feat nine times. In 2002, he won 431 races, visiting the winner's circle 29 percent of the time and hitting the board in 63 percent of his starts. In 2003, he won 410 races at an amazing 30 percent clip, lighting the board in 66 percent of his trips.

Baze currently sits second on the all-time win list with over 9,000 visits to the winner's circle, adding another 321 last year, fifth best in the nation, in an injury-shortened season. As long as he stays healthy, it's likely he'll pass Pincay to become the all time winningest jockey in a few years.

Prior to 2005, he'd won the Isaac Murphy Award, which annually recognizes the country's top winning percentage jockey, every year since its inception ten years ago. He's won over 22 percent of his lifetime mounts and has been in the money 54 percent of the time. He's ridden more than 530 stakes winners, including the current sprinter phenomenon Lost in the Fog.

Considered a "blue collar" rider, he has a tireless work ethic and still makes it out in the mornings to work horses, despite the reputation as more than just a local legend. A former high school valedictorian, he's known as a smart rider who consistently gets his horses in position to win. As a person, Baze is respected as a kind, courteous and humble man.

Without an on-the-board finish in a Triple Crown or Breeder's Cup race, many feel that Baze dodged the high-level competition of other tracks for the safety and security of being the big fish in a small pond. While we'll likely never know how he would've done against the likes of Bailey, Day and Stevens long term on a larger circuit, his winning record is an amazing accomplishment that no one else has been able to replicate.

He was awarded a special Eclipse Award in 1995, commemorating his achievement as the first jockey to win 400 races in four consecutive years. He entered the racing Hall of Fame in 1999 and was honored with the George Woolf Memorial Award in 2002.

Steve Cauthen

Born the son of a trainer in Covington, Kentucky, Cauthen broke his maiden at 16 aboard a horse named Red Pipe at River Downs on May 17, 1976.

In a meteoric rise to the top, Cauthen exploded on the scene leading the country in wins as an apprentice the following season and etching his name in racing history. He set an earnings record with $6 million year as a bug rider, earning the nickname "Million Dollar Man."

In 1978, he became a national hero and an icon for the sport when he won the Triple Crown aboard Affirmed. In a legendary series, he outdueled Hall of Famer Jorge Velasquez aboard Alydar in an epic battle of two brilliant horses. Entering the Belmont with the Derby and Preakness wins behind him, the young Cauthen continued to belie his years as he handled himself like a professional, despite all the pressure and media hype. In the Belmont, Affirmed and Alydar hooked up at the seven-eighths pole and raced side-by-side all the way around. At the top of the stretch, Alydar poked his head in front, but Cauthen responded and the two horses raced down the stretch nose-to-nose as both jockeys threw everything but the kitchen sink into their mounts. At the wire, it was Affirmed winning the Belmont, and the Triple Crown, by a mere head.

Cauthen was rewarded for his remarkable year in 1977 with accolades rarely seen by jockeys. He graced the cover of numerous magazines, made newspaper headlines and was chosen by Sports Illustrated as the 1977 "Sportsman of the Year."

He led the country in wins in 1977 and finished his career with 2,794 victories, winning 19 percent of his rides.

As he physically grew from a boy into a young man, weight challenges led him to try his hand in Europe, where riders are allowed to ride with higher weights. Some worried that Cauthen was a flash in the pan, but he quickly proved them wrong by becoming the first American to win a British jockey championship in 70 years, winning three riding titles in England and won Britain's Lord Derby Award, given to the year's top jockey, three times. He is the only jockey to have won the Kentucky, Epsom, French, Irish and Italian Derbies.

Before hanging up his tack for good in 1993, he rode some of the world's top horses, including Grade or Group I winners Arazi, Diminuendo, Indian Skimmer, Johnny D, Oh So Sharp, Old Vic, Pebbles and Skip Anchor.

Cauthen won three Eclipse Awards in 1977, taking down the prize in the Apprentice Jockey, Top Jockey and Award of Merit categories, a unique distinction not likely to be repeated. He was honored with the George Woolf Memorial Award in 1984 and entered racing's Hall of Fame in 1984.

Gary Stevens

The son of a trainer, Stevens was born in Caldwell, Idaho. As a child, he was diagnosed with Perthes syndrome, a degenerative hip joint disease. An athletic young man, he was a champion wrestler in school, but followed in his older brother, Scott's, footsteps and headed to the racetrack. On May 16, 1979, at the age of 16, he won in his first race at Les Bois Park in Idaho aboard a horse named Little Star.

An intense and highly talented rider, Stevens progressed from smaller tracks to the major circuit in southern California. In 1988, he led the country in earnings, repeating two years later. In 1993, he became the youngest rider to win $100 million. To date, his horses have earned over $218 million, which ranks fifth all time. He's won over 30 races valued at $1,000,000 or more. Stevens has nearly 5,000 victories to his credit so far, including more than 750 in stakes.

Over the years, he's experienced health problems with bad knees and injuries. In and out of retirement at various stages of his career, he's spent time riding in England, France and Hong Kong. He's currently riding back in Southern California, where he's enjoyed most of his American success.

Capturing Kentucky Derbies with Winning Colors in 1988, Thunder Gulch in 1995 and aboard Silver Charm two years later, he's won a total of eight Triple Crown races. He's also won eight Breeder's Cup races.

He's been aboard several top horses, including Horse of the Year Point Given and champions Bertrando, Serena's Song, Silverbulletday, Singspiel and Victory Gallop.

Stevens was honored with the George Woolf Memorial Award in 1996 and the Mike Venezia Memorial in 1999. In 1998, he was awarded an ESPY from ESPN as the year's top jockey. He won the Eclipse Award as the country's top rider in 1998 and entered the Racing Hall of Fame in 1997 at age 34, the second youngest inductee ever. He served as the Jockeys' Guild president for six years.

The well-spoken and highly respected jockey has performed as a racing analyst and television commentator when not in the saddle. In the movie Seabiscuit, Stevens did an admirable job playing the role of George Woolf.

Julie Krone

As the world's greatest female jockey, Julie Krone is the yardstick all great female riders are measured against.

She was born in Benton Harbor, Michigan, and raised on a farm in nearby Eau Claire. The daughter of a riding instructor, she grew up riding horses and winning horse shows everywhere she went. She dropped out of school and went to work at Churchill Downs at age, courtesy of a forged birth certificate, as a groom and exercise rider. She rode her first winner, Lord Farkle, on February 12, 1981, at Tampa Bay Downs. Six years later, she because the first woman to won a riding title at a major track, sweeping titles at Monmouth, Meadowlands and Atlantic City.

In 1993, she became the first female rider to win a Triple Crown race, bringing Colonial Affair home first in the Belmont Stakes. Later that year, she had a nasty fall on the last day of the Saratoga meet. She was thrown from her mount, Seattle Way, and bounced around directly in front of the charging horses. Two is Trouble ran her over, kicking her in the chest. If not for the safety vest, the blow may have killed her. She suffered a bruised heart and ribs and a severely broken ankle in the accident. The crushed ankle required steel plates and screws to repair and left her bedridden. It took her nine months to make it back to the races. When the year was finished, she was awarded an ESPY award by ESPN as the year's top female athlete.

In 1995, she broke both hands in a Gulfstream Park accident. Recovery from that setback was as much mental as physical for the determined rider, as she endured nightmares of racing accidents. Calling herself the "Comeback Kid," she's fought through injuries and adversity all her life.

At 4'10", the diminutive Krone has a crushing handshake that can take a grown man to his knees. With a charmingly infectious smile, she's a tiger on the track and not one to be picking a fight with. Named as one of the 10 toughest athletes in all sports by USA Today in 2004, she's been involved in numerous jockey scrapes, usually getting the upper hand. In 1982, she shoved a jockey off the scales after he'd hit her horse with his whip during the race. Four years later, she punched another rider, bloodying his nose, after he struck her with his whip. The fight carried over into the jockeys' swimming pool, where she swung a lawn chair at him. Three years later, she knocked teeth out of another rider's mouth in a brawl.

On the racetrack, Krone is known as a patient rider. With soft hands, she has the unique ability to gingerly persuade her horses into giving their best. She's racked up 3,704 wins, tops among female riders, capturing 17 percent of her races. Her horses have earned more than $90 million, including 304 stakes races. The list of top horses she's ridden includes Da Hoss, Maxzene, Mr. Greeley and Champion Rubiano.

On August 24, 2003, the 40-year-old Krone became the first female rider to win a $1 million race when set a new track record aboard Candy Ride in Del Mar's Pacific Classic. Two months later, she became the first woman to win a Breeder's Cup race when she piloted Halfbridled home first in the Juvenile.

Krone was inducted into racing's Hall of Fame in 2000. While currently out of racing, it's not a safe bet to assume she won't return to the sport at some point. Well spoken and knowledgeable of the industry, when she's not atop horses, she's done racing analysis and commentary work.

Mike Smith

Born in the land of UFOs, Roswell, New Mexico, Smith is the son of a jockey and wasted no time making it to the track. By the time he was 11, he was riding quarter horses at small bush tracks. He rode his first winner, Forever Man, at Santa Fe Downs in 1982.

The friendly and well-liked Smith won a record 66 stakes, including 20 Grade I events, in 1994 and led the country in winners that year. He's currently ridden over 4,500 winners, banking over $174 million in purse earnings, ranking 10th all time.

When he won the 1991 Irish Two Thousand Guineas aboard Fourstars Allstar, he became the first U.S.–based jockey to win a European Classic.

Winner of the 1993 Preakness aboard Prarie Bayou and the 2005 Kentucky Derby aboard 50–1 shocker Giacomo, Smith has been highly successful in Breeder's Cup races, bringing home the trophy ten times, including the Classic in 1997 aboard Skip and back-to-back scores aboard Lure in the Breeder's Cup Mile in 1992 and 1993.

To date, Smith has won more than 4,500 races, including more than 550 stakes races. He's been aboard many racing stars, including Horses of the Year Azeri, Holy Bull and Skip Away, and champions Inside Information, Sky Beauty and Vindication.

On August 31, 1998, at Saratoga, Smith broke his back after being thrown from his mount, Dacron, and spent months in a full-body cast.

Smith won the George Woolf Memorial Award in 2000, the Mike Venezia Memorial in 1994 and was chosen for the 1994 ESPN ESPY Award as the year's top jockey. He won back-to-back Eclipse Awards as the country's top jockey in 1993 and 1994. Smith was inducted into racing's Hall of Fame in 2003.

Kent Desormeaux

Born in the heart of Cajun country, Maurice, Louisiana, Desormeaux grew up with horses. His father operated a small nearby track, Akadiana Downs. Growing up, the 5'3" young man wanted to be a basketball star.

Once he found his way to the racetrack, it didn't take long for the athletic rider to find success. He won his first race aboard Miss Tavern at Evangeline Downs on July 13, 1986. In his apprentice year, he set a lofty goal of winning 600 races. Riding day and night, he nearly pulled it off, winning 598 in an injury-shortened season.

His outstanding rookie season earned him the 1987 Eclipse Award as the country's top apprentice. While most apprentice riders never repeat their initial success, Desormeaux has gone on to record over 4,600 victories so far, winning 20 percent of his tries and hitting the board half the time. He's been the nation's leading rider by number of races won three times.

He's won two Breeder's Cup wins, taking the 1993 Turf aboard Horse of the Year Kotashaan and the 1995 Sprint aboard Desert Stormer. If not for Gary Stevens' win by a nose aboard Victory Gallop in the 1998 Belmont Stakes, Desormeaux would've won the Triple Crown aboard Real Quiet, after rattling off scores in the Derby and Preakness. He scored again in the 2000 Derby atop Fusaichi Pegasus, among his more than 540 stakes wins.

He's ridden many top champion racehorses, including Risen Star and Pleasant Tap. He was the country's leading rider by purses earned in 1992. With career earnings approaching $200 million, he's cracked the all-time top ten.

On December 11, 1992, Desormeaux was kicked in the head after a fall at Hollywood Park, fracturing his skull and hemorrhaging. Doctors were guarded with his prognosis, and many doubted his return to racing, let alone return to the top of the sport. Determinedly, he returned to the track six weeks later and won in his first race back.

In 2001, he spent time riding in Japan and became the first foreign-based jockey to win a Japanese classic aboard Lady Pastel in the Japanese Oaks.

The pleasant and well-humored rider has enjoyed success doing racing commentary on television and seems certain to be a figure in racing after his riding days are finished.

He was honored with the George Woolf Memorial Award in 1993 and was twice chosen for the ESPN ESPY Award as the year's top jockey in 1999 and 2001. A three-time Eclipse Award winner, Desormeaux entered racing's Hall of Fame in 2004.

* * *

In addition to the profiles of these tried-and-true jockeys, there is a host of riders at the top of the sport today who are poised to move into the ranks of the all-time greats. Among today's strong contingent of riders are the following superstars:

Jorge Chavez

At 4'11" tall, this native of Peru has made a big name for himself after coming to the United States on what was supposed to be a vacation. Chavez has won over 4,000 career races, including over 340 stakes. His horses have earned over $148 million in his riding career.

Chavez enjoyed a remarkable year in 1999, winning Breeder's Cup races aboard Beautiful Pleasure in the Distaff and Artax in the Sprint and earning the Eclipse Award as the year's top rider.

Nicknamed "Chop Chop" for his aggressive riding style, he has been a leading rider in New York and Florida. In 2001, he won the Kentucky Derby aboard Monarchos. Chavez was honored with the Mike Venezia Memorial Award in 2000.

Ramon Dominguez

Dominguez was a successful rider in his native Venezuela before coming to the United States As a high percentage-winning rider, 22 percent lifetime, Dominguez is a rising star among today's jockeys.

He's led the nation in wins in 2001 and 2003, with 431 and 453 wins, respectively. In 2004, he finished second with 383 victories, while winning 28 percent of his races and finishing in the money at a 61 percent clip. He was awarded the 2004 Isaac Murphy Award after recording the highest win rate in the country, dethroning perennial champion Russell Baze. Dominguez finished in the top-ten money earners for the year again in 2004, with purses money totaling $11,506,890.

He won his first Breeder's Cup race in 2004 aboard Better Talk Now, the 27–1 winner of the Distaff. In total, he has over 2,400 wins and 160 stakes tallies.

Victor Espinoza

Like many others that come from south of the border to ride, Mexican-born Espinoza didn't speak English when he came to the United States. It didn't take long for the humble young man, who used to be a bus driver, to figure things out.

In his 2000 breakthrough season, he won the Breeder's Cup Distaff aboard Spain. Two years later, he nearly won the Triple Crown aboard War Emblem. After brilliant rides in the Derby and Preakness, a stumble out of the gate cost Espinoza his chance at the elusive third jewel of the Crown. For his remarkable year, he was the recipient of the 2002 ESPY Award as the top jockey.

A winner of 18 percent of his races in 2004, he finished third in the country with earnings of $15,933,757. His career numbers include over 2,000 winners, 200 stakes wins and $88 million in purses.

Corey Nakatani

A California native, Nakatani has made a major impact on Southern California racing over the past decade, winning titles at all three major tracks in the area.

The athletically gifted rider has won six Breeder's Cup races, including three consecutive Sprints, taking the 1996 version with Lit De Justice, the following year with Elmhurst and again with Reraise in 1998.

In 2004, he won aboard 20 percent of his mounts and finished seventh in the country in earnings with $12,466,557. Nakatani has won over 3,000 career trips to the winner's circle, including 450 stakes on his way to over $160 million in purse earnings.

Edgar Prado

Prado came to the United States after being the top apprentice rider in his native Peru. One of the top riders in racing today, he's accumulated over 5,500 victories and $160 million in career purses. A consistent sort, Prado has won in 19 percent of his races and rewarded show bettors 49 percent of the time.

He may be best known as the spoiler of Triple Crown hopes. In 2002, he brought Sarava home first in the Belmont Stakes at odds of 70–1 to defeat Derby and Preakness winner War Emblem. Last year, he ran down Smarty Jones in the Belmont stretch aboard 36–1 Birdstone to steal the show.

A perennial leader in the jockey standings, Prado led the country in wins three consecutive years beginning in 1997 and consistently finishes in the top 10 of the category every year.

He's finished as the nation's second leading money-winning rider the last three years. His horses earned $18,342,106 last season.

In 2002, Prado was honored with the George Woolf Memorial Award.

Jose Santos

The son of a jockey, Santos was born into racing and worked as a groom when he was only eight years old. He rode his first winner at Hipico Race Track in his native Chile and came to the United States in 1984, already known as one of the best South American riders. Two years later, he won his first Breeder's Cup race aboard Manila, taking the turf race despite dropping his whip in deep stretch. Santos won six more Breeder's Cup races, including the 2002 Classic aboard 43–1 Volponi.

In 2003, he nearly won the Triple Crown aboard Funny Cide. After a great ride in the Derby and a dominating victory in the Preakness, he was outrun over the sloppy Belmont Stakes surface.

Santos led the country in purse earnings four straight years from 1986 to 1989 and has amassed $181 million in purses, ranking eighth all time. He's closing in on 4,000 wins, including 500 stakes wins.

He earned the 1988 Eclipse Award as the country's top jockey and was honored with the George Woolf Memorial Award in 1999. In 2003, he was recognized with the ESPY Award.

Alex Solis

Solis attended Jockey School in his native Panama and moved to the United States in 1982. He is making a comeback from a serious back injury and gaining momentum. When at his best, Solis is one of the top riders in the country, as evidenced by his 11 wins in races worth $1 million or more.

He's a three-time Breeder's Cup winner, taking the 2003 Classic aboard Pleasantly Perfect. His lone Triple Crown win came in 1986 aboard Snow Chief. In 1991, he rode Mane Minister to third-place finishes in all three legs of the Triple Crown.

Despite his back injury in 2004, he still managed to post earnings of over $11 million and ranks seventh all time with over $192 million in purse monies.

A winner of more than 500 stakes races, Solis was honored with the George Woolf Memorial Award in 1997.

Pat Valenzuela

Born in Montrose, Colorado, Valenzuela is blessed with incredible ability but cursed with a history of drug-related suspensions.

He's won seven Breeder's Cup races and two Triple Crown races, taking the 1989 Derby and Preakness aboard Sunday Silence before being ousted in a stirring Belmont Stakes duel with Pat Day aboard Easy Goer and denied the Crown.

In his last full season of racing, Valenzuela won all five Southern California riding titles in 2003, the first to run the table since Hall of Famer Chris McCarron did it 20 years earlier. He finished fourth in both number of wins and earnings nationally in 2003. He has over 3,700 wins and $136 million in career earnings.

Valenzuela returned to the track earlier this year and will have to reestablish his credibility through his riding, horsemanship and clean record. So far, he's off to a great start, competing for the riding title at every racing meet.

John Velazquez

Born in Puerto Rico, Velazquez has become America's top rider, taking the reins over from Jerry Bailey, who ran the table for several years.

As the leading rider on the tough New York circuit, Velazquez has improved his game consistently over the past several years. In the past three years, he's placed in the top ten leading jockey categories, money won and races won. In 2004 alone, as the country's top money winning rider, his horses earned over $22 million. He posted 335 wins, third most in the nation. He crossed the finish line first in 25 percent of his races and hit the board 56 percent of the time. Victorious in 39 stakes races last season, he won nine Grade I events.

"Johnny V" has won six Breeder's Cup races, including scores aboard Ashado in the Distaff and Speightstown in the Sprint in 2004. In total, Velazquez has over 3,300 career wins with 400 stakes victories. His lifetime earnings stand at $160 million and are certain to climb.

In 2003, he won the Mike Venezia Memorial Award. After a brilliant year in 2004, he captured the Eclipse Award as the country's top rider, ending Jerry Bailey's four-year run.

There are several young, fresh faces in jockey rooms across the country who may join the elite riders of our day. While a case can be made for many, here's a few of the more likely stars of tomorrow:

Tyler Baze

Born in Seattle and another member of the large Baze racing family, Tyler is one of the hottest young riders in the country today.

After winning the Eclipse Award as the nation's top apprentice in 2000, he's continued on to post impressive, and consistently improving, numbers. This Grade I stakes–winning rider brought home 239 winners in 2004, good for 17th in the country, and won 17 percent of his races. His runners earned over $10 million racing, 14th best. Baze was off to a flying start in 2005, consistently finding the winner's circle and among the riding leaders in Southern California.

Rafael Bejarano

This Peruvian, Grade I stakes–winning rider led the country in races won in 2004, posting 455 victories while winning 24 percent of his mounts.

He cracked the top 10 in earnings in 2004 with purses totaling over $12 million. He's the top young rider in New York and gaining praise everywhere he rides.

Bejarano, a talented and fearless rider, is getting up on top horses across the country and is certain to be a fixture at the top of the jockey standings for years to come.

Eddie Castro

This young Panamanian rider won the 2003 Eclipse Award as an apprentice and posted impressive numbers in 2004. He improved his 15th place finish in the races won category to 8th best in the nation in 2004, with 270 wins. He won over $6 million in purses in 2004 and appears to have a bright future.

On June 4, 2005, Castro became the first jockey in the United States to ride nine winners on a single race card. Amazingly, he won 9 of 11 mounts on his record-setting day at Calder, including the last five races of the card.

Ryan Fogelsonger

After winning the Eclipse Award as the nation's top apprentice in 2002, Fogelsonger followed up with 278 wins in 2003, fifth best in the nation. While his win total dropped in 2004 to 217, he maintained a high win rate, scoring on 20 percent of his mounts. His horses have earned over $10 million in the past two years.

Pablo Fragoso

An Eclipse Award finalist in the apprentice category in 2004, Mexican-born Fragoso won 10 stakes and three graded events in 2004. Riding much of the time on the tough New York circuit, he finished the year with over $6 million in purses, 25th best in the nation and averaged well over $6,000 per mount, higher than most of the country's top journeyman riders.

Brian Hernandez, Jr.

Hernandez won more races at Keeneland than any other apprentice since Hall of Famer Earlie Fires in 1966. Hernandez, whose father still races, won 243 races in 2004, 13th best in the nation and won 17 percent of his starts. He was recognized as the top apprentice of the year, earning the 2004 Eclipse Award in that category.

John McKee

On his way to becoming a 2002 Eclipse Award finalist in the apprentice category, McKee broke Hall of Famer Steve Cauthen's apprentice records at River Downs and Churchill Downs. After two ultra-consistent years in 2003 and 2004, where he posted earnings over $6 million each year and 210 wins in 2004, two less than the previous season, McKee is poised to make a name for himself on the national scene.

8

OUT OF THE SADDLE

With the burden of carrying the hopes of the trainer, owners and their own financial reward, they compete day after day in a high-stakes, high-risk environment. Over the years, the grind wears them down, both physically and mentally. At some point in his career, the jockey decides enough is enough.

Retirement for most of us is a planned event, a rewarding departure from a lifetime's work into the glorious golden years. For jockeys, retirement often comes without warning and not by choice. The career-ending injury, or complications from years of neglectful health maintenance, may send the rider into premature retirement, one without proper preparation and lacking the foresight of financial, social and emotional planning. Industry estimates show sudden, unplanned early exits from the sport due to injury and illness may be as high as 70 percent.

Jockeys are at risk of riding their last race every time they saddle up. There are so many hazards in the sport. It's not a matter of if they get hurt; it's a matter of when, how often and how badly.

Veteran Hall Of Fame jockey Russell Baze has been fortunate to have been healthy and mostly injury free during his career:

> I've been so lucky to have not been hurt badly like so many guys. Most jockeys retire because they have to, not because they want to. Many of them injured badly and they can't ride any longer, or their injury stops them from returning to the same level of performance they used to ride at.
> I love what I do and if I can't do my best, that's when I'll call it quits.

In the meantime, Baze just continues to write the record book with riding title after riding title.

For those riders who are physically able to sustain a long riding career, at retirement they may find their deteriorated health from years of abuse a grim reminder of the unyielding demands of their profession. Due to the rigorous physical demands of racing, many riders experience health problems after hanging up the saddle. Many suffer back problems, joint pain and complications from years of strict diets and extreme weight reducing measures. Many riders simply wear down over time, deteriorating from the constant wear and tear on their bodies. The price jockeys pay to chase their dreams is a steep one.

A veteran jockey of 23 years, retired rider George Bravo fought against weight issues his entire career:

> It was killing me to make the weights. I was taking diuretics, strong laxatives and heaving all the time. It was pure hell. I didn't even have a reason to hit the hot box, because I didn't have any water weight to lose. I was just dehydrated all the time. I remember being so dizzy and lightheaded sometimes in the post parade, that I don't know how I stayed on. But riding is such an adrenaline rush, you don't ever want to give it up. You'll do anything you can to ride.
>
> I still have some urinary and kidney problems stemming for all the Lasix I took every day for 15 years.
>
> Eventually, fighting the weight just got to be too much and I moved over to quarter horses, where the standard was 124 pounds. I was in hog heaven at the higher weight.
>
> I also ended up with arthritis in my shoulder from so many repeated injuries. I took cortisone shots all the time. Now I have a plastic and titanium shoulder. They basically chopped off my arm, put a new shoulder socket in place and grafted my arm to it.

Similar to Bravo's joint replacement, retired stakes-winning rider Paul Nicolo suffered from osteoarthritis: "My hips just broke down from all the wear and tear over the years. I used to be in pain all the time and walked with a bad limp. It really crippled me up. I finally gave in and had hip replacement surgery on one side and couldn't believe how easy it was. I had the other one done as soon as I could and now I feel great."

Tom Chapman, is a retired Grade I stakes–winning rider and gifted artist. Like most, over the years he suffered many injuries while racing:

> I landed on my head so many times, it may have affected my memory, or maybe it's my age, I don't know. I had five or six concussions and fractured my skull once. I had a herniated disk when I was riding and it flares up every so often and still have some tingling down my arm now and then.
>
> I remember one time when I had been riding for a long time with a sore back. Like most guys, though, I just rode through the pain. I eventually went in to see a Chiropractor and he asked me when I'd broken my back. I didn't even know it was broken.

Retired jockey Tom Chapman spends much of his time now in his art studio (photograph courtesy of Tom Chapman).

Some riders call it quits because they are no longer able to make riding weight. Others may find that as they age, their riding skills decline and they are unable to maintain the competitive edge, leading to a loss in business and income.

With many jockeys entering the racing industry in their teens, they spend most of their adult lives around racing people and in racing's social circles. From dawn to dusk, they're at the racetrack. It's all they know. When retirement comes, they don't know many people outside of racing. Because of this, many lack the skills and confidence to sociale with the outside world.

As professional athletes, jockeys enjoy recognition, involvement and the excitement of competing, and the brotherhood and comfort of the racing community. Once their social circles evaporate, many retired riders suffer from lack of direction and focus in their life. When they leave the game, the loss of self-importance and social status sends many into an emotional tailspin.

Chapman, who hung up his saddle eight years ago, has fond memories of his days in the saddle: "Riding is addictive like a drug or alcohol. After you give it up, it takes a while to come down. You miss the accolades and the back slapping. You don't even realize how much it means to you

8. Out of the Saddle

His masterpiece *Transition ... Jockey to Artist*, portrays his career change (photograph courtesy of Tom Chapman).

when you're riding, but it's really hard to break away from it. I still have dreams about riding. Some retired riders have to get completely away from the sport and seldom go back to the track, while others like to stay very involved in the business and work as trainers, agents, valets or whatever."

Most retired jockeys lack the occupational skills and secondary education for employment outside the industry. Because they lack education, and have little or no other work experience outside the racing industry, many must find work inside the racing world as exercise riders, agents, valets, clockers (timer), trainers or in a racing official capacity.

Dr. David Baron recognizes the difficulty jockeys must have in transitioning from a career at the racetrack: "It's not just the sport; it's their life. Their skills aren't that transferable to other jobs. They lack education, and there's no form of counseling for them. Racing is all that they've done. They just love their sport—it's all they do. It's a rather depressing scenario."

Paul Nicolo feels he's lucky to have found such a rewarding career as the clerk of scales when he hung up his tack: "It's tough when you quit riding. Most of the jockeys don't have much education, and I'd guess that 90 percent of them feel lost in the world when they retire. I was very fortunate to have found this great job as a racing official and am making a good career of it."

Former jockey Tim Malgarini, a veteran stakes-winning rider with thirteen years under his belt, went to work in the racing industry immediately after hanging up his saddle: "I worked as a farm manager, breaking and training young horses at a farm for while, then worked as an assistant trainer for three years."

Malgarini works as an agent for jockey Michael Baze now, but tried his hand outside the industry before being drawn back to handle book for the young rider:

> I tried to get away from racing at one point. I spent a year as the Sports Book Supervisor at the MGM Grand in Las Vegas and also worked at Boeing for awhile, but it was difficult "working for the man." I wasn't used to being on the timeclock and being told what to do.
> As a retired jockey, you miss the excitement of the game. Once it's in your blood, you always want to be a part of that excitement again.

As the paddock judge at Golden Gate Fields and Bay Meadows, retired rider Gary Lawless has worked his hole life at the track:

> I rode for 18 years and loved it, but fighting the weight just wore me down. Dieting and reducing were no fun at all and it was tough on my family.
> When I retired, I had an opportunity to work on the gate crew and worked up to be the Assistant Starter. I worked for awhile as the Assistant Clerk of Scales before taking the Paddock Judge job. I can't imagine doing anything else than working at the track.

Retired jockey and current trainer Vann Belvoir was mucking stalls and caring for six horses as a groom in his father, Howard Belvoir's, barn by the time he was 12. When the young jockey physically outgrew the sport, he hung up his tack after riding for seven years, knowing exactly what he wanted to do:

> Being at the racetrack is all I knew and I always knew, I wanted to follow in my dad's footsteps and train horses.
> Dad helped me get started, and I did well enough to pick up some clients along the way. Winning races helped me attract more clients, and now I'm making the most of my opportunities.
> Having been a jockey gives me some insight other people might not have. I think I have a better opinion of how races develop, what might happen to the horse during the race and what they might benefit from in the future, like stretching out, shortening or how to change their training.

There's a general misperception that jockeys are wealthy athletes, largely because the general public sees the news clips and newspaper articles commemorating the top jockeys victories aboard Kentucky Derby and

Breeder's Cup winners. In reality, it's quite the opposite. Most jockeys are making under $40,000 a year and struggle to make a living. Hence, most riders experience unanticipated financial hardship and adjustment at retirement.

For far too many, what should be the golden years of peaceful relaxation and enjoyment becomes a merciless transition into a world filled with uncertainty, self-doubt and frustration. They may be unable to meet the cost of primary personal needs at retirement age.

While there are many riders who've been fortunate, and wise enough, to tuck anything away while they were competitively riding, most are unable to put money away and are not financially prepared for the transition to life after racing. Even for those who make six figures a year, they often lack the education, coaching or direction to invest their monies wisely. Because there's no retirement program in place for jockeys, they are on their own to plan ahead. Not surprisingly, research shows that retirees who enjoy a smooth transition into retirement, one without worries of financial stability, are generally happier and healthier than those who encounter cash-flow problems.

Stakes-winning rider Joy Scott is now in her mid–40s and realizes her retirement is getting a lot closer than she cares to think:

> When you first start riding, it's like running away from home and joining the circus. You just leave everything behind. Now that I'm getting closer to retiring, I have to think about what I'm going to do when I can't ride anymore. I don't have anything set up as far as retirement goes. I haven't set any money aside. I have to win just to keep going. This is the only thing I know how to do, but I love it.
>
> I've had so many falls, that I don't know how long I can physically keep it up. I can ride just fine, but I have trouble walking and being on my feet from all the injuries. I've had a broken back, legs and toes and bad knees. It all hurts.

The good-humored Scott has a gift with young horses that may offer her some options when it's time to hang up her tack for good: "I hope to have the mental faculties to start another career when I'm done riding. I might try my hand at training or working at a breaking or training facility with young horses."

Retired rider Ray Sibille is one of the fortunate riders to have saved some money along the way for retirement:

> I rode for 35 years and was lucky enough to make some good money over the years and tuck some away for retirement. It's not like I'm going to be able to sit around and do nothing, though, but at least I can take my time looking at options.
>
> So many guys quit school to ride, struggle all their career to make money and retire when they just can't physically ride any longer. They ride because

they love it, but when they retire, they don't have anything else to fall back on. Sadly, many of them are living at poverty level.

Sibille, who suffers from a stuttering disorder, may be best remembered for winning the 1988 Breeder's Cup Turf aboard a horse ironically named Great Communicator. The popular rider retired last summer at the age of 51 to have hip replacement surgery and was the proud winner of the 2005 George Woolf Memorial Award.

Like most riders, Mark Guidry, a 30-year riding veteran, missed out on family activities and wished he would've had more quality time with them during his career:

> When I retire, I'm looking forward to just spending more time enjoying life and being with my family. I've missed out on so much. Because riding demands so much of your time, you just miss out on things like family events, parties and things with the kids at school.
>
> Racing is tough on the body, and it takes a toll over time. The longer I ride, the tougher it gets, and the more I think about retiring. But if you win a couple of races, you feel like you want to ride forever because it's such a thrill. I've been fortunate to have had a great career, but I know the day will come when I decide it's time to call it quits. I'll probably do something to stay in the game, maybe pinhooking yearlings or something.

Phil Teator, an active rider for eight years, recognizes the value of getting an early start on saving for retirement:

> I received some good advice from older riders and a couple of my agents over the years, so I've saved and invested some of my money. I've worked with a Financial Advisor and I have a retirement account set up. Certainly, I could've been smarter when I was younger, but I'm in pretty good shape now.
>
> Most of the young guys don't have the education or the knowledge to know about saving for retirement. When you're young, fast money comes in quick and goes out quick.

Bravo agrees, "The hardest part for riders is saving money. It's not always going to be as easy as it is when they're riding well and making lots of money. They need restraint to not go out and blow it all. They should be putting money away for later."

Despite a high-risk, low-reward occupation that comes with enormous personal sacrifice, most jockeys will tell you they love what they do and wouldn't trade it for anything.

Because they've been used to keeping their problems with weight reducing secretive, many retired jockeys feel embarrassed to ask for any kind of help when they need it. As an industry, racing needs to do more for these incredible athletes. They give so much of themselves for the love of the sport. It's unfortunate we don't do more to recognize their amazing contributions to the sport.

While thoroughbred racing continues to fight for its place in American culture, and its share of the gambling dollar, jockeys will persevere with the ever-changing and challenging times, adjusting to the subtle but necessary changes in the racing industry.

The lore of grand thoroughbreds guided by masterful jockeys, who practice their profession with skill and daring, lives on today as it has for centuries. And for as long as the cry for "riders up" is heard, the fascinating "Sport of Kings" will provide us with thrills, heartache and humanity.

NOTES ON SOURCES

The majority of information used in creating *Jockey* came directly through interviews with jockeys, retired jockeys, agents, trainers, racing officials and other content experts. With their cooperation, courage and passion for the sport, I was able to hear the inside story, learn the secrets and understand the bravery, athleticism and risks that make up the composition of jockeys.

Over the past three years, the following individuals were kind enough to share their time and insight with me: Shannon Albert, Lindy Aliment, Jack Allen, Frank Alvarado, Ron Anderson, Peter Artieda, Rudy Baez, Jerry Bailey, Ryan Barber, Gary Baze, Michael "MC" Baze, Russell Baze, Tyler Baze, Vicky Baze, Rafael Bejarano, Vann Belvoir, Paul Berube, Jeff Bloom, Walter Blum, Gary Boulanger, Paul Bowlinger, William "Buff" Bradley, George Bravo, Joe Bravo, Shaun Bridgmohan, Melody Brooks, Eric Camacho, Jesse Campbell, Dennis Carr, Daniel Centeno, Roman Chapa, Tom Chapman, Travis Church, Grant Clark, Angel Cordero, Jr., Jon Court, Amanda Crandall, Diane Crump, Robert Curran, Jr., Pat Day, Tony DeFranco, Kent Desormeaux, Kenny Doll, Ramon Dominguez, Ed Donnally, Rene Douglas, Francisco Duran, Stewart Elliott, Chris Emigh, Jose Ferrer, Earlie Fires, Ryan Fogelsonger, Freddy Fong, Jr., Rich Fontana, Jamie Fowler, Ricky Frazier, Larry Frazzitta, Jr., Casey Fusiler, Sandi Gann, Frank Garza, Mark Gibson, Steve Goldsmith, John Grabowski, James Graham, Jeff Greenhill, Aaron Gryder, Mark Guidry, Harry "The Hat" Hacek, Darrell Haire, Steve Hamilton, Desiree Hamilton, Joe Hampshire, Ray Harris, Dawn Harrison, Tara Hemmings, Brian Hernandez, Jr., John Hernandez, James "Chris" Herrell, Rosemary Homeister, Jr., Debbie Hoonan, TD. Houghton, Mike James, Sara Jones, Ian Jory, Joe Judice, Kyle Kaenel, Nancy Kelly, Bruce Kravets, Justin Kravets, Kevin Krigger, Greta Kuntzwiler, Chris Lamance, Corey Lanarie, Shane Laviolette, Gary Lawless, Cathy Leaszler, David Lopez, Jason Lumpkins, Frank Lovato, Jr., Mike Luzzi, Thelma Lynn, Tim Malgarini, Kevin Mangold, Felipe Martinez, Tony Matos, Chris McCarron, Scotty McClellan, John McKee, Kenny McPeek, Donnie Meche, Lonnie Meche, Randy Meier, Kathy Melancon, Gallyn Mitchell, Kathy Mongeon, Shelly Moran, Liz Morris, Corey Nakatani, Paul Nicolo, Craig O'Bryan, Doug O'Neill, Perry Ouzts, Dyn Panell, Jerry Parenti, Jr., Billy Pattin, Brian Peck, Todd Pletcher, Rodney Prescott, Ivan Puhich, Karyn Rainey, Adrian Ramos, Chance Rollins, Randy Romero, Ben Root, Mick Ruis, Scott Saito, Jean-Luc Samyn, Victor Sanchez, Dean Sarvis, Jennifer Schmidt, Joy Scott, Joan Scott, Shane Sellers, Ray Sibille, Sherry Simpson, Jere Smith, Jr., Mike Smith (chaplain), Dennis Snowden, Danny Sorenson, Michelle Stanton, Terry Stanton, Joe Steiner, Kelly Summers-Wietsma, Tomey Jean Swan, Phil Teator, Tim Thornton, Ken Tohill, Paul Toscano, John Velasquez, Jennifer Whitaker, Rick Wilson, Randy Wiseman, David Woodcock, Carl "CW" Woodley and Russell Woolsey.

Several experts from the medical field lent their expertise to the book including David Baron MD, Temple University School of Medicine; Jean Bradley Robel, ThD, Anorexia Nervosa and Related Eating Disorders, Inc. (ANRED); Nancy Clark, MS, RD; Brian Davis, MD, University of California, Davis Medical Center; Micky Marquez, PT; Nina Spalek, MD; Gary Wadler, MD, New York School of Medicine; Anna Waller, ScD, University of North Carolina, Injury Prevention Research; and the National Eating Disorder Association (NEDA).

The following agencies provided unique content expertise: Equibase Company, LLC, Horsemen's Benevolent & Protective Association, Jockeys' Guild, National Museum of Racing Hall of Fame, National Thoroughbred Racing Association, Race Track Chaplaincy of America, the Jockey Club, the Jockey Club Information Systems and the Thoroughbred Protective Racing Association.

The *Journal of the American Medical Association* (JAMA) provided the following reference material: *Jockey Injuries in the United States* JAMA, 283 (2000): 1326–28].

The following books were used as a historical reference: *Thoroughbred Champions: Top 100 Racehorses of the 20th Century* (Lexington KY: The Blood-Horse, Inc. 1999) and *Thoroughbred Times Racing Almanac* (Lexington, KY: Thoroughbred Times Co. Inc.).

Equiline.com provided historical and statistical support of jockey racing records.

Lastly, no racing fan or student of bloodlines could live without the decades of reliable news, stories and information provided by the *Daily Racing Form* and *Thoroughbred Times* publications.

INDEX

Adam, Mathieu 110
Agua Caliente 167
Allen, Jack 99
Anderson, Ron 64
Anorexia Nervosa and Related Eating Disorders, Inc. 82
Antley, Chris 26, 45, 76
Aqueduct Race Track 26, 27, 30, 117
Arcaro, Eddie 108, 110, 155, 166–168, 171
Arlington Park 26, 30, 36, 61, 92, 174, 177
Artieda, Peter 11
Asmussen, Steve 94, 143
Atlantic City Race Course 158, 183

Baez, Rudy 148, 149
Baeza, Braulio 10, 171, 172
Baffert, Bob 64
Bailey, Jerry 4, 27, 50, 51, 56, 64, 66, 73, 75, 122, 123, 126, 154, 179, 180, 189
Barber, Ryan 121, 134, 135
Baron, Dr. David 91, 195
Barrera, Laz 19
Bay Meadows 138, 145, 180, 196
Baze, Gary 83, 146, 147, 180
Baze, Michael 124, 149, 150, 196
Baze, Russell 40, 41, 165, 168, 180, 186, 192
Baze, Tyler 22, 119, 120, 180, 189
Baze, Vicky 69, 70

Bejarano, Rafael 109, 189, 190
Belmont Park 17, 27, 36, 62, 109, 139, 143, 165, 174
Belvoir, Howard 196
Belvoir, Vann 78, 196
Bertrand, Mark 83
Beulah Park 44, 148
Birzer, Gary 153, 155
Blair, Paul 43
Bloom, Jeff 77, 78
Blum, Walter 136–138
Boulanger, Gary 27, 28, 40, 154
Bowie Race Track 178
Bradley, Rubel Jean 82
Bradley, William "Buff" 12, 142
Bravo, George 193, 198
Bravo, Joe 12, 29, 126
Breeder's Cup 4, 39, 64, 86, 93, 155, 169, 172, 174, 175, 177–180, 182–189, 197, 198
Bridgmohan, Shaun 34, 35, 135, 143
Brooks, Melody 99, 100
Brothers, Donna 154
Burton, Stacy 34

Calder Race Track 27, 29, 61, 112, 137, 137, 190
Camacho, Eric 39, 40, 60
Campbell, Brian 100
Campbell, Jesse 13, 100
Canterbury Downs 163
Carr, Dennis 55, 117

Index

Castro, Eddie 190
Cauthen, Steve 45, 78, 181, 191
Cedeno, Amir 101
Centeno, Daniel 10
Chapman, Tom 92, 158, 159, 193–195
Chavez, Jorge 186
Churchill Downs 17, 62, 66, 73, 108, 132, 153–155, 183, 191
Clark, Nancy 80, 81
Colonial Downs 88
Conway, Tim 162
Cordero, Angel, Jr. 10, 13, 16, 21, 45, 116, 166, 172, 173, 177
Court, Jon 38, 53
Crump, Diane 67, 68
Curran, Robert, Jr. 163

Daily Racing Form 4, 94, 96, 165
Davis, Dr. Bruce 82, 89–91
Day, Pat 9, 22, 36, 52, 63, 64, 75, 92, 154, 176, 177, 180, 188
DeFranco, Tony 163
Delahoussaye, Eddie 45, 175
Delaware Park 26, 27
Del Mar Race Track 27, 62, 88, 112, 119, 135, 161, 175, 183
Delta Downs 20, 72, 86, 104
Desourmeux, Kent 40, 45, 65, 124, 132, 184, 185
Dettori, Frankie 139
Dickinson, Michael 99
Disabled Jockey Fund 162
Dominguez, Ramon 60, 122, 128, 165, 186
Don MacBeth Memorial Fund 162, 163, 178
Donnally, Ed 35
Douglas, Rene 26
Duran, Francisco 20, 24, 38

Eclipse Award 164–166, 168, 172, 173, 175–182, 184–186, 188–191
Elliott, Stewart 49, 51, 52, 66, 75
Ellis Park 28
Elzey, Steve 47
Emerald Downs 13, 35, 95
Emigh, Chris 42, 135, 136
Equicizer 15–17, 95
Espinoza, Victor 45, 186, 187
ESPN 170, 178, 179, 182–186, 188
Evangeline Downs 20, 76, 104, 175, 185

Exercise Riders 7, 8, 12–14, 19, 33–35, 44, 45, 93, 176

Fair Grounds Race Course 157, 175
Fairmount Park 147
Fairplex Park 33, 178
Ferer, Jose 28, 29
Finger Lakes Race Track 33, 78
Fires, Earlie 43, 60, 190
Fisher, Herb 132
Flint, Steve 32
Flores, David 48
Fogelsonger, Ryan 55, 60, 190
Fong, Freddy, Jr. 60, 61
Fontana, Rich 161, 162
Fragoso, Pablo 190
Francis, Richard "Dick" 134
Frankel, Bobby 13, 49
Frazier, Ricky 90, 138, 151, 157
Frazzitta, Larry, Jr. 87, 88, 117, 118
Fusiler, Casey 38, 39, 136

Gann, Sandi 138, 139
Garden State Race Track 7
Garza, Frank 19, 20
George Woolf Memorial Award 162, 164–166, 168, 170, 172–176, 178–182, 184, 185, 187, 188, 198
Gertmenian, Dr. L. Wayne 156, 157
Gibson, Mark 106
Golden Gate Fields 151, 161, 168, 180, 196
Goldsmith, Steve 44, 46
Gonzalez, J.C. 148
Grabowski, John 33, 78
Graham, James 10
Great Lakes Downs 109
Greenhill, Jeff 47, 48, 53, 54
Grooms 7, 11, 12, 19, 34, 35, 44, 45, 54, 71, 135, 176
Gryder, Aaron 83, 118, 129, 142, 143, 150
Guidry, Mark 75, 76, 97, 198
Gulfstream Park 27, 126, 154, 183

Hacek, Harry "the Hat" 45, 46
Haire, Darrell 154, 156
Hamilton, Desiree 157, 158
Hamilton, Steve 31, 109
Hampshire, Joe 79, 80
Hansen, Ron 74

Index

Harrison, Dawn 159
Hartack, Bill 169–171
Hawley, Sandy 175, 176
Hawthorne Race Course 30, 92, 96
Headley, Bruce 49
Health and Injury 5, 6, 13, 21, 24, 25, 30, 34, 37, 75, 77–93, 95, 103, 104, 106, 113, 117, 118, 127, 128, 145–163, 167, 174–176, 183, 184, 188, 192–198
Hemmings, Tara 29, 68, 69
Hernandez, Brian, Jr. 20–22, 190
Herrell, James "Chris" 32, 84–86, 113
Hialeah Park 27, 68
Hoffman, John 61
Hollywood Park 26, 27, 142, 168, 178, 185
Homeister, Rosemary 28, 29, 117, 139
Hoonan, Debbie 83, 84
Hoosier Park 28, 161
Houghton, Terry "T.D." 79, 151, 152

Ignacio, Rodolfo 47
Indiana Downs 28
Isaac Murphy Memorial Award 40, 164, 165, 180, 186

James, Mike 38
Jockey Agents 13, 21, 28, 29, 43–52, 56, 61, 63, 64, 152, 173, 196
Jockey Club Foundation 163
Jockey schools 10, 19, 20, 178
Jockeys' Guild 6, 65, 68, 92, 136, 146–150, 153–157, 160, 162, 163, 165, 166, 168, 170, 179, 182
Jockey's Room 6, 11, 17, 36, 37, 39, 75, 79, 84, 85, 95–99, 102, 113, 142–145
Jones, Sara 118
Jory, Ian 22
Judice, Joe 119

Kaenel, "Cowboy" Jack 27
Kaenel, Kyle 59
Keeneland Race Course 26, 110, 190
Kelly, Nancy 163
Kelly, Pat 143
Kravets, Bruce 33
Kravets, Justin 102, 126
Krigger, Kevin 58, 59
Krone, Julie 16, 69, 182–184
Kuntzweiler, Greta 31, 67, 105

Kurtsigner, Charles 110, 155, 178
Kusner, Kathy 68

Lamance, Chris 71, 127
Lanerie, Corey 113, 114, 143
Lawless, Gary 89, 90, 100, 196
Les Bois Park 182
Leuszler, Cathy 44, 45
Longacres Park 27, 83
Longden, Johnny 146, 155, 166–168
Lopez, David 79
Lopez, Ray 49
Los Alimitos Race Course 11
Lovato, Frank, Jr. 7, 8, 15–17, 83, 149
Lucas, D. Wayne 19, 93
Luzzi, Mike 50, 70, 125

Malgarini, Tim 196
Mandella, Richard 49
Mangold, Kevin 18, 19, 51, 147
Marquez, P.T., Micky 95
Matos, Tony 45
May, Roy 160
McAnally, Ron 49
McCarron, Chris 42, 43, 45, 93, 159, 161, 162, 177, 177, 178, 188
McCarron, Judy 162
McClellan, Scotty 48, 49
McKee, John 42, 114, 115, 141, 143, 191
McPeek, Kenny 52, 56, 142
Meade, Don 132
Meadowlands Race Track 13, 26, 27, 183
Meche, Donnie 21, 129
Meche, Lonnie 21, 94
Meier, Randy 96, 97, 106, 107
Melancon, Kathy 147
Melancon, Paul 147
Mike Venezia Memorial Award 163, 165, 170, 173, 175, 178, 179, 182, 184, 186, 189
Molina, Juan 114
Money matters 4, 10, 21, 22, 38, 42, 43, 48, 52, 54, 57, 58, 61–67, 97, 98, 137, 153–157, 162, 196–198
Mongeon, Kathy 53
Monmouth Park 29, 183
Moran, Shelly 48
Morris, Liz 60, 61, 92
Mountaineer Park 48, 99, 121, 154

206   Index

Nakatani, Corey 9, 30, 45, 134, 135, 187
National Eating Disorders Association 80, 86
National Museum of Racing Hall of Fame 10, 19, 40–43, 59, 165, 166, 168, 170, 172–185
National Thoroughbred Racing Association (NTRA) 66, 154, 165
National Turf Writers Association 165
Neves, Ralph 145
Nicolo, Paul 98, 193, 195, 196

Oaklawn Park 87
O'Bryan, Craig 30
O'Neill, Doug 52, 53, 56
Ouzts, Perry 22, 42, 113

Panel, Dyn 120
Parenti, Jerry, Jr. 26, 27
Patin, Billy 73, 112
Peck, Brian 127, 128, 153, 156
Pedroza, Martin 142
Penn National 27
Philadelphia Park 5, 29, 69, 121
Pierce, Larry 127
Pimlico Race Track 13, 17, 26, 39, 60, 110, 152
Pincay, Laffit, Jr. 10, 22, 41, 45, 97, 161, 168, 174, 175, 180
Pineda, Alvaro 181
Pino, Mario 60
Pleasanton Race Track 11
Pletcher, Todd 13, 50, 93
Pollard, John "Red" 155
Prado, Edgar 50, 187
Prescott, Rodney 28, 103
Prescott Downs 10, 34, 160, 176

Quinn, Chris 147, 148

Race Track Chaplaincy (RTC) 35, 36, 163
Racing officials 4, 11, 17, 22, 24, 44, 57–61, 72, 95, 98, 100, 102, 104, 106, 107, 112, 114, 129, 134–139, 145, 146, 170, 171, 172, 195
Rainey, Karyn 13, 14
Renick, Sam 155, 166
Retama Park 25, 157
Retamoza, Ernie 114
Richardson, Noel 112

River Downs 28, 115, 181, 191
Robertson, Craig 10
Rockingham Park 13, 148
Rollins, Chance 24, 159, 161
Romero, Randy 86, 87
Rosen, Joe 49
Rowland, Michael 147
Rubin, Barbara Jo 65
Ruis, Mick 9, 30, 116
Ruiz, Arnold 148
Russell, Ben 140

Saito, Scott 153
Salt Lake City Race Track 166
Sam Houston Park 25
San Juan Downs 160
Sanchez, Emanuel Jose 88
Sanchez, Victor 138
Santa Anita Race Track 17–19, 27, 68, 91, 93, 151, 164, 165, 170, 178
Santa Fe Downs 184
Santos, Jose 27, 66, 73, 187, 188
Saratoga Race Course 17, 55, 172, 183, 184
Sarvis, Dean 37, 47, 115, 116
Schmidt, Jennifer 8
Scott, Joan 54, 142
Scott, Joy 158, 197
Seabiscuit 17, 18, 110, 112, 164, 178, 182
Sellers, Shane 27, 65, 92, 100, 153, 155
Servis, John 51, 52
Shoemaker, Bill 22, 161, 110, 167–170, 174
Sibille, Ray 197, 198
Simpson, Sherry 160
Sloan, James "Tod" 115
Smith, Jere, Jr. 32, 99
Smith, Mike (chaplain) 35, 36
Smith, Mike (jockey) 38, 59, 161, 184
Snowden, Dennis 97
Solis, Alex 30, 45, 48, 116, 188
Sorenson, Danny 64, 65, 125, 127
Soumillion, Christophe 39
Spalek, Dr. Nina 95
Sports Illustrated 170, 171, 181
Sportsman Park 96
Stanon, Michelle 25
Stanton, Terry 25
Starting gate 11, 33, 59, 70, 89, 96, 102–109, 117, 118, 122, 126, 130, 148, 150–152, 157, 161

Steiner, Joe 127, 130, 151
Stevens, Gary 17, 30, 45, 51, 59, 88, 155, 180, 182
Stewart, Dallas 32
Suffolk Downs 148, 149
Sunland Park 179
Swan, Tomey Jean 156, 160, 161

Tampa Bay Downs 27, 79, 183
Teator, Phil 56, 57, 198
Thistledown Race Track 10, 27
Thornton, Tim 30
Thoroughbred Racing Protective Bureau (TRPB) 75
Tohill, Kenny 130, 144
Toscano, Paul 112, 113
Transitory business 5, 12, 25–29, 35, 44, 62–64, 155
Triple Crown 32, 45, 49, 51, 52, 64, 66, 76, 78, 110, 166–169, 171–174, 178–183, 185–188
Tropical Park 68
Turcotte, Ron 148, 173, 174
Turf Paradise 30, 46, 59, 139
Turfway Park 28, 47, 48, 67, 109, 113, 115, 127, 147

Ussery, Bobby 167

Valenzuela, Pat 45, 188, 189
Valets 28, 97, 98, 138, 139
Vasquez, Jacinto 10
Velasquez, Jorge 10, 181
Velazquez, John 50, 51, 60, 132, 173, 189

Wadler, Dr. Gary 160
Wales, Travis 46
Waller, Anna, ScD. 150, 151
Warren, Ron, Jr. 157
Weight issues 5, 6, 13, 22, 24, 25, 36, 57–60, 65, 75–93, 98, 99, 150, 175, 181, 193–196
Wietsma, Kelly 65, 66
Wilson, Rick 152, 153
Wiseman, Randy 44
Wittingham, Charles 49
Woodbine Race Track 27, 173, 176
Woodcock, David 162
Woodley, Carl "C.J." 104
Woolf, George 110, 112, 164, 182
Woolsey, Russell 54, 158

Yakima Meadows 180
Yavapai Downs 6

www.ingramcontent.com/pod-product-compliance
Ingram Content Group UK Ltd.
Pitfield, Milton Keynes, MK11 3LW, UK
UKHW042002140426
5217IPUK00015B/941